THE
COGNITIVE
COMPUTER

T H E COGNITIVE COMPUTER

ON LANGUAGE, LEARNING, AND ARTIFICIAL INTELLIGENCE

Roger C. Schank
with
Peter G. Childers

ADDISON-WESLEY PUBLISHING COMPANY, INC.
READING, MASSACHUSETTS   MENLO PARK, CALIFORNIA
WOKINGHAM, BERKSHIRE   AMSTERDAM   DON MILLS, ONTARIO   SYDNEY

Library of Congress Cataloging in Publication Data

Schank, Roger C., 1946–
   The cognitive computer.

   Includes index.
   1. Artificial intelligence. 2. Electronic digital computers—Programming. I. Childers, Peter G. II. Title.
Q335.S386 1984   001.64   84-12326
ISBN 0-201-06443-X

Cover design by Marshall Henrichs
Set in 11 point Palatino by Waldman Graphics, Inc., Pennsauken, NJ

BCDEFGHIJ-DO-8654

Second Printing, December 1984

CONTENTS

v

To my father, Maxwell Schank, who always has wanted me to write a book that everyone could read. And to my mother, Margaret Rosenberg Schank, who thinks that whatever I do is wonderful.

PREFACE

> "When *I* use a word," Humpty Dumpty said, in a rather scornful
> tone, "it means just what I choose it to mean—neither
> more nor less."
>
> "The question is," said Alice, "whether you *can* make words
> mean so many different things."
>
> "The question is," said Humpty Dumpty, "which is to
> be master—that's all."
>
> —*Through the Looking Glass*

A book on computers may seem a strange place to find a discussion of the nature of human thinking and language, but Artificial Intelligence is a strange field. This book is about the nature of human intelligence and what it would mean to have machine intelligence.

In this computer age, questions about what computers can do ought to be considered in parallel with questions about what people can do. There are three important questions for anyone who now uses or who will someday use a computer:

1. What do we have to know about computers in order to live in a world that is full of them?
2. What can we learn about what it means to be intelligent through our development of computers that can understand?
3. How will intelligent computers affect the world we live in?

This book is my attempt to address these three questions. I try to set the computer in perspective, to see it as a machine, a machine with fantastic possibilities. I attempt to allay the fears that those not knowledgeable about computers have upon entering the computer age. To put the computer into the right perspective, we must look at humans. When we think that computers understand, we must consider this idea in light of what we imagine to be the case when humans understand. Knowing how to program in BASIC may not be as important a skill in the computer age as knowing just how advanced intelligent machines are likely to get. In this book I try to give enough information on the problems facing people who are trying to make machines intelligent, so that people who will be affected by these machines will know what is likely to come when.

I am interviewed by various newspapers, magazines, or television shows on the average of once a week. When I decided to get a Ph.D., the last thing on my mind was a career as a media star. I wanted to get far away from the concerns of the average man. I did not want to have to work on something that bored me. I wanted to have fun in what I did, to be challenged, and, most of all, to be in that ivory tower I had read about. I wanted to be a professor because a life centered on ideas appealed to me. It seemed reasonable that a professor at a university would have the opportunity to create ideas without regard for their ultimate utility. Because I was fascinated by the workings of the mind, I decided to explore how people think. I did not enter psychology because the experimental nature of that discipline did not appeal to me. I did not want to run tightly controlled experiments on how people remembered lists of nonsense syllables. I wanted to know how people communicated; how they created new ideas; how they understood the ideas of others. As time went on I found myself, after traveling a rather crooked path, in the field of Artificial Intelligence (AI). What this field encompassed was not agreed upon exactly by any two workers in AI. I was drawn to it because a great many very bright people were in it; because it dealt with computers, which were both new (and therefore exciting) and logical (and thus free of the fuzziness that characterizes so much nonscientific thinking), and because it was legitimate within this field to speculate upon the nature of the mind.

Now, almost 20 years later, I am a professor in a major university, the head of an important AI laboratory, and I do get to work on and think about all the ideas I had hoped I could. My life, however, is not solely concerned with ideas. Two major differences exist between the life I had imagined and the life I live. First, I am not unconcerned with business and money. In fact, I am the president of a private company in the business of selling AI programs. Second, I am not working in an obscure field having to do with the mind. What I say and do is printed quite regularly in the media.

This book, then, has two purposes. First, its intent is to inform the public about the subject of Artificial Intelligence, not from the perspective of a science-oriented journalist, who may or may not understand what he or she has seen and read, but from the viewpoint of one who is involved deeply in the subject. Second, it seems important to ponder the reasons why my obscure field has hit the front pages. The public has discovered AI but is not quite sure what it is. The fact that AI has become a public issue is both important and somewhat sad. It says more about our society than one would realize at first glance.

Despite the massive publicity that Artificial Intelligence has received, the general public does not have a very good idea of what the subject is all about. We have a vague sense of intelligent computers that eventually will take over the world; we even have a general fear or excitement about the possibilities of this happening. Between the opinion that such an occurrence is impossible, and the opinion that it already has happened or is just about to happen, there is a large gap. What is the reality? Is HAL from 2001 already here, or is it reasonable to expect that he will never get here? Is AI just a subject for pointy-headed academics, or will every person need some understanding of AI and computers in general just to be able to cope?

These are the issues that now are discussed by newspapers and by people at cocktail parties. On the one hand, it is nice that people care about such things. On the other, it seems a bit odd that so many people want to discuss their opinions about a subject on which they have so little concrete information.

So, in this book I will try to do what most academics abhor. I will try to boil down twenty years of work on a technical subject into a few pages presented in a nontechnical way. In doing so I hope to inform the public about what the reality of AI is and where the pitfalls and possibilities lie. To do this, I have oversimplified complex ideas, not given credit where credit is due, and generally committed a whole set of what, to an academic, are unpardonable sins. I apologize to my colleagues in AI beforehand, and hope they agree that the goal of informing the public makes bending some of the rules worthwhile.

I do want to mention, however, the numerous people who have worked with me and supported me over the years. Included herein are a set of programs and ideas that took years to develop. As I could not have done very much of what I did without their input I would like to thank these individuals here.

In my early years, I derived much knowledge and counsel from Jacob Mey, Sheldon Klein, and Eugene Pendergraft. At Stanford, Ken Colby and Jerry Feldman were very important to my intellectual development. The ideas and programming ability of my research team at Stanford were critical in changing my own view of the world. The members of that team were Chris Riesbeck, Chuck Rieger, Neil Goldman, Sylvia Russell, Linda Hemphill, and numerous others. At Yale, my students were the heart of my research team. Specifically, I want to mention my Yale Ph.D.s, Jim Meehan, Wendy Lehnert, Rich Cullingford, Bob Wilensky, Jaime Carbonell, Anatole Gershman, Gerry De Jong, Mallory Selfridge, Rick Granger, Mike Lebowitz, and Janet Kolodner. Other people who were not my students, but who were critical in developing ideas and programs, were Steve Shwartz and Mike Dyer. Also, many of my current students have been significant in their help, specifically, Larry Birnbaum, Natalie Dehn, Margot Flowers, Gregg Collins, and many others. A special word of thanks is given to my Yale colleagues who have helped over the years, specifically Bob Abelson, who developed the script concept, and a great deal more, with me.

My work has required a significant amount of financial support, which has come, for the most part, from the U.S. government, specifically the Department of Defense. When one mentions the Department of Defense in a research funding context, there is the usual groan of how scientists are helping make more weapons and such. In fact, the Department of Defense, through the Advanced Research Projects Agency, the Office of Naval Research, and more recently, the Air Force, have been some of the most enlightened supporters of real scientific research in this country. I thank the people who have made those agencies as sensible and significant as they are. I also thank the National Science Foundation for its support over the years.

Various people have taken great pains to help me say what I want to say when I write. Earlier drafts of this book were read and commented on by Larry Birnbaum, Gregg Collins, Kris Hammond, Natalie Dehn, Chris Riesbeck, Diane Schank, Steve Slade, Jim Meehan, and Margot Flowers. Three people spent an extra amount of time helping me. I especially thank Bill Purves, Larry Hunter, and Ann Drinan for their aid.

Last of all, I would like to mention that Yale University is a magnificent place to be a part of. They have put up with me in all my various incarnations, and although it is hard to thank an institution, I hereby do so.

New Haven, Connecticut
March 1984

PART

ONE

CHAPTER ONE

DON'T START THE COMPUTER REVOLUTION WITHOUT ME

Suddenly, computers are everywhere: in the schools, in the banks, in the offices, in the automobiles—even in toys. And just as suddenly, everyone is feeling "computer illiterate." Advertisements for personal computers imply that if we don't rush to buy a computer for our children they will fail in school and never land a job. Adults who have lived happily for years without knowing anything about computers are starting to feel as if they have been left in the stone age. The media bombard the average person with the idea that if he doesn't learn about computers, he is going to be left behind. We are told, even if only implicitly, that computers are frightening devices bound to control our lives unless we learn how to program them. On top of this, the media has begun to sensationalize the imminent arrival of intelligent machines, and apparently has decided that they are going to be *Japanese* intelligent machines, to boot.

This book has one basic message: stop worrying. The computer revolution has not passed you by. In fact, quite the opposite is the case. The computer revolution hasn't caught up to where you are. If you can't use today's computers without pain, then just wait. It is the computers that will have to change, not you.

One might expect a computer scientist to urge people to learn a programming language as soon as possible and to recommend that they purchase the best and most powerful home computer they can afford. A typical personal computer book reminds the reader that one must become "computer literate" in order to succeed, and suggests that the best way to do this is to buy the book and learn whatever computer skills it happens to teach. These books urge you to learn about computers today in order to prepare for the world of tomorrow. But if tomorrow's computers are even worth thinking about, much less waiting for, it is because they will *not* require their users to be "computer literate."

Consider cars and televisions, two machines that play an important role in our daily lives. The main reason they are so useful is that we can use them without having to know anything about the technology that produced them. Computers are likely to affect us in the same ways that TVs and cars have: They will provide entertainment and services, and we will wonder how we ever lived without them. The average person will not have to learn how to program computers any more than he has to learn auto mechanics or TV repair. It's nice to be able to fix your own TV and to rebuild your car's engine; but you wouldn't worry if someone called you *television-illiterate* or *automobile-illiterate* because you happened to be part of the vast majority of people who *don't* fix their own cars and TVs. *Computers intimidate us because we imagine they are smarter than we are.* But a computer really can't do anything unless you, with your human intelligence, tell it exactly what you want it to do, down to the last detail. Anyone who thinks today's computers are intelligent in the full sense of the word has no appreciation of the extraordinary power of the human mind, much less of the real possibility of developing programs that approach human levels of intelligence. If the computers of the future gain any semblance of intelligence it will be because we have begun to unravel some of the mysteries of human intelligence and model them on the computer.

COMPUTER LITERACY

What should we know about computers? One thing seems clear: As computers get better at reflecting human thought processes, they also should become as easy to use as televisions—we will just turn them on and type to them as we would to another person. It is not necessary, therefore, to worry too much about today's computers. Early computing skills will go the way of early car-repair skills, a relic of a period when the users of a new machine had to be experts or devoted hobbyists. Computer literacy will seem as absurd a term as television literacy.

What is "computer literacy," anyway, and what distinguishes someone who is "computer literate" from someone who isn't? Computer literacy means different things to different people. For some it means being able to drop the words *bit* and *byte* into a conversation about technology. To others it means being able to use a word processor. To people who are serious about it, it means knowing programming languages such as BASIC, Pascal, LISP, or APL, and knowing something about computer structure and function. People who know these languages can do only one thing that people who don't know them cannot do: They can write programs. But what kind of programs can they write? Most of today's programming languages are oriented toward mathematical and statistical operations. Computers have been programmed for these kinds of operations since they were first developed, mainly because engineers and mathematicians were the original developers of computers. But the average person doesn't have mathematical and statistical operations to perform, so even if everyone learned these programming languages, they would have no reason to write programs in them. The average person might become *computer literate*, but he would have nothing to say.

An in-depth knowledge of computers, programming languages, and programming techniques is almost irrelevant for the average person. Unless you have some programs that you really need to write, you needn't bother learning a programming language.

There is one very good reason to learn programming, but it has nothing to do with preparing for high-tech careers or with making sure one is computer literate in order to avoid being cynically manipulated by the computers of the future. The real value of learning to program can only be understood if we look at learning to program as an exercise of the intellect, as a kind of modern-day Latin that we learn to sharpen our minds.

The centerpiece of any computer program is the algorithm it uses to accomplish its task. An algorithm is quite simply a recipe, a set of step-by-step instructions for completing a process of some kind. (The problem of processes and algorithms is examined in Chapter 4.) Learning how to formulate an efficient algorithm in order to solve a problem sharpens the mind. Programming can develop your intellect and show you the benefits (and problems) of step-by-step reasoning. If you want to learn programming as an intellectual adventure, fine; the process certainly will develop your reasoning skills.

The media can't seem to get away from the idea that we are about to make a sudden leap from the Apple computer to some version of the HAL 9000 electronic monster depicted in Arthur C. Clarke's *2001: A Space Odyssey*. In order to understand what leap we are talking about here we should take another, less apocalyptic, look at the computer and the average person.

THE COMPUTER AND YOU

The main reason for the average person to care about computers is that they might contribute to daily life by providing some kind of service. We all know, for example, that computers allow large businesses and institutions of every kind to keep their records straight, with incredible speed and efficiency. Sadly enough, the average person only becomes aware that some business is using a computer to handle transactions when something goes wrong. Computers can break down, just as any of our machines can. Their circuits can overheat and deteriorate, and they can be destroyed by magnetic fields and fluctuations in electrical power. There's the story of the broken electronic banking machine that ate the same customer's bank card and refused to let him make withdrawals or deposits three times in a row. The customer finally pulled out a revolver and shot the machine six times. However, billing errors that arrive in the mail are rarely computer errors; they are usually errors on the part of some human involved in programming or data entry. Somewhere along the line, the wrong instructions were given—a decimal place was moved or a key was pressed twice by accident.

These things don't happen to everybody; nor do they happen all the time. Most of us never have to be bothered with the knowledge that all our purchases, banking, insurance, medical records, air travel, telephone service, and other utilities are kept track of, and properly handled by, computers. Computers contribute to our ease and well-being, since we don't have to stand in line or wait eight weeks for a phone to be installed and connected, and can be billed easily and promptly for exactly what we owe.

A COMPUTER IN EVERY HOME: SIDE-EFFECTS

Some of the best and most appropriate uses of computers in the home are really side-effects of computer technology: games, word processing, and sending personal letters over computer networks. Computer scientists have had such toys available to them for years. What has changed is that now computers are small and cheap. The average person can have his very own computer sitting on a desk at home. He can take advantage of the side-effects of the computer age that computer scientists have developed for their own use.

What else can someone who isn't a programmer do with a computer? Why isn't he using the real power of computers, namely, to run programs that perform a necessary task? Why are games, word processing, and computer mail the primary things that today's computers can do? Does the lack of *computer literacy* prevent the average person from doing more with the computer? What can a computer-literate person do with a home computer?

Today's computers can only be addressed in severely restricted and prescribed ways. This is why someone who wants a computer to make everyday life easier in some way will quicky become frustrated. *Computers do only what they have been programmed to do, and this essential fact of computers will not change.* Any intelligence computers may have will result from an evolution of our ideas about the nature of intelligence—not as a result of advances in electronics.

To understand this distinction we must discuss the difference between *hardware* and *software*. A good analogy here comes from television. When you buy a television, it is only as interesting and valuable as the programs that run on it. Certainly, the electronics of the box (the hardware) contribute to the overall quality of the reception and the sharpness of the picture. But if there are no worthwhile TV programs to watch, the TV set gets packed away in the attic.

It is the quality of the programs that really matters. (The fact that the word "programs" occurs in both cases is not accidental.) So, the same goes for a computer. If you can't find any good software for it to run, the computer hardware will just lie there gathering dust. The biggest difference between programs for TV and those for computers, in this respect, is that with computers you can write your own programs. If you can do the work necessary to write your own programs, you also had better have a need to use the programs you write, or the result will be equally superfluous. The computer will do what you tell it to do, assuming you know how to tell it, what to tell it, and really want it to do what you told it to do. This is true for all computers, regardless of size. The big computers used by businesses to handle large amounts of data and perform complex calculations are really just as restricted as the small home computer. If all a giant computer has been programmed to do is handle the payroll, customer and employee records, or to solve equations used in designing the wings of supersonic aircraft, then those are the only things it will do. A computer that can do these things is very *powerful*, but its level of understanding is no greater than that of a small home computer. Their larger size means they are faster, have a greater memory capacity, and thus can run more sophisticated programs—not that they are in any sense "smarter." Big computers don't generally disappoint their users the way home computers can because their users tend to be highly paid professionals who do not have such grand expectations.

We might defend the home computer by saying that people can do their home finances on them, but most home finance software isn't a big step up from a ledger and a hand calculator. More importantly, if you don't already know quite a bit about home finance, the current software isn't going to teach it to you. Most commercially available software is written for people who need specific programs to keep track of numerical data in their area of expertise. The smaller the computer, the more restricted will be the software it can run. Most people don't have accounts to keep track of, or hundreds of clients and employees to deal with. In a much more down-to-earth vein, home finance has got to be one of the least interesting things people spend their time doing, whether with pencil and paper or with the smartest computer we can imagine.

Another possible justification for the home computer is that people can learn to write their own programs for whatever they want. There are some problems with this, however. Most people have good reasons for not becoming programmers. They don't have the time; they hate the kind of detail that programming involves; they have more interesting things to do. Putting a computer in every home will become unsatisfying once the novelty has worn off—unless these computers can provide interesting and valuable services for the average person who is not a programmer, who isn't going to become a programmer, and who never will need to write the kinds of programs that professional programmers do using today's programming languages.

THE HOME COMPUTER: WHAT IT UNDERSTANDS

When you buy a computer, big or small, its understanding is limited to programming languages such as BASIC, Pascal, COBOL, and FORTRAN. These languages are really only programs themselves, and all programs are known as *software*. The software for these programming languages translates the programs you write so that the computer can execute them. The computer also can run programs, written by someone else, which do some specific task. If you type words or sentences that are outside the language the software enables the *hardware* to understand, you will get no response—the computer will not understand you.

If you ask the computer to help fix your broken lawnmower in the language that comes naturally to you, by typing in, *My lawnmower won't start. Can you help me fix it?*, the computer will respond with the same error message it would use if you had asked it to help you create a good recipe for sweet-and-sour pork:

WHAT?

Unless you have found some lawnmower-repair software or Chinese cooking software (assuming such software existed) for your computer, it will not understand you when you ask it for help in repairing your broken lawnmower or in making dinner.

In order to respond appropriately to such a question a computer must first of all know enough English to understand what you have asked. On top of that, it must know something about mechanics or Chinese cooking. But the computer you can buy in a computer store hasn't been programmed with principles of internal combustion engines or of Chinese cuisine. It doesn't even recognize the words you have used. The reason for this is simple enough: No one has been able to figure out how to program this level of understanding very well.

The language a personal computer *can* understand is very primitive: There are perhaps two dozen commands that the computer has been programmed to recognize. For example, if you type,

BASIC

the computer will wait about a second while it loads a program that allows it to interpret commands written in the programming language BASIC, the first line of which tells it to respond with

READY

Now you may type commands that are "written in" BASIC, a very primitive programming language. Again, there are but a handful of commands—LIST, RUN, SAVE, DELETE, CATALOG, and so on—the computer will understand. You might set out to write an interesting program, but it could involve only the operations that can be expressed in BASIC. It quickly occurs to you that the number of expressions the computer can interpret is very limited indeed. Interacting with this computer is going to mean using a vocabulary of at most a few dozen expressions and symbols.

You could program the computer to play games; however, you are impatient, and you didn't buy a computer because you like programming. It would take you hours just to write a tic-tac-toe program. Besides, game programs written in languages like BASIC are very slow and take up a lot of space in the computer's memory. Most game programs you can buy in the store are written in machine language, a far more complicated and far less English-like programming language than BASIC. It takes weeks to learn machine language well enough to write a good game program using it. So, you run back to the store to buy some ready-made game programs and educational programs, but even these will bore you after you've run them a few times. The home computer isn't powerful enough to run very interesting programs. The game software you buy is really just a series of commands someone else has written down, and running the same program again and again is like reading the same book over and over—the more you read it, the more predictable it becomes. You might just as well have bought a video cassette recorder and some good movies. You have learned rather quickly that today's personal computers lack the ability to transform our lives, as is implied by their manufacturers in full-color advertisements.

Before we dismiss the phenomenon of home computers entirely, we have to note that there really are some potentially valuable uses of home computers. One is the educational software that we mentioned in passing above. There is the potential for an educational revolution there, and I'll discuss this issue further in Chapter 9. A second is word processing. No one who writes a great deal will be buying ordinary typewriters for very long. Once you have used a good word processor, it is hard to stop.

The last, and perhaps most important potential use, doesn't have to do with home computers exactly. One of the most useful features of a home computer is its capability of tying into other computers. Computers that have large amounts of data stored in them, from data about stock prices to data about sports records, could be accessible to anyone at home who has a computer terminal. What prevents this access now? First, these data bases aren't readily available to individual consumers. The second problem is that even if you can find a data base that is of interest to you, you have to learn a "query language" in order to access it. Once you need to learn ten different query languages in order to use ten different data bases, your enthusiasm quickly fades. Getting the information you want can be very arduous indeed. The solution? Read on.

LANGUAGE: THE REAL PROBLEM

The real problem with today's computers is that they don't understand us when we use language the way we are used to. When we sit down in front of the computer, we can tell right away that we aren't interacting with an intelligent entity that understands our words in the ways we intended. How can we tell when the computer understands what we say? How do we determine that the home computer understands even the restricted language it has been programmed to understand? How do we know that our personal computer has been programmed to understand the words RUN, LIST, SAVE, and DELETE? By the simple fact that when we say RUN, the computer runs the program we are currently working on, and when we say SAVE, it stores the program and lists it when we say CATALOG. The extent to which the computer *understands* is precisely and only the extent to which it responds to what we say in a way we expect.

For example, when we type in,

Bill cried when Mary said she loved John.

what is it that assures us the computer does not understand us? How do we know it doesn't have the intelligence to associate any meanings to this sentence? Because it doesn't respond, or responds with an error message, such as

WHAT?

But what if the computer had been programmed so that it could respond to the example sentence in one or more of the following ways?

Bill, Mary, and John are characters in a story.
Bill is sad.
Bill probably loves Mary.
Bill probably thinks Mary doesn't love him anymore.
John probably loves Mary.
Does Mary love Bill?
How are Bill and John related to Mary?

If the computer could give these responses, we would assume that it had understood what we said, at some level. The level of understanding might be very shallow indeed. For example, it is very easy to write a program in BASIC which will respond only to the sentence, *Bill cried when Mary said she loved*

John, with any or all of the phrases above. But we immediately would notice that merely changing the sentence to *Bill cried when he heard what Mary said,* brings back the telltale sign that the computer doesn't understand:

WHAT?

There is a difference between merely matching or displaying a set of English sentences in response to a specific initial English sentence and *understanding* the meaning of such a sentence. But what is the dividing line? When does mere pushing around of meaningless symbols inside the computer become understanding? If it were possible to get a computer to respond reasonably to sentences such as the above, could it be said to *understand* them? We already have created programs that enable a computer to respond to such phrases at fairly deep levels, in different syntactical arrangements, and with different expressions for the same events. It is hard to claim that the computer understands what *love* is or what *sadness* is. It is hard for most people to claim that they understand what *love* and *sadness* are. But we can claim that we have made a significant step in getting the computer to make the kind of connections and inferences that most people would make when given the same sentence. A person given the sentence *Bill cried when Mary said she loved John* might well respond with some of the examples given above. He would be unlikely to respond with phrases such as

> Bill must be a dentist.
> Bill's shoes are too tight.
> Mary's new car gets good mileage.

Indeed, if he did give such responses, we would assume either that he had not understood what we had said; or that he knew these things really were relevant in some way that we did not; or that he was being funny; or that he was unintelligent, or even insane. The point is that there are certain responses to even a short phrase out of context such as *Bill cried when Mary said she loved John,* which humans arrive at through processes that can be modeled on a computer.

With all this in mind, we can see why a computer would have to have very sophisticated language processing software in order to respond to a sentence such as the one we have been discussing. There is no way we can expect programming language software such as BASIC, Fortran, or COBOL to understand English. Programming languages are not simply highly stripped down versions of human or "natural" languages. Programming languages allow *only one* way to say things, with a specified syntax and a very limited vocabulary, allowing no ambiguity. Programming languages enable the computer to understand instructions for moving various symbols around, and to decide the order in which such commands should be executed. It is not possible, in a programming language, to discuss something, voice an opinion, or elaborate a point. The representation of abstract ideas and of concrete events is the province of natural languages alone.

The computer's ability to understand anything is merely a function of our ability to program it to do so. If we can program it to understand English and to respond to sentences and stories with the kind of logical conclusions and inferences an average human would make, this would be quite an achievement. But before we even tackle such a problem we will have to learn how humans understand such sentences and form their responses to them. What is language and how do humans use it? What does it mean to understand a sentence? How do humans interpret each other's messages?

HUMAN LANGUAGES

Language is a complex phenomenon that can be seen, on the one hand, as a fairly rigid framework for expressing ideas and, on the other hand, as a flexible representational system that allows a speaker to express anything he wants. We constantly are saying things to each other and understanding each other at different levels and in varying ways and degrees.

Humans use thousands of mutually incomprehensible languages. While most people use the Arabic numbering system, most do not, however, speak Arabic, Greek, or even English. Within the group of English speakers, the majority would agree on what the word "horse" represents (although the tiny minority of horse experts, trainers, and breeders would differ greatly in their understanding of what *horse* represents). But it is very unlikely that two people would ever agree on what the word "love" represents. In general, the most problematic "things" we try to represent are distinctly *human* things or ideas, such as "justice," "virtue," "democracy," "beauty," and so on. No two humans have the same views or feelings about these "things," and this fact severely limits our understanding of one another when we use these representations. Our views often are simply too complex and too diverse to put into words or representations that another person can fully understand. As if this didn't complicate things enough, we also change our views and feelings about these kinds of things as we grow older and have more experiences. At every turn we change our minds and contradict ourselves. Perhaps it is a great miracle that anybody understands anybody else at all, even when the subject is limited to horses.

With all this in mind, the goal in getting a computer to understand a natural language such as English clearly cannot be to get a computer to understand what "love" or "truth" or "beauty" are and then tell us the answer. No human really understands what any other human means when he uses these words or tries to explain what they mean, so it indeed would be surprising if a computer could exhibit this level of understanding. The fact that people don't understand these abstract concepts in the same way doesn't prevent people from understanding the more practical, everyday uses of language to communicate wants and needs. You don't have to understand what "truth" or "beauty" are to ask a traffic cop how to get on the highway. But you do have to have a basic ability to understand the cop's language.

Much of our communication concerns concrete and simple concepts. We understand statements like *Pass the salt please* and *I'm hungry* without too much difficulty. Programming a computer to process this portion of our communication just the way we do is possible and is potentially of great use.

UNDERSTANDING IN ACTION

Imagine that we open a strange book and read the following sentence:

> Yellow dreams sleep unembarrassed in the trajectory of the
> expedition.

We could say that this sentence doesn't mean anything, even
though it conforms to the rules of English grammar and syntax.
We also could say that we cannot make sense of it; that it is
nonsense. We might note that the sentence *is* language, and not
just random markings of some chemical caused by geological forces.
We might assume that someone might have constructed it with
one intention or another, and that it could mean something after
all. If we determine that it has no meaning, then we ignore it and
go on with whatever else we want to do in life. But if we decide
that the writer of this sentence had something in mind that we
can interpret, we face the task of *understanding* it. How do we go
about doing this?

Our ability to understand language—that is, our intelligence—allows us to say almost anything we want about this sentence. To begin with, we easily could associate or relate various
things to the sentence and come up with many possible meanings
for it. For example,

> Dreams are yellow because they often happen at sundown.
> *Yellow dreams* are actually little alien creatures from outer space,
> who need sleep like any living thing. The expedition could
> be on a trajectory because it is really a kind of projectile fired
> from a cannon.

Obviously, there are many possible interpretations of the sentence. While the above associations aren't even compatible, we
can continue to try to make sense of the passage. We could write
a whole page of meanings for the passage and invent a story
around it. Our intelligence is flexible enough to enable us to say
literally anything we want about it. We are story writers whenever we read, even without taking up pencil and paper. Someone
might protest that the story isn't a *true* story because it refers to
things that don't exist. But someone just as easily could say that
there never has been a truer story. Someone might say that the
sentence above isn't truly a story, but rather a poem in one line.

Our ability to understand the sentence lies in just how we

associate meanings and add our own ideas to help find a meaning for the original sentence. In order to understand the sentence we had to use quite a substantial amount of knowledge—knowledge of dreams, sunsets, emotions, sleep, ballistics, and so on. New meanings for the words *yellow dreams* and *expedition* even were created in an effort to make sense out of the original sentence, based on our knowledge of the possibility of *alien creatures* and of an *expedition* which might be on a trajectory because it is in fact the name of a bullet or projectile. Someone reading this may have already made a connection between *alien creatures* and *expedition*. The expedition might be on a trajectory not because it is a bullet but because it is a group of people in a spaceship who are searching for the alien *yellow dreams,* who might be *unembarrassed* because they sleep in the nude but have not learned guilt. And all of this from the original sentence, *Yellow dreams sleep unembarrassed in the trajectory of the expedition!*

We understand what we read by adding it to what we already know; a new meaning is always a product of a previous meaning. Understanding a sentence involves all the knowledge we have so far acquired about what goes on in the world. The more knowledge we have about the world, the more experiences we have had, the better equipped we are to find possible meanings for whatever sentence, paragraph, poem, or story might come our way. Language is not in itself knowledge, but it is a medium for expressing and organizing what we think we know, which is really only what we believe or feel at any given time. When we decide a sentence has a meaning and start to look for it, we are saying to ourselves, *Whoever wrote this sentence has some knowledge and this sentence must be his or her attempt to communicate this knowledge.*

The phrase "language understanding" is really very misleading because we don't understand language per se. We can understand only *particular uses* of language, such as in the above example. The most important elements of our understanding process have little to do with the rules of language as they have been discovered by scholars of linguistics. If all we relied upon were "the rules" of language (whatever we might say they are) then everyone would understand the same sentence the same way. The simple fact that two people can understand the same sentence in completely different ways should tell us that there is far more to language understanding than decoding the syntactic structures that a given language uses.

Language understanding is a highly individual process. We understand by relating the meaning of a sentence to our own knowledge and experiences. This is why getting another person to understand exactly what we mean when we say something is often such a challenge. We all have different experiences and consider different things to be possible or true. We don't all have the same *knowledge*. We don't all have the same desires or the same beliefs. Every person's knowledge is different from every other person's, even people who think they agree about everything. Some people know that abortion is a bad thing; some people know it is not. Some people know that God exists, some people know He does not. Our knowledge is really what we have learned and experienced over the course of our lives. A fourteen-year-old who has never had a good teacher and can't read *knows* that school is a frustrating bore, while one who has had inspired and caring teachers all her life *knows* that school can be challenging and fun. What we know is really only what we have learned through our experience of the world. The reason we all have different knowledge is simply because we all have had different experiences.

Imagine that you are doing a close friend's laundry. When you empty all the pockets a scrap of a torn-up letter falls out with the following sentence on it:

Bill cried when Mary said she loved John.

Imagine also that you don't know who Bill, Mary, and John are, and that the rest of the letter is missing. It would be easy to say that this sentence has much more meaning than the *yellow dreams* sentence. It is simple to conclude that Bill loves Mary and that he is very sad because she loves John; that John loves Mary; that Mary might not want to see Bill anymore; and that Bill might try to pick a fight with John because he is jealous. But it is equally simple to conclude that John is Bill's brother who has just died in an accident, and Bill has been moved to tears because of Mary's expression of love. In forming these interpretations we employ our knowledge of such things as psychology, love, the male ego, why humans cry, and of some of the possible situations where such a scene could take place—all of this based on what we have experienced ourselves. We can make many assumptions about the surrounding facts, and could continue to make them all day. Mary might be Bill's mother, and John might be his father, whom Bill hates for taking up his mother's time. With our immense storehouse of experiences to use in interpreting the sentence, the possibilities are endless and we could generate an entire book simply by searching our experiences and free-associating them to this sentence.

If we think about it for a moment, it really is quite crazy to infer that Bill cried because of Mary's words, *I love John*. There are probably hundreds of people who wouldn't have cried when Mary said these words. But we know that people don't generally cry unless they're emotionally excited for some reason, and when we think of a reason for Bill to be emotionally excited in the above sentence, based on what we know about people from our own experiences, we hit upon the inferences we discussed above. It wasn't the event of Mary saying *I love John* that caused Bill to cry, but the event of Bill thinking sad things as a result of believing that Mary loves John. In simple terms, we use our knowledge of what can cause what to interpret the sentence. Imagine that the sentence had been even less informative:

Bill cried when he heard what Mary said.

How are we able to interpret this sentence? What is the process we go through in concluding, for example, that *Mary must have said something awful*, or *Mary said she hated Bill*, or *Mary said Bill's wife had died*? We know of many things Mary might have said to Bill to make him cry. However, most people's experiences of what can cause what would make it very difficult to imagine that Bill cried because Mary said *pass the salt please* (unless, of course, she had previously been mute—there is always an "unless" in understanding).

Now imagine that you find another scrap of the letter and discover that the sentence above had been preceded by the following passage:

Bill is passionately in love with Mary and can't stand the thought that she is married to John, who often comes home in a drunken rage. Mary has been seeing Bill in secret for weeks, but she's frustrated by his oversensitive and depressed character, and tired of his incessant demands that she leave John. She's tried to tell Bill that she loves him, but not the way she does John. She told him how much she wants to help John get over his alcoholism. Bill cried when Mary said she loved John.

You now have much more knowledge about the circumstances of the scene as it originally was written. In simple terms, you have a *context*. The chances of arriving at the story above after reading only the last sentence out of context are very slim. Context makes it much easier to understand a sentence, and since most sentences, whether written or spoken, have some kind of context, we don't waste our time trying to make every single likely inference based on all the experiences we have had that could possibly relate to the situation. When we are told by a friend that *Bill cried when Mary said she loved John,* we usually know the people involved and why such as chain of events might occur. We already know the context, and can rapidly form high-level assessments of what is going on and why. If we didn't know the people involved, we would respond with a slew of questions— *Who's Bill? Is he in love with Mary? Is he a crybaby?* and so on. In both cases we would *understand* the sentence, but the difficulty of making meaningful interpretations of a sentence out of context would compel us to ask some questions in order to create a context.

Now that we have more of the story, our picture of what is happening can be much more detailed. In effect, we use our experience of the entire paragraph to understand the last sentence. We also use our own storehouse of personal experiences to understand the paragraph and to evaluate the scene as a whole. For example, based on some experience we might think it unlikely that Mary would see Bill at all if she didn't love him, or that she would be so devoted to a husband who is an alcoholic. But someone else who had had such an experience might think it plausible, normal, and likely that Mary be able to love John and not Bill. Someone might conclude that Bill is too emotional and demanding and that Mary is just as well off staying with John, if she loves him and thinks he can get better.

WILL COMPUTERS EVER UNDERSTAND AS WELL AS WE DO?

This discussion should give some idea of just how complicated the knowledge is that we bring to bear in the process of understanding everyday sentences. Do computers need all this knowledge in order to understand English sentences? It seems clear that they do. How, for example, could a machine really be intelligent about advice that it might give, in any area of expertise, without possessing a thorough understanding of the consequences and effects of its decisions? How will machines help us find whatever information we need without our first having to teach them everything they need to know to read and to understand what they read? Is it all hopeless then? Should we give up on intelligent computers as merely a fantastic idea in the science-fiction writer's mind? No. Our progress in getting computers to understand language has thus far demonstrated that there is a real prospect of creating intelligent computers that can understand and respond to almost anything we might say to them. It won't happen tomorrow, but it will happen.

Computers are and will be an important part of our lives. The computer is an electronic device whose development is still in its infancy. Its value to us lies in its potential uses, and one of its most important potential uses is in the modeling of human intelligence. The key to improving the usefulness of computers for everyday people is in the development of programs that enable the user to ignore the computer's inner workings, and to ask whatever he wants without having to learn anything more than where the on/off button is located.

Computers that can understand us when we use our natural language will shape the lifestyles of the future and, more importantly, change the way we view ourselves. Learning about some of the key problems in our effort to get computers to understand language is far more valuable to the average person than learning to program in BASIC. We must look at what this effort can teach us about being human, and what the impact of intelligent computers on our lives will be.

This book has a twofold message for people who want to know what computers can conceivably be made to do. First, intelligent machines *are* possible. Second, they are not here yet, nor will they be here in the very near future. It is very hard for the nonspecialist to assess the world of difference between what is here now and what will be available in the future, particularly when everyone from moviemakers to TV newscasters wants us to believe that we already have very intelligent machines. A person in today's world does not need computer literacy. What is needed is the ability to differentiate reality from overstated claims. It is important to understand what kinds of intelligent computers are possible in principle, and how the computers of the future will affect us and the world we live in. A computer revolution may indeed be taking place, but it is a very *young* revolution.

This book is an effort to clear up some of these confusions. What is relevant about today's computers? What is important to know about tomorrow's world of *intelligent* computers? What must happen in order to make intelligent computers? How will the world we live in be affected as we progress from today's computers to those of tomorrow? And, most importantly, why should we care?

CHAPTER TWO

REVOLUTION
OR
EVOLUTION?

The automobile is a piece of technology that bears great similarity to the computer in its history, its ability to transform the whole of society, and its impact on our daily lives. When cars were introduced in the earliest part of this century, and when computers were introduced in the latter part, people felt that something tremendously new and important was afoot, something that would transform their world. In both cases people developed extremely hostile views on the one hand, and wonderous excitement on the other.

The first users of cars and computers had to struggle to make these completely new machines operate within the limits of the systems that were designed for an earlier world. Even though the first cars were actually just motorized versions of the horse and buggy (minus the horse), the majority of people were not prepared for these vehicles. Drivers of the first automobiles had to solve innumerable problems: The cars had to be crank-started, primed, choked, and shifted by hand; oil had to be changed daily. Driving was so complex and strenuous back then that the car owners who could afford to do so often hired a driver, and sometimes even two. The imagination that created cars was grounded in what was most familiar to that era, consequently, automotive technology developed very slowly.

The computer industry's perspective suffers from the same lack of creativity and long-term vision. Computers are severely limited by the world views and ideas that have preceded them. The current shakeout in the computer industry demonstrates that manufacturers weren't capable of competing even on an unsophisticated level. Those companies that didn't make sure they came out with a little more memory, a little more software, a little better graphics every four months or so went bust. This shakeout proves once more that the average American is just a little smarter and a little more demanding than the manufacturers must think. American consumers already are bored with what computers can do at the moment; yet we are still naive about what computers could do in the future. In this impressionable condition, we are being urgently counseled to become computer literate, and are being warned that the Japanese fifth generation project might spell disaster for the American computer industry. As I explain later on in this book, it is my contention, however, that there are more significant issues in the world of computers for people to concern themselves with than merely learning to program or how to compete with the Japanese.

Another similarity between the computers and automobiles is the extent to which their earliest users had to become experts in the technology behind the machines in order to operate them. Those who were successful at learning the new concepts and techniques that went along with the first cars and the first computers became the first true believers in the new technology. The early car driver was more than just a driver; he became, by necessity, an expert on the principles of internal combustion. Early computer users had to know everything about the internal structure of the computer, from knowing where to plug long cables, to replacing vacuum tubes and programming the machine to do even the most rudimentary tasks.

As cars and computers became more widely used, supporting technologies evolved, transforming the car expert and computer expert into a car driver and computer user. With a few simple modifications today's cars can be operated by the handicapped—a very important indicator of just how far we have come since the days when you had to be rather athletic and technically informed just to *start* the car. Even though computers are in their infancy, these kinds of supporting technologies already have started to emerge. Today's computers rarely require new circuits; they don't break down as frequently as the very first computers did, and can restart themselves when they do. Even children now can learn to use a computer.

Most importantly, both automobile and computer technology have promoted an overwhelming revolution in society. We only began assessing the long-term effects of the automobile once it already had made significant changes in our society. Similarly, it is nearly impossible to estimate the ways in which we already have been affected by computers, let alone what the long-term effects of this technology will be.

The people who build and use computers today, from the big machines used by corporations to the home computers used by kids and their parents, maintain the same *Model-T mentality* as the early users of cars. We tend to think that the Apple or the IBM PC is the computer we are going to be using for the next 50 years. We look at popular software today as if it is the software we will use for the rest of the century. We must realize that computers are in their infancy.

ARTIFICIAL INTELLIGENCE

The nature of the computers of the future, and the impact they will have on our daily lives, will be determined by what happens in the field of Artificial Intelligence both in the next few years and in the next several decades. Intelligent computers are likely to have a much greater effect on our lives than dumb ones, and developing intelligent computers is the sole province of Artificial Intelligence research currently underway in a few universities and some industrial laboratories.

For a long time Artificial Intelligence had been an elite subject, studied by those few who were the possessors of both massive computing power and a curiosity about the nature of thinking. As computers became more available to the general public, the natural curiosity that most people have about themselves as people can lead most anyone to wonder what exactly one has to do to get a machine to reason. This book is more about Artificial Intelligence than it is about computers. The reason is simple enough. To understand what computers can really do, in the long run, one must understand Artificial Intelligence.

*Artificial Intelligence (usually referred to as AI) is perhaps more difficult to put in perspective than the computer itself. AI tends to be an elusive subject. Artificial Intelligence is best understood as an **evolution** rather than a revolution.*

There are several subfields of AI research, including robotics, automated vision, automated problem solving, expert systems, and natural language processing. The goal of natural language processing is to give the computer the ability to understand natural language. My colleagues and I at Yale stress this aspect of AI research. This subject area addresses fundamental issues about the nature of what it means to understand in a way that other areas of AI do not. Being able to communicate with computers in our own language will change the whole nature of who gets to use computers and what they will be able to use them for.

Today even the most user-friendly, commercially available systems only respond to a few English-like words in very restricted ways. Any novice who has begun to use a computer has spent a huge portion of time trying to find out what words the computer has been programmed to recognize. The work of learning the restricted language that today's computers recognize is so frustrating to most people that the computer manufacturers have had to develop "touch" screens with pictures (usually referred to as icons) representing the user's command options. This somewhat decreases the computer's opacity to the new user, since a symbol can be seen for each possible command. But whether we must type in the word "delete" or press a picture of a garbage can, the idea that computers can be intelligent or might understand our language the way we do seems a far-off notion. Nevertheless, we are being given the impression by the media that intelligent computers are here and that they will be in control in the future.

We should neither praise nor denigrate computers. Computers themselves are really not the issue. If we want to understand what the prospects for intelligent computers truly are, and how these computers will affect our lives, we have to look at ourselves, not computers.

PEOPLE ARE AMAZING, NOT COMPUTERS

The power of the human mind is much more impressive than the power of the computer. Intelligence is an incredible, complex combination of the ability to formulate an idea; the ability to draw an inference and interpret the meanings of others; the ability to develop a personal belief from one's own experiences; the ability to formulate a goal, and a plan to achieve that goal; the ability to learn, to change, to create, and so on. These are the fascinating questions of human intelligence. AI forces one to find out what all the questions are, and to address them all; it is an intrinsically *human* subject.

The goal of building an intelligent machine forces one to deal with the fundamental problems of human intelligence. A computer is a machine that executes instructions. It does just what it is told. When a computer carries out such instructions it does so only because someone has given it, in gory detail, a complete specification of every step of that process. If the programmer has left out even one tiny step in the process the program won't work, and the instructions will not be followed. The computer serves a valuable purpose in Artificial Intelligence research precisely because it assumes nothing. It forces the researcher to think of everything in an attempt to build a model of any human task. It is in this *thinking of everything* that the interesting aspects and intellectual power of AI lie.

WHY LANGUAGE?

Getting a computer to understand language, to learn from experience, and to make important connections in what it reads sheds light on how humans do so, and vice versa. Artificial Intelligence thereby probes the ancient problems of the philosophy of mind.

Natural language processing will eliminate the need to become computer literate or to learn even one programming language. Although AI researchers hardly can claim to have solved all the problems of human intelligence, they are beginning to be able to apply some of the early parts of the solution to real-world problems. We currently have the ability to endow a computer with a mechanism that enables it to make sense of some simple sentences we type into it (see Chapter 7). We haven't even begun to envision all the possible applications of these systems in the daily lives of people in the real world.

Products derived from AI research have just started to emerge and the world is starting to take notice. At the same time personal computers are becoming ubiquitous and people are concerned that technology is somehow getting beyond their grasp. We are at a pivotal point in the computer revolution; unfortunately, we don't know how to tell the reality from the hype.

The moment that new ideas and methods from AI research started to come out of the universities and to be developed into marketable systems, big articles in news magazines appeared with titles like "The Thinking Computer is Here." Even unfinished research programs written in the universities have been touted as "intelligent." This kind of press has the potential to mislead everyone (including the AI researchers themselves) into thinking that AI researchers have solved all the puzzling questions of human intelligence. We have built programs and prototypes that model some parts of intelligent reasoning and language understanding within a restricted area. But we haven't even come close to building a complete model of human understanding and intelligence; nor has the computer industry taken the best approach to developing products from what we have discovered so far.

No standards currently exist for assessing the intelligence of a machine. This is an utterly new problem for society, ushered in by the computer and AI research. Ten years ago we simply did not need such standards; today, we do. How do you tell the difference between a real understanding system and a personal computer that has the word "smart" on its box? People are always approaching me with fantastic stories about someone in some garage who has built a household robot that understands you, cleans your house, puts your kids to bed, reads them a bedtime story, and greets friends and strangers at the door. When I tell them it's a lie, they ask me how I know. I explain to them that there are certain stages we have to go through in modeling these forms of human understanding, and that the leaps in scientific understanding about the nature of thought that are required will take many years of very hard work.

We need some idea of what levels of machine intelligence are possible and what intelligent systems might actually be built over the next 30 years. If we are going to be interacting with these machines, we will have to understand them, and this means knowing precisely to what extent they understand us. AI researchers explore the basic questions of human intelligence and build models of intelligence on computers. They are engaged in an ongoing intellectual adventure, a continual thought-experiment. In order to see how AI can change our conception of the computer and of ourselves we need to examine its evolution more closely.

THE EVOLUTION OF ARTIFICIAL INTELLIGENCE

Artificial Intelligence has been an academic discipline in a handful of universities for almost 30 years. But AI really began the moment the first computers were developed. The history of Artificial Intelligence inevitably recounts the saga of the ways that computer scientists and others have grappled with the problem of getting a computer to be intelligent. The constantly changing definition of Artificial Intelligence reflects the different approaches that AI researchers have taken over the years.

Early AI researchers felt that if they could get computers to do things that intelligent people could do, such as playing chess or proving mathematical theorems, then that would *be* Artificial Intelligence. People who are good at chess are usually quite intelligent. So, the argument ran, it follows that if you can get a computer to be good at chess, then the computer can be said to have some intelligence too. Researchers in the 1950s assumed that intelligence lay in logical and mathematical thought, as if these were the only critical elements of human intelligence. (This may have had something to do with the fact that many of the early AI researchers were initially trained as mathematicians.) But an important aspect of intelligence is not that a genius can play the logical and mathematical game of chess but that people who are not considered to be very bright can talk, learn, understand, and explain their experiences, feelings, and conclusions. Talking is incredibly complicated. A man with a low IQ is not stupid. He's incredibly intelligent compared to other animals and present-day computers.

These early AI reserachers were determined to get a computer to play chess. They began by telling the machine how to compute every possible move and countermove for each turn, to see which combinations of moves led to the best result. When computers became more powerful, that is, faster and with larger memories, the chess programmers were able to make their programs consider more and more of the possible outcomes for every move they made.

Chess programs began to get very good. But the moment people succeeded in writing good chess programs, they began to wonder whether or not they had really created a piece of Artificial Intelligence. The programs played chess well because they could make complex calculations with extraordinary speed, not because they knew the kinds of things that human chess masters know about chess.

Such programs did not embody intelligence and did not contribute to the quest for intelligent machines. People don't go through every possible outcome every time they move; they intelligently produce far more sophisticated algorithms than we have yet been able to figure out how to give a computer. A person isn't intelligent because he or she is a chess master; rather, that person is able to master the game of chess *because* he or she is intelligent.

It isn't the limitations of computers that prevent us from creating chess-playing computers that use sophisticated human-like algorithms. It is just that AI researchers haven't yet figured out what those algorithms are.

Today, AI researchers have started to ask questions about the real nature of human intelligence. We are trying to define precisely what it means for humans to understand, to learn, to think, and to change over time. This seemingly simple shift in approach actually makes a profound difference for the definition of AI and for the course of AI research. Rather than concentrating on a specific task, such as getting a computer to play chess, we are addressing the essential theoretical and philosophical questions of human intelligence. This attitude reflects the two basic approaches to Artificial Intelligence research that have evolved so far: the product-directed or technological approach, and the theory-directed or scientific approach.

The product-directed approach is essentially a throwback to the early days of AI research. The early chess programmers were product-directed in their approach insofar as they felt that if they only could produce a chess-playing computer, it would be intelligent. The product-directed approach is concerned mainly with the technology of getting computers to do a range of things that are quite fantastic in human terms. Since this technology embodies some form of *intelligence* it naturally could be seen as a part of AI. But it is sometimes rather tricky to draw a line between a technological advance that is AI and one that is not.

Advances in AI really do have the possibility of creating significant changes in our lives. With simple new technologies, what you see is all you get. A chess-playing computer will not have as many cosmic and long-range effects. A computer that solves complex problems in general, conversely, would have possibilities that could make any computer revolution very real. It is important to be able to tell the difference.

THE AI LABEL

What is often touted as a breakthrough in AI may only be an advance in creating some particular technology. A product-directed researcher feels that a computer that could do A or B would be *intelligent*. When this researcher finally gets a computer to do A or B, the task itself is demystified. What once seemed complex and intrinsically human all of a sudden seems to be simple and mechanical because a computer has done it—and in an uninteresting way at that. So, one more problem slips away from the scope of AI.

Artificial Intelligence is redefined every time we get closer to developing a well-structured theory of mind. AI constantly evolves a new set of questions about what and why people do what they do. Each attempt to answer these questions increases our knowledge of what we are after; at each stage, we find out more about what we didn't consider properly at the previous stage. It is even difficult for AI researchers to agree on what constitutes a legitimate advance in AI. We cannot label every advance in software or robotics as AI. The central problem in AI has little to do with expert systems, faster programs, or bigger memories. The ultimate AI breakthrough would be the creation of a machine that can learn or otherwise change as a result of its own experiences.

TOWARD AN INTELLIGENT COMPUTER

The theory-directed approach to Artificial Intelligence concerns the representation of knowledge, learning, and human thought processes. We are concerned with finding out what people know, how they use what they know, and how they learn what they know. We are also interested in testing our theories of mind by constructing models of mental processes on a computer.

In its theory-directed mode, as was pointed out before, Artificial Intelligence is really just a new term for the ancient enterprise of the study of mind, which must be tested at every stage. The only way to know that we have developed an accurate theory of natural language processing is to create a program or build a machine that tests the theory. One can see what goes wrong with one's initial theory, and then improve it. AI thus is very close in spirit to philosophy, linguistics, psychology, and a host of other fields—except that AI tests its hypotheses on a computer. AI researchers build models, see what goes wrong with them, and move on to the next project that expands the scope of the earlier one. Each project teaches us what the next one should be by showing us what we have forgotten or misunderstood.

EXPERT SYSTEMS

The distinction between product- and theory-directed AI, between technological and scientific AI, is a new one and is not accepted by everyone in the field. The distinction between these two approaches is important because AI's recent debut in the public arena has centered around an outgrowth of product-directed AI, namely *expert systems.*

As a descriptive term used by AI researchers, an expert system is a fairly clearly defined type of program. But, like most AI terms, the words "expert system" are loaded with a great deal more implied intelligence than is warranted by their actual level of sophistication. The popular use of the term by the media also tends to give people the impression that an expert system is equivalent to a human expert in a given field, or that all AI is concerned with is the construction of expert systems. Neither of these is the case.

Today's expert systems are, for the most part, derived from the product-directed approach to AI. They are products designed to respond to demands from particular industries, and are not a test of anyone's theory of human cognitive processes. The programmers who devise these systems interview real human experts in the particular technical field and even occasionally become experts themselves in order to create the expert system.

Expert systems are not innovative in the way that real experts are; nor can they reflect on their own decision-making processes. The builders of expert systems try to reduce an expert's knowledge to a set of if/then rules in a program. The program interacts with a user in such a way as to guide the expert system through its chain of rules until it reaches a conclusion. Consider a hypothetical medical expert system for diagnosing liver cancer. It asks the doctor for an orderly set of data about a patient—vital statistics, blood test results, liver function tests, abnormal cells, and so on—and draws a conclusion by using the rules it has been given. Its rules might allow it to conclude *the patient has cancer,* but if you ask it *What's cancer?* or *What do you think may have caused it?* it will respond in a very non-expert way:

WHAT?

Such a program can have rules for diagnosis and still not understand, in any real way, the nature of the domain within which it is dealing. It works according to some of the *rules* of medicine, but it can *only* work according to the rules. The expert system is organized, but it has no self-organization ability and it cannot change as a result of its experiences.

Expert systems are horribly misnamed, since there is very little about them that is *expert*. They are an application of current AI work on finding out what kind of knowledge people have and how to represent that knowledge. To some extent, they do capture the knowledge that various experts have and thus can be quite useful in certain circumstances. But the reason we value human experts is that they can handle a situation in which events have taken a new twist, one that doesn't fit the textbook rules. Expert systems, while potentially useful, are not a theoretical advance in our goal of creating an intelligent machine. Real intelligence demands the ability to learn, to reason from experience, to *shoot from the hip*, to use general knowledge, to make inferences using gut-level intuition. Expert systems can do none of these. They don't improve as a result of experience. They just move on to the next if/then rule.

Useful expert systems can be written for some fairly straightforward applications, such as determining whether someone meets the requirements for a bank loan, because we really can come close to compiling all the details that go into making such decisions. There isn't as much experience-related decision making, nor critical learning, in devising an insurance policy for a person as there is in medicine, because policy rates and exemptions are more or less literally interpreted, or should be.

Unfortunately, expert systems have been hyped beyond all recognition to the point where they are hailed as the vanguard of intelligent machines that are just around the corner, which they are not. We might, in a decade or two, develop "expert systems" that actually do approach human cognitive abilities within a certain field, but not if we oversell what we have today. These systems are bound to disappoint potential users because expectations for them are so high.

Suppose you wanted to create a program to help you cook. Your first instinct might be to buy several highly acclaimed cookbooks and systematically store all the recipes they contain on a personal computer. But the value of a computer program that stores hundreds of recipes would be the same as the value of having many cookbooks, no more and no less. It might be nice to have a computer terminal on your kitchen counter instead of lots of books, but that is a matter of personal taste. Such a program would no more be an automated chef than the cookbooks would be a "printed" chef.

It would seem logical that the more recipes we could store in this program, the more potentially useful the program would be, if only by saving the kitchen from the clutter of books and magazine clippings. Computer memories are now large enough so that we could easily store 1,000 or even 10,000 recipes. But there is one serious problem here: organizing the recipes so that you can find them when you need them. A computer (or, for that matter, a normal cookbook) with a thousand recipes in it has to have some kind of indexing system to make it easy to find the recipes you want. Distinguishing important index categories from unimportant ones is part of what any computer programmer must think about if he wants to make such a recipe program useful. With a poor indexing scheme, the more recipes the program has, the slower it would be in finding the one you want.

One common non-AI indexing scheme is called "keyword" indexing. It indexes a recipe under a handful of key words that appear in it. You might index recipes under national style, ingredient, time of preparation, food group, or any number of categories. Some elements of each recipe are obvious candidates for entry into the index, such as the main ingredient or the spices used. Other elements of a recipe are useless as index categories. If you want a recipe for beef, you might get 1,000 recipes if you used the keyword "beef." Narrowing it down from there would be an arduous task. One classic problem in such systems (called *information retrieval systems*) is that they can provide too much information, which can be even more annoying than getting too little information. You'd probably end up going back to your favorite cookbook in which you know there are a dozen or so reliable beef recipes. If you have to do this, the computer hasn't contributed much to your lifestyle, has it?

What would an AI program be able to contribute to such a situation? A content-based indexing scheme might be developed that depends on the categories people commonly use for describing the meal they want to prepare, such as *a spicy Chinese beef dish*. An AI version of this recipe collection would enable the organization of the recipes in such a way as to make them more easily accessible and more potentially useful. Or, we could program the computer to scan each recipe for certain items, such as tofu, peppers, or hamburger meat. Instead of reading a long index and then telling the computer which entries we want, we simply could sit down at the computer and type *broiled whitefish* and the computer would display the names of dishes with broiled whitefish. We then would type the name of a recipe that sounded good and it would be displayed instantly. If we spent enough time at it, we might even program it so that one could type *whitefish/ shallots* and receive only the recipes of whitefish dishes flavored with shallots.

AI people currently are developing good classification schemes, and some day we may see an application of these techniques that would allow a computer cookbook to be on every kitchen counter. Today's personal computers, however, don't have enough memory to be useful as massive storage devices. There are plenty of computers available that are big enough, of course, but they are much too expensive to make us want to replace a good collection of $20 cookbooks. As soon as it gets cheap enough to build them, we probably will see such devices. Yet, like expert systems, such work is a spinoff of AI.

If we want a computer cooking advisor, we have to develop a computer that really *knows* about recipes and cooking. The problem has nothing to do with the number of recipes we can store. A cooking advisor might not have *any* recipes stored. What it would have to have is the ability to create a recipe on demand. A computer chef wouldn't know 1,000 recipes. Instead, it would know principles of cooking. You could tell it what ingredients you have available, and it would reason on the basis of what it knows about cooking. It would create rather than recite a recipe for dinner. It would explain in great detail how you should prepare the dish, and answer any questions you might have, even elementary ones such as *How do you broil something?*

Such a program would have to have an enormous amount of information; yet this information would be entirely different from a list of stored recipes that any computer can print out on a screen. A cooking computer advisor would have to understand the rules and principles of cooking for every national style and personal taste, from Thailand to Mexico and from nouvelle cuisine to macrobiotics. When you ask it, *What do I cook for dinner?*, it replies, *Well, what do you have in the house?* You could tell the computer, *I have a chicken, onions, mushrooms and tomatoes.* It would put the ingredients together in combinations that make sense to it. It might ask *Do you want stuffing?*, *Do you have rice to go with it?*, *Do you have tarragon?* and so on. You could tell the machine anything about your eating habits, for example, *I hate tarragon, I'm allergic to gluten,* or *I'm on the Scarsdale Diet.* You would only have to tell the machine once, and it would never again bother you with tarragon, gluten, or high carbohydrates. The machine would be a great help to anyone trying to stick to a restricted diet because it can create new and interesting meals, enough for an entire family of picky eaters. Indeed, such a machine could teach you a great deal about cooking. If you invited five people for dinner and all you had in the house was peanut butter and jelly, you would have to go shopping. But before you went, you could consult the computer chef, tell it what you felt like cooking, and ask it what ingredients you should buy. It would create a recipe, tell you just how much to buy for the number of people you were serving, and suggest a good wine. Owning a machine programmed to do this would be like having resident master chefs in all the major cuisines.

The computer cooking advisor represents the level of intelligence AI is trying to program into computers *today*. The underlying principle of this effort is that to write this smart cooking program, you don't have to know about computers, you have to know about *people*. You have to discover the knowledge about cooking that real cooks use when they decide what to cook and how to cook, and you must formulate this knowledge in a way that can be programmed into a computer. If you learned a few *principles* of cooking, without memorizing a single recipe, you might have an extremely valuable knowledge of cooking. You would be more intelligent than before. In the same way, an intelligent *computer* chef has to know *human* principles of cooking.

The general approach of AI today should be to discover the thought processes that humans use for various intelligent activities and to program computers to perform these processes. AI will produce software that will, in fact, transform our lives. A recipe program that is just an indexed library doesn't change anyone's life. But a recipe program that arrives at a recipe based on individual requirements and tastes can change people's lives, not drastically, but in a fun way.

Like the car, the television, and the telephone, computers eventually will be so commonplace that we won't even notice them or think about them that much. Using the computers of the near future will come as naturally to us as driving a car or turning on a television. We just will talk to them and they will answer. We won't have to log in, or even punch keys. They will be voice activated and will become attentive when we address them and ask them something. They will be programmed to respond to a wide range of questions the average person might need answers to. Do you need a certain book? Tell the computer *I'm looking for a book.* It will respond, *A book on what subject? On dinosaurs,* you may reply. The computer will communicate with the public library computer to get its file of all the books on dinosaurs, and then go through it with you until you find one that suits you. It will display text and photographs, even moving images. You could easily spend 20 or 30 minutes just looking at card-catalog entries under *dinosaur* at the library, but a computer with a general language understanding ability could summon all the books on a certain subject to your home in a matter of seconds and help you analyze them. In a library you might spend hours getting books out and flipping through them to see if they are worth reading in depth. But an intelligent computer might enable you to select a few good books out of hundreds in seconds. It wouldn't just store the text of these books. It would be able to read them and to perform cognitive tasks with what it read.

All of this is not as far away as one might think.

CHAPTER THREE

UNDERSTANDING AND INTELLIGENCE

We really have no standards for measuring intelligence other than by observing the behavior of something we suspect is intelligent. A rat that gets through a maze very fast and remembers the correct route is considered to be more intelligent than one that is slow and forgetful. We cannot help but assume that a child who understands college physics is more intelligent than one who cannot understand simple arithmetic. Most children can learn simple arithmetic. Most children cannot understand college physics. We find ourselves speaking of intelligence in terms of understanding.

What does it mean to *understand* college physics or, for that matter, simple arithmetic? Understanding generally implies an active process of interpretation. Two people might be *intelligent* but that doesn't mean they *understand* each other. Many *intelligent* humans do not *understand* one another—husbands and wives, parents and children, capitalists and communists, and so on. Two people or two groups might not understand each other because they speak different languages, or because they cannot agree on something—some set of words or values, or the interpretation of some representation. They might have conflicting views and feelings. They might not identify with one another. People sometimes *feel* they understand each other when in reality they do not understand each other's views at all.

Understanding seems to be a very complicated notion.

UNDERSTANDING UNDERSTANDING

Understanding can be seen as responding to a stimulus of some kind. We have toyed with the idea that when a computer responds to certain commands or symbols at any level, in a consistent way, it can be said to *understand* at that level and with a given consistency. We know that most computers only respond to a few different words, symbols, or typed instructions, such as LIST, RUN, SAVE, + and = . From a certain point of view, namely that understanding means responding appropriately, today's computers *understand* these words or symbols. When these words are typed the computer will respond with *output.*

And yet the concept of understanding is more complex than just stimulus/response. It is very difficult to estimate the level at which someone or something is understanding us. How can we tell whether a computer has understood a newspaper article on the Middle East when we type it onto the screen? Would the computer be understanding if it responded *This is a newspaper article on the Middle East*? If we then typed in an article about a coup in Chile and the computer responded, *This is an article about a coup in Chile,* the computer would appear to understand at some level. How would we detetmine that level? By asking it questions and observing its output. We would have to discover just how deeply it could understand what we were saying. A human can understand the words LIST, RUN, and SAVE on many levels and within a huge context or structure. We have far more ways of interpreting these words than computers do. We can understand stories and essays in which thousands of different words are used in millions of different combinations.

Each of us would understand one of these stories differently from one another. Understanding is a highly individual process. Our individual experiences can so affect our understanding that we can seem to *misunderstand* when we are really just understanding *differently*. Two people who read the same newspaper article on a subject as broad as the Middle East can produce strikingly different interpretations of the article. The two readers need not be of different ethnic or religious origins in order to disagree. It isn't necessary that one person be a Palestinian and the other an Israeli. Two Jews from Brooklyn are quite capable of coming to blows over their different interpretations of the situation in the Middle East. Palestinian factions have spent much of their time waging wars on one another over *their* differing understanding of what various actors in such stories are doing and why.

Whence comes all this difference of opinion? Why does everyone misunderstand? Because everyone has their own individual set of goals by which to measure and judge such things as Middle Eastern affairs. Even if we were to decide that one person's understanding was *better* than another person's understanding, this would still only be *our* understanding of the situation. If we really think about it, the problem is not that people don't understand a given subject or situation, but that they don't understand it in the same way. Every individual has his or her own individual understanding based upon his or her own experiences. This has the effect of convincing us that other people, who have had different experiences, misunderstand the world completely.

Understanding what other individuals say and how other individuals feel is a much more complicated activity than understanding how to bake a cake. To get a glimpse of some of this complexity, let's look at the example of reading a story. Millions of people have read the novel *The Catcher in the Rye* and have understood it. Thus, there are millions of ways to read this book, or any book for that matter, and no two people will read it in exactly the same way. Just as people use different words for the same feelings, people often use exactly the same words to describe completely different feelings and thoughts.

At the simplest levels of understanding, everyone would probably agree that *The Catcher in the Rye* is a book, and that it is written in English. Most people would say it is well written, but some might say it is written poorly or simplistically. Some might say it is one of the greatest novels ever written, and some might say it's just a common piece of fiction. Some might call it adolescent trash. The question is not whether these people are right or wrong, or whether they agree or disagree; the question is to what extent they can understand each other's views.

If we consider how many possible things there are to understand in this world—books, poems, newspapers, religions, moral beliefs, emotions, laws, taboos, political ideologies, scientific doctrines, ethnic groups, sexual practices, artistic styles, television shows, commercials, and so on, we might ask, *How can two individuals ever understand each other's feelings and views about anything?* Besides being a compelling question for any person to ask, this question is obviously very important for AI research, because if we don't know how people understand people, it will be very difficult to get computers to understand people.

Understanding between humans is certainly more complicated than just responding to stimuli or learning some new activity. To begin with, suppose that understanding another person simply requires knowing what the person is talking about—being able to find a meaning for his words. If a friend came back from five years in Nepal and told you that he had joined the Hare Krishna faith, you would understand what he meant on a superficial level only if you had heard of *Hare Krishna*, knew that it was a *religion*, and had a general idea of what religion involved. But just how much more deeply could you understand your friend's new religious views? If you were somewhat religious yourself, you probably would understand his views better than someone who treated a religion of any kind as a big joke. You at least could identify with that part of your friend's religious leanings that corresponded to your own. You might ask your friend various questions to see just how deeply religious he had become. If you found out exactly why he had become a member of Hare Krishna, and could identify with his story to the point of imagining yourself becoming a Hare Krishna person under the same circumstances, given the same feelings, then you might be able to understand your friend at a very deep level.

Understanding other people involves *empathy* and *identification*—putting oneself in the position of the other person. We can identify very strongly with others of our species, and to a lesser degree with higher mammals, in proportion to their intelligence and human characteristics (chimpanzees, dolphins, apes, and dogs are easier to identify with than snakes, clams, or frogs). We can have empathy for someone who has had similar experiences and who, because of those experiences, has developed similar values, beliefs, methods of processing information, goals, and other mental processes. We can understand others in light of our understanding of ourselves.

Let's consider this another way. Understanding consists of processing incoming experiences in terms of the cognitive apparatus one has available. Our *cognitive apparatus* has two main components: the actual brain itself (the hardware, really) and the knowledge or information it contains (the software). A person brings to bear the totality of his/her cognitive apparatus in an attempt to understand the world, fellow humans, and personal mental processes. What this means in practice is that people understand things in terms of their particular memories and experiences. Specifically, this means that people who have different goals, beliefs, expectations, and general lifestyles will understand identical episodes quite differently. There is an unavoidable relativism to our understanding of the world. This is not simply a matter of differences in people's positions in space and time; it is relativism between different structures of knowledge. The more different people are, the more different will be their experiences and the knowledge these experiences allow them to form. Only when people share certain dimensions of experience will they tend to perceive experiences along those dimensions in a similar fashion.

We might consider that if two people were to live through exactly the same experiences, their empathy or understanding of one another would tend to be almost complete, leaving aside, for the moment, genetically determined differences in their brains and native intelligence. Living through exactly the same experiences is, of course, absolutely impossible. When two humans understand each other it is because they have searched their own very individual experiences and feelings and have been able to see their very different experiences in similar ways. There is an old French maxim: *Tout comprendre, c'est tout pardonner* (to completely understand is to completely forgive). If you really understand why someone does the things he or she does, to the extent perhaps that you can see yourself doing them or actually have done them, then you can forgive them for everything they do. You don't agree with them, but you can understand them at a very deep level. Such understanding is difficult to achieve. It takes a great amount of effort and intelligence to carry out such identifications. It thus is rare for two people to achieve such deep levels of understanding. Understanding is really a spectrum of relative degrees and levels.

THE UNDERSTANDING SPECTRUM

At one end of the spectrum, we have what we shall call COMPLETE EMPATHY. This is the kind of understanding that might exist between twins, very close siblings, very old friends who know each other's every move and motivation, and other rare instances of kindred spiritedness. At the opposite end of the spectrum are the most basic levels of understanding, which we call MAKING SENSE. At this level of understanding, events that occur in the world are interpreted by the understander only in terms of a coherent but highly literal and restricted structure, without reference to any other understander.

MAKING SENSE ———————— COMPLETE EMPATHY

The endpoints of this spectrum can be described loosely as, on the one hand, the understander saying to herself, *Yes, I see what is going on here, I know what it is about* and, on the other hand, her saying, *My God, that's exactly what I would have done, I know precisely how you feel.*

One way to illustrate these levels of understanding would be to think of the typical old Western, one with perhaps two or three central characters and whole armies of cavalry and Indians. When we watch dozens of Indians and cavalrymen bite the dust, we MAKE SENSE of what is happening. We know what is happening in a detached, simplistic, and clinical sense. One of the big controversies regarding the sociology of television centers around precisely this issue. We might be rooting for one side over the other, but unless we are very sensitive we don't feel much when we see these scenes. We don't understand them very deeply. Yet when one of the central characters is wounded or loses his loved one we identify strongly with him and understand him at much deeper levels. Why? Because we know much more about him. His cares and hopes, his desires and fears have been the focus of the film, and we have put ourselves in his place to some extent. We come much closer to the level of COMPLETE EMPATHY with the main character because there is much more material about his life for us to relate to our personal experiences. If the film were to portray the despair of the families of all the dead cowboys and Indians (assuming this were possible in two or three hours) it would probably be too painful to watch. If we were shown all the consequences in these Westerns, we would identify with all the characters and, to some degree, perhaps even the horses. In short, to understand people you have to know about them, about what they do, about what they feel, about what they want, and what they say.

Two individuals might approach COMPLETE EMPATHY if the experiences of the individuals involved had caused very similar memory structures to have been created. The two individuals would understand each other in terms of their own memory structures. Given a set of similar goals and beliefs, individuals might process new episodes in much the same ways. The above caveat is very important. Similar experiences with different goals and beliefs still would result in a different understanding of the events, a lack of COMPLETE EMPATHY in understanding. By the same token, seemingly disparate experiences could lead to the formation of strikingly similar memory structures.

The more completely goals, beliefs, prior experiences, and memory structures are shared, the better the understanding between two people can be. At the opposite end of the spectrum, MAKING SENSE requires simple recognition of the terms used and the actions performed. It doesn't involve the kind of analysis and identification required for COMPLETE EMPATHY. If a friend came over to your house and suddenly burst into tears, you could MAKE SENSE of the situation by determining that he was sad and questioning him as to why he was so sad. You would understand why he was crying at the level of MAKING SENSE, but you would have COMPLETE EMPATHY for him only if you could relate what he told you to very similar memories and experiences of your own. You would have to put yourself in his place by analyzing your experiences relative to his and by allowing your memory structures to change as a result of this new experience.

What level of understanding can we hope to program a computer to achieve? Computers are not likely to have the same feelings as people, or to have the same desires and goals. They will not "be" people. The complete empathy level of understanding seems to be out of reach of the computer for the simple reason that the computer is not a person.

Given that most people fail to understand each other, it seems no great calumny to admit to the likely failure of computers to achieve this level of understanding. This does not mean that AI people will hit the unemployment lines, because there is plenty of work to be done just getting computers to MAKE SENSE of the same kinds of things of which humans can make sense. Just getting a computer to MAKE SENSE of the sentence, *Bill cried when Mary said she loved John* is very difficult. It is easy to assert that computers never will be programmed to become emotional or sentimental when reading such a sentence (and there may be good reasons for not wanting computers to become emotional or sentimental). They certainly can be programmed to MAKE SENSE of such sentences, but they won't share the human experiences of being in love or of being sad. Computers will fail to understand humans in the same way that an unmarried aunt might fail to understand her niece's desire to get a divorce. Intelligent entities, whether people or computers, can, at best, MAKE SENSE of experiences they have never had. As a more universal example, no one but a handful of astronauts (except maybe skydivers) has a deep level understanding of what it's like to float around in zero-gravity. We all can make sense of it but we won't have COMPLETE EMPATHY for an astronaut's description of floating in space unless we do so ourselves.

Computers can and do share some experiences with people. When you read a news story about terrorism, you don't feel that just because you and the terrorist share the feature of being human that you really *understand* the terrorist's actions or his views. Having past experiences that involve human feelings facilitates important dimensions of your understanding of a story, allowing you to experience it in your own way. Likewise, an intelligent computer would have its own particular set of experiences of reading and remembering terrorism stories, in addition to the principles and details of international terrorism which have been programmed into it. It would read and analyze new stories and form valuable inferences and connections using its vast number of stored memory structures. In a real sense, the computer's own past experiences could equally well be said to facilitate important dimensions of its understanding of new stories. The computer's past experiences would be different from people's past experiences, and even from other computers' past experiences. The intelligent computer would have some measure of individuality, not a human individuality, but an individuality nonetheless. Any truly intelligent computer would change over time as a result of its experiences. Its understanding of a certain story at one time would be different from its understanding of the same story at some later time.

COMPUTER UNDERSTANDING

If we make any progress in the next few years, it will be toward more sophisticated levels of understanding. We have already made great technological strides at the level of MAKING SENSE. We have developed computer programs (some of which are illustrated in Chapter 7) that interpret text in the way that a dispassionate observer might interpret it. But we are far from approaching the kind of deep-level understanding that is typical of an understanding that is truly empathetic. Computers are unlikely to experience the deepest levels of human empathy. The computer could be made to relate its understanding of your feelings and desires to its understanding of another, previous user's feelings and desires, or to its memory of your desires at an earlier session. It thus would use its past experience, but not with the level of personal involvement that humans can achieve.

The immediate question is not whether we will ever go that far with machine intelligence, but where we can aim in the short term. What level of understanding can we hope to successfully make computers reach in the next ten years? The answer is somewhere in the middle of the spectrum, at a point we can call COGNITIVE UNDERSTANDING.

MAKING	COGNITIVE	COMPLETE
SENSE —————	UNDERSTANDING —————	EMPATHY

A computer which understands at the level of *Cognitive Understanding* will be able to do some of the following things:

1. Learn or change as a result of its experiences.
2. Relate present experiences to past experiences intelligently, i.e., by making useful comparisons and by picking out important and interesting relationships.
3. Formulate new information for itself—come to its own conclusions based on experience.
4. Explain itself—say why it made the connections it did, and what *thought process* was involved in reaching a conclusion.

Keep in mind that we are talking about the middle of the spectrum, not the deep-level end. Human intelligence has proven to be so complicated that 2500 years of philosophic inquiry and 100 years of the neurosciences have been unable to crack its secret mechanisms. If we can imagine a computer that could become an expert at something simply by sitting in a classroom and listening to a professor lecture, and by reading hundreds of books, we would have a computer that approaches human levels of intelligence. Such a computer would, in effect, program itself based on the knowledge we presented to it.

There is no straight and narrow path to our ultimate goal. Each time we test our theories about intelligence, learning, and understanding we discover entire worlds of possibilities we previously failed to consider. AI is such an excellent field for studying the workings of the mind precisely because our theories about its workings are ruthlessly tested at every stage, forcing us to consider issues that at first it seemed safe to ignore.

In this way, the practice of AI continually informs the theory of AI. Our progress at every stage usually yields some piece of useful technology, such as an expert system, a natural language front-end for a computer, or a robot. These things are all mere steps along the way. Some AI workers focus on creating new technology to meet specific immediate demands, which is fine. But the exciting thing about focusing on the scientific or theoretical side of AI is that technological applications emerge from each little attempt to make machines smarter, even from failed attempts. The gap between *pure* and *applied* research is much smaller in theory-directed AI than in other sciences. In the course of testing our theories of human mental processes by trying to get machines to replicate those processes, we constantly produce new possibilities for practical applications.

No question in AI has been the subject of more intense debate than that of assessing machine intelligence and understanding. People unconsciously feel that calling something other than humans intelligent denigrates humans and reduces their vision of themselves as the center of the universe. Dolphins are intelligent. Whales are intelligent. Apes are intelligent. Even dogs and cats are intelligent. Our assessment of the intelligence of an entity depends entirely on our definition of intelligence in the abstract. The simplest and perhaps safest definition of intelligence is the ability to react to something new in a nonprogrammed way. The ability to be surprised or to think for oneself is really what we mean by intelligence, and with that definition it is easy to say that computers may some day have it. The real issue is *how much* they can have; how they might get it; whether they actually had intelligence or were just simulating intelligence; and how we would know the difference.

THE POOL-SWEEP THEORY
OF INTELLIGENCE

People who have large swimming pools often purchase a device called a pool-sweep, essentially a motorized float with long tentacles that sweep the bottom of a swimming pool. It has to be *programmed* to the shape of the pool, and then simply is left to do its work. When someone sees a pool-sweep in action for the first time, it looks very smart. It appears to go after the dirt and make its way around the pool as if it were being steered by a little man. It is indeed programmed in the sense that it has been given a set of instructions and it follows them. When we think of something as being programmed we imply that it is in some way *intelligent*, certainly more intelligent than something that hasn't been programmed, or that cannot be programmed. People are fooled initially by the pool-sweep, and only see it for what it is after being told that it's *just programmed* for one pool, and if it were placed in a different pool it wouldn't work.

In a similar way, people can be fooled initially into thinking that computers are really smart or intelligent. But even though a computer you can buy today *appears* to know what to do when you type the word LIST, it doesn't *understand* the word LIST and has no idea what the word LIST means to you. It could just as easily have been programmed to make a list when we typed the word FOOT or GRAND PIANO.

Computer hardware has no mind of it own. We have to give it one. Asking the question *Can computers be intelligent?* means asking *Is there software available that allows this machine to seem to act intelligently?* A computer is only a piece of hardware; it just sits there, waiting for some instructions to follow and some experiences to understand. The only way it can interpret what you say, read between the lines, and make reasonable conclusions is if someone figures out how to write software that does these things. The computer is waiting for humans to learn how to program the processes that embody intelligence.

Imagine an intelligent computer that has been *programmed* to read Russian newspapers and analyze them using its knowledge of Russian history and politics, or an intelligent computer that has been programmed to create recipes. These machines also would be *just programmed*, but they would be programmed thoroughly and comprehensively within a certain field and would be able to analyze information and effectively reprogram themselves whenever necessary in accordance with what they have experienced in their respective fields. They could in some sense learn from their experiences and make high-level conclusions that only experts in Russian foreign policy or Cordon Bleu chefs could appreciate or challenge.

You could ask the Russian foreign policy system questions like *What's going on in Afghanistan,* and it would give you its most recent analysis of the Russian occupation from news articles and intelligence reports it had been given to read. You could ask it *What prevents the Russians from pulling out?* It would explain to you every major reason why the Russians might not want to leave, from their desire for a stable satellite to their domestic use of propaganda about the Afghanistan invasion. It's easy to see that this machine would be no less *programmed* than a pool-sweep, even though its program would be far more complex and would understand an almost indefinite number of different scenarios and combinations of information.

Would such machines be *intelligent?* Obviously, the answers depend entirely on our definition of intelligence, and there are really two ways in which AI considers the question of intelligence in machines:

1. THE PRAGMATIC QUESTION:
    If all you want to do is create a machine which can fool 100 percent of the people into thinking it is intelligent 100 percent of the time, what do you have to do?
2. THE PHILOSOPHICAL QUESTION:
    Is the machine really *intelligent* or *just programmed?* Have we created or merely imitated intelligence?

PRACTICAL INTELLIGENCE

There is much to be said for the pragmatic question and for AI's approach to it. After all, it really is impossible to distinguish a computer that can fool all of the people all of the time from a human that can do so. People are fooled by politicians, doctors, generals, lawyers, businessmen, and experts of every kind into thinking that they are intelligent. If a computer could be programmed so that its responses were indistinguishable from those of a human, we would probably believe that the machine was as *intelligent* as a human. If this seems radical, we should consider that before we demand of AI that it explain how we are to determine that a *machine* is intelligent, we should ask ourselves how we determine that a *human* is intelligent.

When we ask *What is intellligence?* we are really only asking *What does an entity, human or machine, have to do or say for us to call it intelligent? What are the signs of intelligence?* These are very difficult questions to answer. They are among the central questions being wrestled with in psychology, philosophy, and anthropology. Many people have found their own answers for these questions and are ready to be the supreme arbiters of what or who is really *intelligent*. If we just wanted to examine the ramifications of this question, never mind find an answer for it, we would have to write two or three volumes of very dense philosophical prose. For now, let us grant the skeptics their day and admit that AI has not yet come to terms with this question any more than other disciplines.

INTELLIGENT OR
JUST PROGRAMMED?
A PHILOSOPHICAL QUESTION

We have stressed that all a computer can do is run programs. This is true, and it is an aspect of computers that will not change suddenly with some new development in computer science. No matter what the advances in computer engineering may bring—bigger memories, more sophisticated architectures and systems, faster computing—the essential fact that a computer runs programs will not change. What will change is the intelligence of the programs we write for computers to run.

The fact that anything a computer might be made to do would be *"just a program"* doesn't denigrate it. A person is just a program, too, in a way. To the extent that a person's behavior at any time is a function of his experiences, he has been indirectly *programmed* by his experiences (or, directly by parents or school). What we do at the present time tends to be a function of what we have experienced in the past. This does not mean that if everyone were subjected to the same experiences they would or should behave the same way. People are different, both in terms of native intelligence and in terms of their experiences. It is precisely because we are in some sense *programmed* by our experiences that we all behave differently and with such incredible diversity.

From a certain point of view then, humans are also *just programmed*. And from this point of view a computer is just a very slow, very literal, very spineless human. It also is just programmed, but it never rebels against its programmer. Perhaps if we could program absolutely everything into a computer, its intelligence indeed would be indistinguishable from that of a human. It would be both intelligent and just programmed.

We can take the practical approach to the matter of the intelligence of our Russian history computer and our master chef computer by asking some provocative questions: Would we expect the computer expert on Russian history and politics to be able to give us a half-decent recipe for Hungarian goulash? No. Would a computer chef even have a loosely formed opinion on the Soviet invasion of Afghanistan? No. But how do we know that a *human* expert on Russian history and politics is intelligent?

If we asked him for a good recipe for veal parmigiana and he told us that he couldn't cook, would we say that he was unintelligent? If we asked a French chef for his thoughts on Soviet foreign policy, would he be stupid if he said that he doesn't care about it and instead offered us some soupe aux legumes? Judging from their outputs, none of these computers or human experts would fool anyone if asked to respond to questions outside their expertise.

Imagine a very complex pool-sweep that has been programmed to look at *any* pool and decide how to clean it efficiently. You could just set it down next to any pool and it would look at it and decide how to clean it, based on its knowledge of pools and its principles of pool cleaning. The intelligence here would be in its ability to see and recognize dirt. This pool-sweep would be just like our intelligent computer chef or Russian policy advisor. It would be very intelligent with respect to what it has been programmed to do, but lost outside of its specialty.

If we accept the fact that most humans have only a few areas of real expertise, it doesn't seem so surprising that computers will be similarly limited in scope. It takes years of learning and studying to become an expert on Soviet foreign policy or a master chef, and not all humans are able to become experts. Most of us aren't really experts at anything, although we all have things we do best. Creating a computer that understands Soviet foreign policy or the principles of cooking is a very long and complex task—certainly no less complex than the task of training a human to do so.

So far we have been evaluating computer intelligence on the basis of response, or output. But, ideally, the test of an effective understanding system is not the realism of the output it produces, but rather the validity of the method by which that output is produced. Unfortunately, there is no way to test the intelligence of an entity by evaluating its processes. From the practical point of view, it is difficult to cut open either the machine or the human to see what either of these entities does when understanding or thinking. Doing so usually destroys the organism. Examining the *hardware* doesn't tell us much, anyway. No one yet has been able to pinpoint the location of any particular piece of knowledge in the brain. Where is someone's knowledge of his or her birthday stored, for example? In which group of synapses or neurons are the words *April 17, 1958* stored? In a philosophical vein, we do not examine the innards of other people in order to establish that they are understanding us. Most of the time we take it for granted that others like us have the ability to understand, if only because, judging from their outputs, they *are* like us and respond just as we do in familiar situations.

Determining intelligence solely from output isn't any easier than doing so by examining the process by which the output was produced. From the practical point of view it is extremely hard to test people's intelligence, even in tightly controlled experiments, because of the wide range of their possible experiences prior to the experiment. From the philosophical point of view, we don't administer intelligence tests to our friends, lovers, children, or parents to see whether they understand us. What do we go by, then, in taking it for granted that others are intelligent and understand us at some level?

There are times when we do try to assess a human's ability to understand. Schools, certain industries, the military, psychiatric hospitals and other institutions attempt to evaluate human intelligence using a variety of testing methods. From this we simply might conclude that the methods that are good for the human are also good for the computer. But people who place their faith in such testing methods are in for a shock. And the problem is reversed in the case of computers. If all we had to do to make computers intelligent was to enable them to pass some conventionalized test of intelligence, we would have intelligent computers by the thousands. It is probable that we could create a machine that would get consistently high scores on the SATs. But we are left with the rather dull observation that such a machine would not be particularly intelligent. It would be a specialist at taking the SAT, a test that supposedly predicts performance in college, but if you sent the machine to college it would be very disappointing. A machine could get 800 on a verbal SAT and still not have anything interesting to say. It is extremely difficult to assess intelligence, human or machine, from performance on standardized tests, and we should realize that we don't even know what questions to ask in order to determine the intelligence of someone or some thing.

OUTPUT IS ALL WE GET

We thus are faced with a dilemma. We would rather use something other than output to tell us if a system really *understands.* Output, however, is all we reasonably can expect to get. Despite the fact that setting out to assess the intelligence of an entity using *any* method at all is a highly dubious pursuit, it may be that evaluation of output is the most effective approach we have for estimating the degree of understanding of both humans and computers. In the end, any system, human or mechanical, is judged by its output. We do not take apart a human to look at his insides in an effort to establish that his understanding mechanisms are of the right sort. Nor is it clear what the right sort of mechanisms are.

Reliable methods for evaluating the intelligence of an entity based solely on outputs would be of utmost importance in the case of an encounter with advanced extraterrestrials. We would have no understanding of their civilization or their physiology, and the sheer problem of communication with such entities would limit sharply the accuracy of our assessment of their intelligence. Our basis for evaluating their intelligence would rest solely on the outputs we received from them, and their understanding of us would rest solely on our output to them. With precisely these considerations in mind, NASA scientists affixed a gold-plated plaque etched with information about earth to a Pioneer spacecraft. This information is formulated to perform two very difficult tasks: First of all, to signal extraterrestrials that the plaque *is* in fact output from an intelligent entity; and second, to be understood easily by another intelligent entity. The designers of this plaque are depending on any advanced life form to be able to make the crucial decision to treat the plaque as output, and not as a mere sheet of metal, and to be able to understand that output. The spacecraft is itself an output, and we also are assuming that the intelligence of extraterrestrials would enable them to see this. We can think of intelligence as the ability to see a crucial difference between the Pioneer spacecraft and some other piece of interstellar debris. Similarly, when we discover such things as the Rosetta stone, or a notched bone in a prehistoric cave, we are able to make the crucial decision that these *are* outputs from intelligent creatures, and not random etchings or markings produced by geological forces. How do we know the outputs of intelligence when we see them? By analogy to ourselves. The more an output looks like something we might have produced, the more willing we are to label it as resulting from an intelligent process.

INTELLIGENCE TESTING

Given that evaluating output is a poor but necessary method of assessing intelligence, what guidelines can we create for the evaluation of intelligence from output? The understanding spectrum is a fairly good yardstick for estimating the intelligence of either a computer or a human. We can judge the intelligence of either of these sources of outputs in terms of a place on the understanding spectrum. For example, there are at least three fairly distinct levels of understanding that we can differentiate based solely on the outputs formulated by the entity in question, be it human or machine:

MAKING SENSE
     input: news from the UPI wire
     output: a summary of the newspaper story

COGNITIVE UNDERSTANDING
     input: a set of stories about airplane crashes, complete with knowledge structures about flight, airplanes, and the circumstances of air travel
     output: highly informed conclusions about what may have caused a recent crash

COMPLETE EMPATHY
     input: remarks about a personal problem
     output: thoughts that indicate that the person to whom you are talking appreciates your situation and can help you by explaining his/her similar experiences

It is possible for computers to MAKE SENSE of what they

see because we can give them rules for how to produce certain outputs on the basis of having processed corresponding inputs. COGNITIVE UNDERSTANDING is harder because it requires us to understand how people come to new conclusions about the information they process. COMPLETE EMPATHY, however, may be beyond our capabilities. One reason that empathy-level understanding may be impossible for a computer to handle is that human output at the level of COMPLETE EMPATHY cannot easily be put into words or representations. What happens when the output is a kiss or a backrub, or a wonderfully cooked dinner, or a vase of flowers? Humans process output of many kinds simultaneously, which is just a dry way of saying that we have human bodies and use every part of them to communicate. It is very difficult to imagine a computer that could understand fully a story about being kissed or hugged and how wonderful this feels at the level of COMPLETE EMPATHY. Machines *can*, however, be made to understand such stories at the levels of MAKING SENSE and of COGNITIVE UNDERSTANDING. To illustrate the distinctions between these levels one more time, here are outputs at the three levels at which an entity might understand the input of a tender story of kissing and hugging.

INPUT:
Did I tell you about what happened with Mary last night? We were at this party drinking and talking about nothing in particular and all of a sudden we weren't talking anymore and I noticed her face was right near mine. She moved closer and we kissed.

OUTPUT—MAKING SENSE:
You and Mary were at a party. You were close to each other. You kissed each other. You didn't talk while kissing.

OUTPUT—COGNITIVE UNDERSTANDING:
Mary must like you. From what you've told me about other women you know, she is more assertive than they are. She must have felt good being with you at the party.

OUTPUT—COMPLETE EMPATHY:
That's like what happened with Cindy and me after the party. She came up to me and asked if I could give her a lift, and while we were in the coatroom she threw her arms around me and started kissing me.

Obviously, no computer is going to understand this story at the level of COMPLETE EMPATHY for the simple reason that no computer is every going to go to parties and get kissed and hugged by people. At the level of COGNITIVE UNDERSTANDING, however, a computer could make very sophisticated connections and conclusions, and could have a very complex verbal knowledge of what love, kissing, and hugging were like. It would know everything about kissing and hugging that had originally been programmed into it, and also would learn more about these things from its experience of listening to many human stories. Given the right programming and enough experience, it might understand what happens when all that kissing and hugging leads to other things.

Understanding does not fall into one of these three distinct levels all the time. Most of the time it is very fuzzy and hard to assess, as we have been saying all along. What other guidelines can we develop for evaluating intelligence from output? One very practical guideline might simply be called the Imitation Game.

THE IMITATION GAME

One of the first people to propose that the imitation of humans would constitute a valuable test of intelligence was Alan Turing, who proposed a test called the Imitation Game. (Turing was a mathematician who also was one of the world's first and most important computer scientists. His proposed test was published in the early 1950s.) Turing felt that the question *Can a machine think?* was meaningless, and couldn't really be answered properly. In place of this question, he suggested that if a person failed to distinguish between a man imitating a woman (via teletype), and a computer imitating a man imitating a woman, then the machine would have succeeded in the Imitation Game.

One of the interesting facets of Turing's Imitation Game is

UNDERSTANDING AND
INTELLIGENCE

that it requires that the person doing the testing be able to tell the difference between a man and a woman using only output appearing on a teletype machine. The implicit assumption is that there *are* differences between the responses of men and women that are discernable by teletype. Given that the problem is to get a computer to do as well at imitating a woman as a man, then the task is to get a computer to imitate a human as well as possible in its answers. Turing's test doesn't actually depend upon men and women being discernably different, but on a computer's ability to be indistinguishable from a human in its responses.

Turing never said that machines would be *thinking* if they played the Imitation Game successfully. He just said that successful imitation was an appropriate test of computer intelligence. In the subsequent history of Artificial Intelligence, two general lines of criticism on this issue have been taken up. One has been that machines never will duplicate actual human thought processes, and the other is that no matter how well they might imitate human responses they could never be said to truly *understand*. The claim is often made that the Turing test will never be passed and that even if a computer did pass it, it wouldn't prove that the machine could understand. Turing himself disagreed with the claim that it would not be passed, and regarded the second claim as meaningless.

Many aspects of imitating a human can be taken into account within the context of the Imitation Game. We can decide whether the outputs of the computer are similar to what would be arrived at by the average human. But by far the most compelling problem is that of determining just how deeply the computer could understand some input. Just as we should suspect any human who says the same thing over and over, or who sticks to a programmatic ideology, we would have to be suspicious if a computer were to do so. We would have to be on the lookout for restricted areas of understanding. We could try different formulations of the same input to see whether the entity was understanding at a fairly high level or just repeating a set of programmed responses. But how could we be sure that the machine was *really* understanding what we said, and that its responses were not merely programmed by someone who anticipated all our suspicions?

The fundamental difference between a system that merely

produces the right output and one that could be called an *under-standing system* is that an understanding system would *know what it is doing*. An intelligent program must not only do interesting things, but must also explain why it does them. Understanding means being able to relate what one is currently doing to what one has done previously, to explain one's own processes and conclusions.

If a computer could explain what steps it went through in responding to an input, it would know itself much better than many people. How could we assess such self-awareness from output? How could we tell if the machine really knew what it was talking about? We could devise an Explanation Game to supplement the Imitation Game.

THE EXPLANATION GAME

Let's look at a program that can play the Explanation Game at the level of MAKING SENSE. A famous program created by Terry Winograd in the early 1970s, called SHRDLU, manipulated blocks by responding to English commands. It could obey English commands such as *Pick up the red block next to the green pyramid*. One of the most impressive aspects of SHRDLU was that when asked why it had performed a given action, the program could explain its causal sequence of actions. It could say that it had moved a block in order to clear a space for another block, and so on. At the end of its chain of reasoning, it had only the initial command given by the user, at which point it responded, *I did that because you asked me to*. This latter response became well-known and was psychologically very appealing, precisely because of the questions it raised about intelligence.

Although it was not put this way at the time, one of the reasons why Winograd's program was much appreciated was because it understood at the MAKING SENSE level on the understanding spectrum. It understood its world of blocks as well as a human would. It would not have passed Turing's Imitation Game test because it understood nothing but blocks. Yet, within its own blocks world, it passed the Explanation Game test at the level of MAKING SENSE. It knew what it had done at any given stage.

SHRDLU was certainly more intelligent than a program that could not explain its own actions.

Each point on the understanding spectrum should have a corresponding set of requirements for the Explanation Game. A program that appears to exhibit a given depth of understanding also must be able to account for its own output at that given depth of understanding. It must be able to explain how it forms its responses at each level. Any program that effectively explains the steps it has gone through understands at the level of MAKING SENSE. At the level of COGNITIVE UNDERSTANDING the program must be able to explain why it came to the conclusions it did, what conclusions or lines of reasoning it rejected and why it rejected them, and how previous experiences influenced its response. The machine must be able to answer the question *How do you know?* at the level of understanding that a schoolteacher would reasonably expect from his students.

If we think back to SHRDLU's interesting final explanation, we can imagine a bright young schoolboy replying *I did that because you asked me to* when called upon by his Dickensian headmaster to explain his actions or thoughts. Why don't we think of such a situation as very educational? We prefer children to give *intelligent* explanations for what they do. We don't just want them to repeat what we say. We want them to understand. We must tell children *why* they should brush their teeth if we don't want them to reply, *I brush my teeth because you asked me to.* If we want machines to understand well enough to give a good explanation of what they do, we will have to tell them the reasons for doing things.

At the deepest level of understanding, that of COMPLETE EMPATHY, there is no more general test than the Explanation Game. Any system purporting to understand at this level would have to satisfy its examiner in the same way that a human would satisfy him in a similar situation. The machine would have to explain, in highly personal and intimate terms, why it had made the choices and decisions it made. Since human choices and decisions at this level are highly influenced by such things as emotion, mood, instinct, desire, and feeling, not to mention unconscious material from childhood, machines are unlikely to do well at this level of the Explanation Game. Machines will not understand us or themselves very well at this level. No machine will have undergone enough experiences, and reacted to them in the same way as humans do, to satisfy anyone that it really understands people at the level of COMPLETE EMPATHY. One is extremely lucky if one meets one or two people in one's entire lifetime who satisfy this criterion.

Another way to test whether a computer passes the Explanation Game at each level would be to tell the computer a joke. A program that only explained what had happened in a joke would be understanding at the level of MAKING SENSE. A program that actually understood that it was a joke, to the extent that it could explain what the punch line meant, what other similar jokes or situations it knew and so on, would be understanding at the level of COGNITIVE UNDERSTANDING. Finally, a program that actually found a joke funny, that belly laughed because of how a joke related to its own particular experiences, and then expressed a point of view about life which it was only just realizing, would have understood at the level of COMPLETE EMPATHY.

WHERE ARE WE GOING?

AI programs that take computers towards COGNITIVE UNDERSTANDING already have been developed. Can we pass that point? And if we can, how will we know when we have passed it? Beyond the level of COGNITIVE UNDERSTANDING, the question of what constitutes *adequate* performance in the Imitation Game and Explanation Game becomes one of personal taste and feeling rather than of science. Is this level of understanding good enough? Artificial Intelligence researchers, as well as those who might use computers for important tasks, will be very pleased to achieve the simulation of COGNITIVE UNDERSTANDING in machines. It is unlikely that we will get machines to do well at the Imitation Game or Explanation Game beyond that level on the spectrum; it is by no means clear that we should even want to do so. Although people will benefit greatly once we have achieved COGNITIVE UNDERSTANDING in machines, most people probably will prefer that whatever COMPLETE EMPATHY they receive comes from humans. AI is an attempt to build intelligent machines, not people.

UNDERSTANDING AND
INTELLIGENCE

With the objective of developing intelligent machines, ones that understand at the level of COGNITIVE UNDERSTANDING, some obvious questions arise: Where do we begin? What do we know so far? What do we still need to learn about understanding? What problems have yet to be solved? What does the attempt to build a humanlike device tell us about being human? And what will a world full of intelligent machines be like? These are questions I will try to answer in the remainder of this book.

PART

TWO

CHAPTER FOUR

WHERE DO WE BEGIN?

As I've suggested, computer literacy is like Latin: It strengthens the mind. While science has traditionally asked "What is there?" and "Why is it the way it is?" computer science asks, "How does it happen?" Writing a program forces us to specify in exacting detail how to do whatever it is that we want the computer to do.

Artificial Intelligence is the attempt to describe the processes of our mental life. Our goal is to specify the "How" of thinking. Process is what human thought is all about. Process is what computers are all about. And process is what computer literacy ought to be about.

AI AND PROCESS

Computer programming demands the skill of reducing a complex process to a set of step-by-step instructions. Most computer scientists spend a great deal of their time devising efficient algorithms for complex calculations. They attempt to find the *processes* for accomplishing whatever task they are concerned with using the smallest amount of computing time, and invent algorithms as well. But the goal at this point in the history of AI is not speed or reduction of steps. AI researchers are still trying to determine the processes that comprise intelligence so that they can begin to develop computer algorithms that correspond to human algorithms for understanding.

The human intelligence mechanisms we use in everyday life aren't always the most efficient ones, or the ones most applicable to a computer. Consider the algorithm that a three-year-old might use in order to count to 20: *Take off shoes; locate leftmost foot; locate leftmost toe; add one; locate toe to right; add one; continue until big toe; find next foot; locate rightmost toe; etc.*

A computer scientist wouldn't seriously consider solving the problems of touch and sight before attempting to find an algorithm for counting to 20. But an AI researcher might do exactly that, not in order to solve the problem of counting, of course, but to gain insight into the fundamental processes involved in intelligent problem solving. Efficiency can be the main idea when the algorithms one needs to develop are understood. But in AI we are dealing with much more complex processes that are very difficult to pin down. In the whimsical example above, an AI person would start by asking how the child determines what a foot looks like, what a toe is, what left and right mean, how to take off a shoe, and how the child infers that he should take the sock off as well. A three-year-old who can execute the above process doesn't show how intelligent he is because he can count to twenty. His intelligence is exemplified by his ability to tell his big toe from the rest of his body and remember where it is in relation to his other toes; he is intelligent because he can tell when he is being talked to and can use words as names for things.

These seem to be ridiculously simple processes. What would we think of an adult who had to be told how to locate his big toe? Even a very stupid adult is far more intelligent than most other entities in the world. It is far more difficult to create algorithms for these processes than for mathematical computations. Although the problem of developing computer programs that can count by use of fingers and toes is very difficult, it pales by comparison to the difficulty of the processes that AI researchers currently are working on.

Here is a more familiar example of mental processes at work:

1. A former student comes back after a few years and says: *I think I want to become a doctor.*
2. I reply: *What does your father do?*

What processes are involved here? It would be easy to develop an algorithm that told the computer, Any time you see the sentence *I think I want to become a doctor*, print *What does your father do?*. The "real" algorithm is surely more complex than merely firing off a prestored response to a given pattern of letters. What are the steps in coming up with a response in such situations?

To begin with, I might have used my knowledge about why people tend to decide to become doctors and what factors influence career choices. I might have considered past experiences with students and looked at my own feelings vis-à-vis my career choices. I had to estimate what kind of guidance or response was expected of me based on my perception of how confident, insecure, proud, humble, up-tight or laid-back the former student was. I might have known that his father was a great physician admired by his son, or that his father was a monster and was forcing his son to become a doctor. If the student appeared to be the shy and guarded type, I might have responded by saying *Great! When did you decide that?* to get the student to reveal more about his decision so that I would be better equipped to advise him about it. An extremely complex set of mechanisms already seems to be at work here, and we have only scratched the surface of the problem of process. We are really nowhere near the formulation of a step-by-step *process.*

The process of formulating any kind of response to a sentence uttered in a real human context involves a huge amount of knowledge of every sort: our past experiences, what we learned in school, our observations about people and things, even things we learned as children. How can AI programs begin to describe the steps in this process? The process of forming even a short response to a short statement, as in the above example, contains thousands, maybe even millions of steps, yet the human mind executes them in a fraction of a second.

While the human mind is truly a magnificent information processor, it does not allow great insight into its own processes. We don't really know how we *think*, despite thousands of years of self-analysis and introspection. The simple fact is that we are unaware of most of the processes we go through in forming our thoughts. When children or adults think, they go through processes whose steps they cannot even begin to fully describe. The success of Artificial Intelligence research depends on the discovery and modeling of those thought processes.

When a child is asked why he has said something, he often replies, *Because!* When asked the essential question *Because what?* he elaborates on his thought process by declaring, *Because because!* Children really don't have access to their own reasoning processes. The observation that a child's thought is imperfectly developed is unimportant and probably obtuse, since it is *childish thinking* that somehow always produces intelligent adults. It may even be that reaching adulthood constitutes a loss of certain learning abilities; after all, children often make connections which adults cannot make or which they find morally repugnant or taboo. Adults often are no better at describing their thought processes than are children. When an adult is asked to describe the process by which he arrives at a particular response, he can often be very inarticulate, as the examples below, taken from a man-in-the street-interview conducted by a Connecticut radio station, would seem to indicate:

> Are you concerned at all about the Soviet warships off the coast of Oregon?

> Yes, I'm concerned about their presence there, but I think I'd be a little more concerned if they were there and nobody knew about it.

> I expect that there's no more reason to be concerned about warships off our coast than there is for the Soviets to be concerned about our warships which are certainly off of theirs.

> No, I'm not, because I believe that we have subs off the Baltic Sea and I don't think that they're too worried about that. It's just a deterrent.

> Yes, I would think that those are something of concern, but I have confidence that our state department knows what it's doing in reference to that matter.

> No, I'm more concerned about the Angolians and the Iranians. That seems a lot more volatile.

THE AI RESPONSE

When we formulate a response to a remark, *What's step one?*, the very asking of this question illustrates why AI is such a difficult field. Who can tell how many steps this process takes, and where we even should begin? And how would we know if we were right? To get a computer to come up with reasonable responses to sentences, we will have to know all the steps in the *process* of understanding, thinking, recalling, and speaking, at an extremely specific level of detail.

Each step in the process can itself be a process. For example, the first step might be to decode the sounds that were made by a speaker in such a way as to realize that they formed *words*, that they are directed at me, and that I must find the meaning of these words and interpret them in such a way as to figure out an overall intended meaning.

Of course, these and other processes that we shall discuss have been the subject of scientific inquiry in one form or another for centuries. But theories that were developed before or without computers tend to be too vague to be used as the basis for computer models. Computers force us to address the problem of process which in turn forces us to be much more specific in what we consider to be answers to a problem. This specificity has helped us notice problems that had previously escaped the attention of researchers in other disciplines.

The notion of process changes the nature of what can be considered acceptable theories of the mind. What are meanings? How does one draw inferences from propositions? What is the nature of intention? The computer forces us to look at these questions from a process point of view and subsequently changes our perspective. If we propose a step-by-step description of a mental process in the form of a computer program, the computer tests our proposed theory of that mental process. If it does what we expected, then we have taken a step in the right direction. Most of the time, however, our programs surprise us by failing to do what we expected. They reveal the flaws in our initial conception of the processes involved in whatever it was that we are trying to model. We go back to the drawing board with a new, usually broader, conception of the problem. AI can be seen as a continuing evolution of theories about mental processes slowly converging on a correct theory.

Let's return to the problem of the particular process we have been considering, namely formulating a particular response. What was my first step in creating my response to my former student? Obviously, I didn't begin by asking *What's a doctor?* or trying to remember the student's favorite sport. I already have a good picture of what a doctor is, and something, some *process,* prevents me from wasting time determining whether the student's favorite sport has anything to do with his career choices. My very first step might have been to understand that this conversation is about the student's career goals and ultimately about values in life. I could have begun by examining information in my memory relevant to these broad issues. I might also bring to mind information in my memory about this particular student, especially recalling how unsure the student had been about his interests and career goals, and how impressionable he had seemed. From there I might have jumped to information I have about how to advise students using general principles about human psychology learned in advisory situations. For example, I might have decided that he really wants to be told by someone with authority what he should do. In order for me to decide such a thing, I must consider particular prior experiences that relate to this kind of situation. From there I might jump to my memories of other students who had had similar problems. I might remember another student who had to be compelled to examine what was really behind his career decisions before he was able to take full responsibility for them. I might then try to assess whether the student is strong enough to face such realizations and the responsibility they demand, or whether he really can't face anything except a pep talk. Based on this assessment, I might decide to prod the student into analyzing his career choice rather than simply agreeing with it.

Establishing a connection between the student's statement and my response requires that we outline a process, though we have been rather vague about it here. It is quite conceivable that I might be wrong in any or all of the assessments and comparisons used in the process of coming up with the response, "What does your father do?" The student might reply that his father runs a restaurant, and that he has decided to become a doctor after volunteering at a hospital and learning quite a bit of what medicine is all about. The details of this example, are, of course, irrelevant. I mention them here only to point out that the most important problem of human intelligence which AI researchers attempt to tackle is establishing specifically what the processes are that constitute human reasoning.

Human thought processes are so complex and so detailed that without a computer one could never know if all the step-by-step details of a proposed theory of mental processes actually do what they are supposed to do. The computer model serves to reveal the holes and gaps in his theories. It forces him to formulate his thoughts on how humans think in as precise a manner as possible by continually sending him back to the drawing board.

LEVELS OF DETAIL: MAJOR LEAGUE AND LITTLE LEAGUE

Suppose you asked me how to become a major-league baseball star. You would expect me to answer with some kind of list of requirements and things you should do (assuming I knew how it could be done). Quite simply, you would expect me to give you a *program* for becoming a major league baseball star. Here is one *program* I could give you:

> You become a great hitter.
> A major league team spots you.
> The team hires you.
> You hit home runs.
> You sign autographs.

This algorithm describes a process, but at a very high level. And it's fairly accurate in the sense that if you were able to execute each step, you would become a star baseball player.

You might have a problem with this program, however. You might complain that the execution of the steps isn't clear, that I've left out all the steps in between. You would be quite right in asking me to give more information: How do you become a great hitter? What's a home run? How do you play baseball? How do you hold the bat? If I answered these questions in more detail, I would be giving even more programs—smaller, more detailed ones that are subroutines (smaller programs in service of another program) of the first five steps, which are themselves subroutines for becoming a major-league baseball star.

The point of all this is that at the highest levels of description everything can be stated simply, since it assumes all the lower levels of understanding. The five steps to baseball stardom I gave above are simple to read and memorize, but understanding what they mean and being able to carry them out requires a familiarity with all the lower levels of detail assumed in each step. You would have to have a high-level of understanding in order to follow the steps.

Now, if I were to offer you a program for becoming a major-league baseball star at a very low level of detail, it might start with the following steps:

Put on your socks and shoes.
Put on your pants.
Go to a baseball stadium.
Find a piece of wood of the correct weight and size for batting.
Swing it in an arc to hit a leather-covered sphere of string.

At this level of description it's going to take a long time to describe how to become a home-run hitter. I would have to describe how the ball moves, how to stand when hitting, timing, placing the ball, running the bases, how to make the pitcher lose his cool, and all the other fine points of baseball. These steps would be accurate in the sense that if they were understood and carried out they might produce a major-league baseball star (assuming the pupil also had the requisite physical abilities). But if someone who is already a major-league baseball star read all these steps, he might find them to be inappropriate and probably even incomprehensible. While he may be aware that he always puts on his pants before he plays, he may not be aware of the exact angles and thrusts associated with throwing a ball accurately.

We do not have to dredge up or formulate all the steps down to the very lowest level of detail every time we want to do something. While we can easily perform many highly complex activities, we have a fairly difficult time understanding in step-by-step terms just what it is we are doing. When we read we are understanding at a very high level of description. We don't even think about lower levels of description—in simple terms, we are *unconscious* of them. When we go to a restaurant, take a bike ride, or go fishing, we don't go around analyzing and rehashing everything we do right down to the level of what brain waves to set off.

Programming a computer to understand and follow a step-by-step program is much more difficult than getting a ten-year-old to do so. First off, a ten-year-old understands English, while a computer can only understand commands written in a programming language. A computer's experience is extremely limited; it doesn't have the background knowledge about fun, games, sports, competition, language, or even physics that a ten-year-old has. The computer starts out at the very lowest level of detail there is, and must be told everything. A computer can follow step-by-step programs at these extremely low levels of detail far better and faster than a ten-year-old. But try programming a computer to hit a nice slow underhand pitch in one afternoon of little league practice. Many people who coach little league have had the satisfaction of seeing a ten-year-old nonhitter become a hitter in one afternoon, relying only upon ten or twelve programmatic verbal steps and perhaps a demonstration from the coach and, of course, the amazing ability to learn from experience. Clearly people have some advantages over machines.

Let's get back to the problem at hand, namely, answering the question *How do you become a major-league baseball star?* An AI researcher who also is a little league coach on weekends might have to answer just such a question from an eager ten-year-old. The AI person would immediately ask himself: What's the right level of description for becoming a home-run hitter in the case of this ten-year-old? He would have to estimate how much baseball the kid knew from playing with friends, watching TV, reading *Sports Illustrated*, and so on, and would respond at some level that the child might understand. He might decide that a ten-year-old is not likely to understand certain aspects of professional baseball, such as the politics of being spotted as a free agent, looking for an "in" at a club, and so on. Every little league coach consciously or unconsciously goes through exactly this process of deciding on which level of detail to explain baseball to children. Some little league coaches are more sensitive to their kids than others, and some are more articulate. Some use demonstration and some prefer verbal descriptions. But only a little league coach who was also an AI researcher (in reality or at heart) might spend her time trying to understand how these levels are determined and why they're important. These are the aspects of language, description, and learning that interest people in AI (as well as contemplative little league coaches).

Certain levels of understanding are harder to accomplish than others. Take the example of a hypothetical computer command, LIST. We might use it to make a list of data such as the batting averages of the players on a baseball team. We type into the computer LIST REDSOX, and we are given a list of the batting averages for the Red Sox. It turns out that in computer programming, lists are needed so often that almost all computer languages contain some kind of list command. It tells the computer to remember the stored locations of certain data such that it will display the first item next to the second item, and the second item next to the third, and so on. The LIST command is a set of step-by-step instructions at a very low level of detail which the computer follows in the process of making a list.

At its most basic level, all a computer can do is turn switches on and off and light up dots on a TV screen. If we had to tell it what switches to flick and what dots to light every time we wanted it to do something, computers wouldn't be very useful. Fortunately, programming languages allow people to use a higher level of description to communicate the processes they want executed on the computer. The language allows the computer to understand a higher level description by providing a process for translating it into the on/off low level description that is built into it.

PROGRAMMING LANGUAGES: WHAT THE COMPUTER DOESN'T NEED TO BE TOLD

A programmer translates what he wants the computer to do into terms that it understands. Usually this means translating one's wishes into a high level programming language. If the programming language on your computer could execute a command called

TAXABLE INCOME after you entered in all of your financial information, it is because someone else has spent the time figuring out how to explain all the steps in that operation in a lower-level programming language.

We don't have to articulate or think about all the levels of detail in everything we do. We don't think in terms of muscle movements and synaptic messages when someone asks us to shake hands. We learned to shake hands at one time, but we no longer remember or think about the details of the operation unless circumstances force us to. HANDSHAKE is a program we execute without breaking it down in terms of all its intricate details, such as locating the hand to be shaken, putting our hand in exactly the right location and exerting the right amount of force in the right direction. When we learn to play tennis, we are told to *swing* the racquet instead of being given a detailed set of muscle movements to execute. A good tennis teacher tries to "program" us in a fairly high level programming language, namely English, rather than in a lower level one that is much harder to use, such as a description of the physics of muscle movements.

The operations that a computer can execute are embodied in the programming languages it can understand. Any time you wish to break new ground in computer understanding you have to figure out how to explain everything to the computer in terms it already can understand, namely, a programming language at a lower level. A programmer is someone who is familiar with the levels of understanding which computers so far have been given. He knows how to give the computer instructions which it can interpret at the levels it already knows. A computer scientist is someone who attempts to find new ways to get computers to execute programs more efficiently or new ways to enable people to communicate with computers more effectively.

In contrast, AI researchers attempt to raise the level of understanding that computers have. We are trying to make computers understand people who aren't computer scientists. AI is raising the minimum level of explanation that computers require so that the computer doesn't need to be told all the surrounding details every time we say something to it.

One way to explain all this would be to look at an actual programming language. But since most programming languages were written for computers to read, it is best for our purposes to invent a new, hypothetical programming language that is read easily by people. This language has the same basic style as most programming languages.

Imagine that you have a two-year-old child who has the understanding ability of an average digital computer instead of an average two-year-old child. (The processing ability of a two-year-old's brain so far exceeds that of a computer that this hypothetical comparison is a bit demeaning to the child, but we will let that go for the moment.) Our hypothetical two-year-old responds to a set of commands exactly the way a computer would. He has no mind of his own. He does exactly what he is told to do, but he only understands commands in the programming language he knows. We can only tell him to do things in terms of his programming language, by defining new commands in the terms that he already knows.

Let's assume that the child's programming language has in it the following command with the following definition:

MOVE (bodypart, direction, speed)

The child/computer knows the names for the parts of the body, can recognize directional words, and has a scale of speeds at which it can move. To get our child/computer to move a bodypart we must say MOVE, followed by the name of a bodypart, followed by a direction that we want it moved toward, followed by a speed of the motion. There are a few other commands in the two-year-old's programming language:

GRASP(object)
START(action)
STOP(action)
OPEN(object)
REPEAT(action)

Using this handful of simple commands, we can begin to create more complex ones. What kind of complex commands do we want to create? If we tell our two-year-old *Eat!* it won't know what to do. We don't want to have to spoon feed the two-year-old forever, so we set out to define EAT:

```
EAT(food) = REPEAT(
            START (MOVE(hand, food1, slowly))
            STOP ((MOVE) (when hand is at food))
            GRASP (food)
            START (MOVE (hand, mouth, slowly))
            STOP ((MOVE) (when hand is at mouth))
            OPEN (mouth)
            START (MOVE (hand, inside of mouth, very
                   slowly))
            STOP (when in mouth)
            OPEN (hand)
            START (MOVE(hand, food2, slowly))
            REPEAT ((MOVE (teeth, food, slowly)(until
                   chewed))
            REPEAT ((MOVE (throat, food, slowly)(until food
                   in mouth gone)))
            (until food is gone from plate))
```

Fortunately, we don't have to tell a real two-year-old all this to get him to eat. He has powerful instincts that compel him to do the right things with his mouth and swallowing mechanism from the moment of his birth. But if we did have to tell a two-year-old how to eat, the above program would be woefully inadequate. The above program has not been *debugged* and it needs to be.

Any program needs two different kinds of *editing* to fix errors and problems. The first kind of debugging, *linguistic debugging*, means making sure that everything you said to the computer can be understood by the computer. We need to make sure that all the statements in a program are valid statements in the programming language we are using. For example, we haven't defined what *food in mouth gone* might mean in the eating program. The programming language as we defined it does not know what to do with those words. We haven't explained what *until* means, or *when*. The programming language contains three actions, MOVE, GRASP, and OPEN, but it doesn't know what *chew* could mean.

Writing a set of instructions in a programming language is similar to trying to translate something into another language, such as French. If you know how to write French properly, there's rarely a problem. But if you don't, an understanding problem arises that resembles the situation with our two-year-old/computer. The Frenchman who is to understand your bad French is an intelligent human being. He can attempt to figure out what you meant when you said something even in very bad French. He uses his own knowledge of the world and of what you as another human might want to say to help himself make sense of what you said.

Our child/computer, conversely, has no knowledge of the world to help it figure out what you meant when you said *until chewed*. The machine will just fail to understand you, period, the way a Frenchman might if he wasn't too interested in what you had to say in the first place. If you write Fortran badly or BASIC carelessly, you are on your own. The machine will not tell you, *Hey, you left out a step between lines 73 and 74*. If we had a computer that possessed enough knowledge to say this kind of thing to us, it could program itself.

This introduces a second kind of debugging, conceptual debugging, that involves the restructuring of poorly formed thoughts. Conceptual bugs are incomplete commands that don't tell the understander everything it needs to know to do something right. These are more difficult to locate and to solve than linguistic bugs. An inexperienced programmer often assumes that the machine will know what her intentions are and thus will fill in the steps she left out and will behave reasonably.

The eating program for our two-year-old has quite a few serious conceptual bugs. The programmer assumed that the child/computer would know that he should close his mouth after opening it. But the two-year-old/computer doesn't know to do that, so his mouth would remain forever open. Also, when a hand is opened to put food in one's mouth, it has to be closed again in order to leave the mouth. People know this, of course, but a machine does not. Another conceptual bug involves repeating the action of the feeding until the food is gone. After the command

MOVE(hand, food2, slowly)

there is no statement anywhere that says this action should be stopped so that the food can be grasped, or that the whole process of getting the next morsel of food to the mouth should be started, or that it should be timed in concert with the original food getting swallowed, and so on. If we ran this program, the child/computer's hand would go right through the plate on the second try and never stop.

In trying to explain to a computer something we take for granted, like eating, we are struck with the vast complexity of our most primitive actions.

AI programmers spend most of their time determining what might seem like obvious conclusions. Again and again, AI researchers have had to grapple with the same kinds of mundane problems that arose in the example of our two-year-old computer. We spend most of our time coming to conclusions that seem quite trivial. Examining the details in the processes we use in our daily lives is tedious and time-consuming work. It isn't very earthshaking to discover that you have to tell the computer what *chewing* involves, or how to grasp a piece of food and let go of it at the right time. But no computer program, and no person for that matter, will seem very intelligent without a clear grasp of the obvious.

TALE-SPIN

It took a great deal of time for AI researchers to realize exactly how much of their effort had to go into structuring our mundane world knowledge in such a way as to make that knowledge usable by the computer. After all, getting computers to play chess or to prove theorems doesn't require detailed world knowledge. But speaking and understanding does. As AI began to focus its efforts on getting a machine to *understand,* researchers ran straight into the problem of getting what is obvious to us to be obvious to the computer.

One of the best examples of work that demonstrated the need for such knowledge—and the difficulty of finding out exactly what that knowledge was about—was the program called TALE-SPIN. TALE-SPIN was written during the time that I had small children. I found myself making up stories, usually involving animals, to entertain my children at bedtime. The more stories I invented, the more I became fascinated with the nature of that invention process. At the time, our research at Yale was involved with attempting to understand the human planning process well enough to help us in our effort to get machines to understand stories that involved planning. We had written a number of programs that could read stories and paraphrase them or make inferences about what was happening in them, but we hadn't written a program that made up stories. I began to think about this problem with one of my graduate students, James Meehan.

TALE-SPIN, a program that makes up stories about animals, was written by James Meehan as a part of his doctoral dissertation. It was part of a larger effort on planning, as I have said, but it is worth considering here because it illustrates the problems involved in getting a machine to have general world knowledge, and shows how we gradually refine our theories of process until we get one that works.

In TALE-SPIN, Meehan concentrated on telling the computer in great detail about how bears might plan to get some honey, how they might try to avoid getting stung by bees, and how animals might plan their way out of the various situations that were set up for them. This work went very well. The program could generate hundreds of animal stories using its basic knowledge of the elements needed to construct a story, the elements of planning and the achievement of goals, knowledge of language structure and various modes of expression, as well as problems of personal interaction and general world knowledge.

The important thing to stress about TALE-SPIN is that it invented stories on its own. The stories weren't *canned* by us in any way. That is, stories, pieces of stories, or even sentences did not exist in the computer before the program started. The designers of the program created knowledge structures and a set of rules on how to use those structures. The program was then able to create a cast of characters and a set of situations that were problematic for those characters. We wanted to see if the program could generate some already extant stories, such as those of Aesop, using just the mechanisms of how a story ought to proceed.

In debugging TALE-SPIN, we learned a great deal about how we generate stories and how we make sense of the stories we hear. TALE-SPIN generated a great many terrible stories on its way to becoming a good story teller. These *mis-spun tales* in fact represented serious conceptual bugs at the time. Each bug was fixed, gradually, over time, but they illustrate precisely what it is that AI people have to learn in order to get machines to understand what we say.

Here is the first of the mistakes that TALE-SPIN made:

1. One day Joe Bear was hungry. He asked his friend Irving Bird where some honey was. Irving told him there was a beehive in the oak tree. Joe threatened to hit Irving if he didn't tell him where some honey was.

The computer doesn't seem to know what it has just said.

One of the first problems we faced in writing AI programs was getting the computer to have knowledge of what it has done. The computer has to be capable of understanding its own creations. In this particular case, the machine created an answer to a question it posed to itself in the course of figuring out how the story should go. But we had forgotten to give the machine the ability to interpret its own sophisticated answer.

The computer was capable of answering the question *Where is honey found?* But it could not look back at *beehive* and see that that is where honey can be found. It couldn't interpret its own answers. It concluded that Irving Bird had refused to help Joe Bear. We had to tell the machine more about beehives in order to allow it to understand that the answer it itself created was acceptable.

2. One day Joe Bear was hungry. He asked his friend Irving Bird where some honey was. Irving told him there was a beehive in the oak tree. Joe walked to the oak tree. He ate the beehive.

Unfortunately, when we made the above change we failed to do it correctly. Since the program contained a conceptual representation for *source of food* we merely told it that *beehive* was one. *Beehive* is indeed a source of food, but we forgot to mention that *source as container* is different from *source as object*. Finding a refrigerator will do when you are hungry, if you know to look inside it, and not to eat it. None of this is obvious to a machine.

In the early TALE-SPIN programs, all the action focused on a single character. Other characters could respond only in very limited ways, as in answering direct questions, for example. Unless you remember to put it into the program, you cannot get one character to *notice* what another character has done. Because of this error, TALE-SPIN created the following story, which was an attempt to produce "The Ant and the Dove," one of the Aesop fables:

> **3.** Henry Ant was thirsty. He walked over to the river bank where his good friend Bill Bird was sitting. Henry slipped and fell in the river. He was unable to call for help. He drowned.

This was not the story that TALE-SPIN set out to tell. Henry wasn't supposed to drown. TALE-SPIN decided to have Henry fall into the river so as to create the central problem of the story. Part of the TALE-SPIN's model of a good story was that it had to have a central problem and a solution, a rather simple literary theory that we all learn in school. Had TALE-SPIN found a way for Henry to call to Bill for help, this would have caused Bill to try to save him. But the program had a rule that said that being in water prevents speech. Bill was not asked a direct question, and there was no way for any character to just happen to notice something. Henry drowned since the program knew that that's what happens when a character that can't swim is immersed in water. Later, we added some rules about noticing unexpected changes of location so that Bill could rescue Henry.

The rule, *If A moves B to location C, both A and B must end up in location C*, which seemed reasonable at the time, was incorporated in TALE-SPIN when it made the next mistake. We also gave the program a rule that if a character is in a river, he will want to get out because he will drown if he doesn't. Since computers require very specific rules, as we have seen, this information was actually given to the computer as: If a character has legs it might be able to swim out, if it has wings, it might be able to fly away, and so on. Also, there were rules that said that if a character had friends, he could ask them for help. These all sounded reasonable. However, we also told the computer that a character falls because gravity moved that character. The juxtaposition of all these rules produced the following story:

> **4.** Henry Squirrel was thirsty. He walked over to the river

bank where his good friend Bill Bird was sitting. Henry slipped and fell in the river. Gravity drowned.

Since gravity had neither legs, wings, nor friends, and had been moved into the river when it moved Henry Squirrel there, its death was inevitable. To fix this conceptual bug, we changed the representation of the concept *fall* to a force *acting on* an object rather then one *moving with* an object.

Once we began to give characters an awareness of their surroundings in order to get them to notice things, the following problem occurred:

5. Once upon a time there was a dishonest fox and a vain crow. One day the crow was sitting in his tree, holding a piece of cheese in his mouth. He noticed that he was holding the piece of cheese. He became hungry, and swallowed the cheese. The fox walked over to the crow. The end.

We were trying to set up the initial situation so that the computer would make up a story like Aesop's "The Fox and the Crow." The fox had the ability to trick the crow out of the cheese, and since he would want the cheese when he saw it, we expected that the story might come out right. But when he got there the cheese was gone, since the crow also had a sense of awareness. This was fixed by adding the assertion that the crow had eaten recently, so that even when he noticed the cheese, he didn't become hungry.

6. Joe Bear was hungry. He asked Irving Bird where some honey was. Irving refused to tell him, so Joe offered to bring him a worm if he'd tell him where some honey was. Irving agreed. But Joe didn't know where any worms were, so he asked Irving, who refused to say. So Joe offered to bring him a worm if he'd tell him where a worm was. Irving agreed. But Joe didn't know where any worms were, so he asked Irving, who refused to say. So Joe offered to bring him a worm if he'd tell him where a worm was . . .

This is an example of a conceptual bug that causes an infinite loop. To debug this problem, we had to teach the computer some more about how to achieve goals. Specifically, we had to tell it not to give a character a goal if he already has it but to try something else. If there isn't anything else to try, then we had to explain that the goal can't be achieved.

As the program grew, we gave it even more rules: If a character is hungry and sees some food, he will want to eat. If a character is trying to get some food and fails, he will get sick from the lack of food. If a character wants some object, then one option he has is to try bargaining with the object's owner. One story that resulted from this new information:

> 7. One day Henry Crow sat in his tree, holding a piece of cheese in his mouth, when up came Bill Fox. Bill saw the cheese and was hungry. [Bill has just been given the goal of satisfying hunger.] He said, "Henry, I like your singing very much. Won't you please sing for me?" Henry, flattered by this compliment, began to sing. The cheese fell to the ground. Bill Fox saw the cheese on the ground and was very hungry. [Satisfying hunger is about to be added to Bill's goals again.] He became ill. [Because satisfying hunger was already a goal of Bill's, it can't be added again. Hence, Bill fails to satisfy his hunger, so he gets sick.]
> Henry Crow saw the cheese on the ground, and he became hungry, but he knew that he owned the cheese. He felt pretty honest with himself, so he decided not to trick himself into giving up the cheese. He wasn't trying to deceive himself, either, nor did he feel competitive with himself, but he remembered that he was also in a position of dominance over himself, so he refused to give himself the cheese. He couldn't think of a good reason why he should give himself the cheese [if he did that, he'd lose the cheese], so he offered to bring himself a worm if he'd give himself the cheese. That sounded okay, but he didn't know where any worms were. So he said to himself, "Henry, do you know where any worms are?" But of course, he didn't, so he . . . [And so on.]

The fix here was simple enough. We just had to add the rule that dropping the cheese results in loss of ownership.

Although TALE-SPIN used rather crude rules to establish an

Aesop's world of talking animals with human attributes, the program illustrates that the development of an understanding system requires a constant effort to find out what is going on in the world that we are modeling. The more complicated that world is, the more complicated it will be to find out exactly what processes and knowledge are part of that world. AI may indeed be the science of the obvious, but the obvious has the rather challenging ability to be very difficult to fully describe. While we seem to find it so easy to understand our own languages, we find it almost impossible to explain just how we do so. If we want machines to understand us, we will have to explain how we understand language in process terms.

EASY TO UNDERSTAND, BUT IMPOSSIBLE TO EXPLAIN

Imagine that you had set yourself the goal of programming a computer to understand sentences that deal only with the concept of trade and exchange, buying and selling, giving and taking, or transfer of possession in general. You are not trying to get it to understand Shakespeare, but merely to understand what is going on in sentences like:

John sold Mary a book.
Jim and Tom traded baseball cards during lunch hour.
Dick bought Walt's bike.
Lisa exchanged dollars for francs at the airport.
Hank and Tim swapped fishing stories.
Rich gave Susan a kiss in return for her help with his
    homework.
Burt gave Joe a black eye for calling him a name.

We already can see the difficulty of our task. No one has any trouble understanding these sentences, or coming up with obvious conclusions such as *Mary paid for the book* and *John didn't want the book any longer*. But how do you explain all this to a computer? The verbs in each sentence seem similar enough (*buy, sell, give, take, trade, exchange*), yet what is happening in each of these sentences differs greatly.

We don't imagine, for example, that Burt handed Joe a black eye that had been cut out from someone's face with a knife. We imagine that Burt socked Joe in the eye. We don't imagine that Hank and Tim swapped printed, bound volumes of their fishing stories, but that they told their stories to each other in turn. These verbs, and the concepts or visualizations which they evoke in these contexts, are evidently quite complicated. If we merely substituted the phrase *transfer of possession* for the verb in each of the above sentences, some of them would make sense and some would be real nonsense. How could Rich *transfer possession* of a kiss after Susan had *transferred possession* of help with Rich's homework? We could imagine that Rich scraped someone else's kiss off his own cheek and wiped it on Susan's cheek, but this is not really what happened. People easily make assumptions that give them the right sense of the words they encounter in a sentence, but how can we get a computer to make those seemingly effortless assumptions?

Understanding language, even such simple language as is used in the sentences illustrated above, requires knowledge of the concepts underlying what is being talked about. This isn't as obvious an idea as it seems. Early efforts in getting computers to be able to use natural language focused on what we might call the *dictionary/grammar book approach.* The idea was that in order to get a computer to understand sentences, you needed to program into it all the possible dictionary definitions of trade and exchange, in all its possible uses, and then simply program the computer to break up new sentences into grammatical units of subject, predicate, object, indirect object, and so on. The computer was then supposed to take new sentences, break them up, match their parts with the dictionary, and then spit out the matching meanings. But the dictionary definition of trade in all its possible uses is enormous. We would have to begin by teaching the computer to understand all the different uses of the concept of trade—trade as a job, trade as exchange of commodities, trade winds, trade-ins, trade-talks, trade-papers, trading cards, and so on.

This is certainly *not* the way in which humans understand sentences. What people know that enables them to speak and understand seems to be intimately involved with the notions of *meaning* rather than form. They use what they know about possession to help them understand sentences that involve that concept. Again, we face the crucial questions: How do humans understand these sentences? What is the process? What's step one?

Let's look at this question another way: How would you explain to a child what possession is? Children know only that something is *mine*. They only imagine that they possess something which they can actually hold in their hands and control, and they can't see possession as limited or subject to change. Small children cannot imagine that something might be removed from their hands and left alone, and yet still be *theirs*. They typically refuse to relinquish a cherished possession even for the short time it takes to get their pajamas on or to bathe them, despite solemn promises that their possession will be returned to them when bath time or pajama time is over. Children understand possession at a very basic level, without all of the abstractions, refinements and nuances which must be learned in the course of growing to adulthood in the company of other humans.

All the forms of trading, giving and taking we are discussing have a very strong underlying element to them, a meaning which we intuitively understand but which seems to elude us when we try to put it into words. These words generally seem to refer to the concept of transfer of possession or ownership. We know about possession and giving and taking intimately—we have a range of experiences which have taught us to understand all these different instances of a concept which is really quite difficult to put into words. What we mean when we say something is not necessarily reflected in a particular word. We can indicate transfer of possession in Chinese or Greek, or in a gesture. In countries with many different tribal languages, entire markets are organized in which all communication takes place in gestures for the simple reason that the traders cannot understand each other's words. What visualization or intuitive conceptualization enables us to interpret these *events* in all their varied forms?

If we want to get a computer to interpret varying usages of these concepts of trade, exchange, buying, selling, giving, and taking then we are going to have to provide the computer with some set of concepts that correspond to the ones that humans have. We will have to find basic conceptual elements that a computer can use to interpret sentences such as those above. We have to find out exactly what concepts we use to understand the world.

CHAPTER
FIVE

ENGLISH
FOR
COMPUTERS

If the most important thing for people to understand about computers is *process,* the most important thing for computers to understand is *English* (or any other natural language). Computers will really only become useful for the average person when they can be used by people with no training at all. We want the computer to understand what we say. We want the machine to anticipate our intentions. When we ask the computer to do something, we don't want to have to tell it any more than we would have to tell a normal person. If we have a financial adviser program and we say to the computer, *Gimme my tax liability,* we don't want it to respond with *I don't understand 'gimme.'*

English itself is only a small part of the problem. As the TALE-SPIN program demonstrated, the problem is *knowledge.* You can't talk about what you don't know; getting a machine to understand English doesn't simply involve nouns and verbs. Understanding sentences and stories in any language requires considerable knowledge of the world. The only way computers will understand us when we speak or write is if we program them to understand all the levels of detail that are encompassed in simple human utterances, such as *Get me some toast.*

If a machine doesn't have background knowledge that relates to what you are talking about, it can't understand you. An utterance such as *Get me some toast* should trigger an organized and restricted set of expectations. We would expect the speaker to want to *eat* the toast. We would be surprised if he put it in his wallet or used it to prop up the leg of a wobbly table. Understanding *Get me some toast* requires a huge amount of knowledge that doesn't appear anywhere in the sentence.

Imagine that you hire a Martian as a servant. He says he knows English, but when you ask him to get you some toast, he responds, *What's toast?* You explain to him that it is bread that has been seared in an oven, and he disappears to the kitchen for fifteen minutes. To your horror, he comes back with a large smoking mass of burned plastic and smoldering bread. You scream to him that he should take the slices of bread out of the plastic bag before toasting them. He returns having simply placed a stack of slices in the oven, toasting the top and bottom slices on one side only. You tell him that he should toast them individually. He returns holding a severely charred piece of bread, barely a cinder of carbon. You then explain very calmly to him that toast isn't cooked for so long, that it has to be lightly browned.

This nightmare could go on and on. The Martian servant isn't doing anything wrong; he just doesn't know all the steps involved in carrying out your request. He doesn't know anything about toast or cooking or bread, or eating habits, and has no expectations about what one does with toast. He has to be told the process you want him to carry out at the most excruciating level of detail.

If we don't want our computer to behave like the Martian servant, we will have to provide it with all the details required to understand us when we speak or write. To understand the sentence *Get me some toast*, it will have to know what toast is, how it is made, and that the speaker wants to *eat* the toast.

Understanding any word is difficult. For example, consider the following sentences that employ "get" in what seems to be the same kind of sentence as *get me the toast:*

Get me some baskets. (Said by a coach to a basketball
   team.)
Get me some help.
Get me some shoes.

It may be obvious that the Martian is to take the action necessary to make toast and bring it to the speaker, but in the three sentences above no "making" is required and the bringing of a physical object only occurs in the "shoes" sentence. Our Martian has to understand English to the extent of being able to understand what people might want, and that it no easy matter.

Understanding any sentence, therefore, requires the computer to figure out how to carry out the necessary steps of the action at hand. It must be able to fill in missing details that apply to the context of what it reads. And since none of this knowledge is *present* in the sentence, an intelligent computer has to *infer* it all from context. For example, suppose that next to the toaster was a fresh sandwich that the Martian had recently made. We would expect an intelligent processor to know enough about the goals of the speaker to know that he might be hungry and that this sandwich might be seen as a reasonable, if not improved, substitute for the toast. The Martian, and any computer, must know enough about the situation it is in to be able to infer the goals of the speaker with whom it is interacting. *Making inferences* about what might be true, in addition to what was explicitly stated, is crucial to understanding. Here, we are not talking about *logical inferences*. There is nothing *logically* true that says that someone who asks for toast is hungry. But people understand other people by assuming such things, and computers have to have the ability to do the same.

MAKING INFERENCES: A SIGN OF UNDERSTANDING

A computer that reads sentences and makes inferences about likely circumstances and conclusions must understand sentences at a fairly sophisticated level, at least at the level of MAKING SENSE described in Chapter 3. If a computer could read many different stories, formulate general principles and conclusions, and change these principles and conclusions whenever necessary, it would understand at a level very close to COGNITIVE UNDERSTANDING.

A great many problems in AI have to be solved before computers approach COGNITIVE UNDERSTANDING. It is quite a substantial challenge just to get computers to deal with meaning, to interpret potentially ambiguous usages of the same words, and to paraphrase what it has understood.

THE AMBIGUITY PROBLEM

Words can be highly ambiguous. Almost everything we say has many possible interpretations due to both the multiple meanings of individual words and the many possible ways that words can combine. Consider verb ambiguity in the case of the word *gave:*

1. John gave Mary a book.
2. John gave Mary a hard time.
3. John gave Mary a night on the town.
4. John gave up.
5. John gave no reason for his actions.
6. John gave a party.
7. John gave his life for freedom.

Looking at the first example, we might think that to get the computer to infer that *Mary now possesses a book* when it sees the word *gave*, all we have to do is tell it to find the indirect and direct objects in a sentence with *gave* and slap the words *now possesses* in between them, yielding *Mary now possesses a book*. This very simplistic algorithm is easy to write. But a computer that has been programmed with such a simplistic algorithm would respond to example 2 by saying *Mary now possesses a hard time,* to example 3 by saying *Mary now possesses a night on the town,* and to example 4 by saying *Someone now possesses up.*

This "simplistic program" identifies parts of sentences, takes them apart, and stitches them back together. It is not *understanding* what it reads in any sense. If you asked such a program *What's a book?* or *What will Mary do with the book?* it would have no answer. A computer programmed in this way would treat *book* as a direct object or a part of speech, and would see it no differently from *chainsaw* or *Brooklyn Bridge.* If a computer is going to understand what it reads it has to know, intimately, about people and books and giving and taking.

Now consider ambiguity in the case of the word *hand:*

1. John had a hand in the robbery.
2. John had a hand in the cookie jar.
3. John said, "Hand me a cookie."
4. John is an old hand.
5. John gave Mary a hand with her luggage.
6. John asked Mary for her hand.
7. All hands on deck!
8. Look Ma! No hands!

A computer programmed to understand the word *hand* as *a five-fingered appendage used for gripping* would understand that John in sentence 4 is an old five-fingered appendage, and that in sentence 6 he asked Mary to chop off her five-fingered appendage and give it to him. In sentence 7 the computer would infer that a ship was to be laden with five-fingered appendages, and in sentence 8 the computer might think that the speaker was showing his newly amputated forearms to his mother.

How are we going to get a computer to understand all the different usages of *hand?* What the computer "sees" is the same in each of these sentences—we don't spell *hand* differently in every different context. How are we clued in to its different meanings? We understand the meaning of a word in a sentence only after we analyze the entire sentence and relate it to things we already know. One problem here is that the meaning of a sentence is often more than the sum of its parts.

When we see the words "cookie jar" in sentence 2, we know that John *having a hand* in it has a different meaning from John *having a hand* in the robbery. We think of "cookie jar" as a material object, a glass or ceramic container into which one puts one's hand to get a cookie, and then withdraws one's hand. We think of "robbery" as something very different—the act of taking something from someone else's possession by force or cunning—and that having a *hand* in the robbery means participating in it. We don't think of "robbery" as a glass container into which one's hand can be placed. Nor do we think that someone can *participate* in a "cookie jar."

Where did we learn such subtle distinctions? Experience. But experience of what? If not direct experience of events involving cookie jars and robberies, then at least experience in reading about them abstractly and having others contribute to our knowledge of these things by correcting us when we spoke about them. We can't really understand what robbery is at the level of COMPLETE EMPATHY until we have actually experienced it. All our experiences of "robbery," ranging from what we have been told about it to memories of actual *events*, come into play when we read sentences about robbery. Sentences and stories only have meaning to us insofar as they represent *events* we have experienced (or have read or heard about) and can therefore understand. If a computer is going to understand all the different ways we have of talking about an event, it must be able to formulate an underlying representation of such events. The computer has to get back to the event.

PARAPHRASING: ANOTHER SIGN OF UNDERSTANDING

When we are told *Mary punched John,* we can easily paraphrase the sentence in many different ways, and even in different languages. We usually don't remember the original wording of stories. Our memories are not attuned to words but to ideas. Our ability to remember a story *at all* depends on our ability to form an underlying conceptual representation that is *not* tied to any words or dependent on one particular sentence. As an example, try to recall the first paragraph of this chapter. If you have been reading carefully, you may remember the ideas presented there. The words, unless they were particularly catchy, are likely to have long since disappeared.

When we read three or four similar newspaper articles about an event, such as an auto accident or an invasion in the Middle East, we are able to understand what happened despite the different ways in which the event has been described. If we are asked to recount the stories we have read, we might do so without using any phrases actually appearing in the stories. Ironically, remembering stories and paraphrasing them requires that we *forget* the words originally used and that we invent our own way of saying the stories to ourselves. We conjure up a wordless picture of what is going on in a sentence. Sometimes this isn't possible because of the obscurity of what we are reading; because of our lack of experience with the events in the sentence; or because the sentence involves an abstract concept. But we always use the gamut of our personal experiences to create a highly individual understanding of whatever we read.

Each person understands a particular story differently. This is just another way of saying that no one really reads by memorizing the actual words in a story. What he *remembers* is his own individual version of the story, what the words mean to *her*, the inferences and expectations they arouse in *her*. One task in AI, strangely enough, is to get the computer to *forget the words*.

We don't simply want the computer to forget the particular words; we also want it to remember *what happened*. This is the key to Natural Language Processing. We have to formulate some primitive conceptual tools for understanding stories. We want the computer to make inferences, to disambiguate different uses of the same words, and to understand an event described, no matter how a human paraphrases information. An understanding system, whether human or computer, has to depend on a *conceptual representation of events*, not on particular words or sentences.

CONCEPTUAL REPRESENTATION

We tend to see the world in terms of the events that take place in it. These events usually involve one or more *actions*, which we describe using the many verbs in our language. We can think of concepts which don't involve actions, such as a fine spring day, or a rock, or a fire hydrant. It's easy to say that a rock doesn't perform any actions because it just sits there and doesn't move. But we have to stop and remember that the descriptions *just sitting there* and *not moving* both refer to *actions*.

It is extremely difficult to describe an event without describing actions as well. We can say the words *rock* and *fire hydrant*. But somehow the word *rock* itself doesn't tell us much about rocks. We have to use *other* words. A fire hydrant *means* the set of actions that are called up when there is a fire. It refers, in an implicit way, to the need to stop fires from destroying objects by soaking those objects with water. If we want to describe a fire hydrant in a useful way, we must do so almost entirely in terms of actions. What can one *do* with a fire hydrant? What *comes out of* a fire hydrant? What's it *made* of? What's a fire? The actions involved in the concept of a fire hydrant are discrete and unique in that they differ from those involved in the concept of a telephone or an electric drill.

A crucial feature of any computer understanding system is going to be the way it represents actions occuring in the events it reads about. In order to make the correct inferences, the computer must have a system of conceptual representations for the kinds of actions we speak and write about.

Before devising such a system, we first must determine what events people talk about most. We have to examine precisely what actions can take place in the world and what words we use to talk about those actions. We want to tell the computer about the actions at the roots of the verbs we use. For example, what kinds of actions are really involved in instances of the verb *give?* Are they always the same? We have to tell the machine what actions are involved in the sentence *John gave Mary a book* as distinct from the actions in *John gave Mary a hand with her luggage.* Besides using the same verb for different actions, we use a great many different verbs to depict very similar actions. How do we tell the machine that one verb refers to an action that is almost, but not quite, exactly the same as the action of another verb?

We have seen that *give* and *take,* and *buy* and *sell,* are somehow related in a way that *eat* and *fall* or *walk* and *think* are not. It also seems that *give* is somehow related to *trade,* and that *trade* and *exchange* are related. How can we represent this relationship concretely enough so a computer can make use of it? A list of correspondences or synonyms (the "easy" approach taken by so many of today's programs advertised as "knowing English,") will not do. We could say that buy is like sell, but it isn't when we use "I'll buy that" to mean "I believe you." We could say that trade is equal to two gives, but it isn't when we say that a man has learned a trade. We could say that words like earn and pay have to do with jobs and money, but so, too, do make (as in "make money"), get (as in "how much did you get"), and take (as in "what was the take?").

Computer understanding is not going to be achieved using words themselves as the representation of the meanings of those words. Although it may seem plausible to have computers treat words as symbols to be matched to other symbols, people don't do this and computers shouldn't go through enormous lists of word correspondences in order to understand sentences.

Any meaning representation system, either human or mechanical, must make explicit exactly what the relationships between concepts underlying a verb are. If some set of verbs relates to the idea that someone got something, received something, or took something, regardless of the actual verb used, then that underlying concept of possession change should stand on its own as a concept.

The value of treating "possession-changing-action" as a concept in a meaning representation is that whenever a word refers to it, knowledge we have about changes of possession can come into play. In this way, the verbs *trade, buy, exchange;* the nouns *gift, present, theft;* the phrases *make a donation, buy a stock* can be understood by reference to the same primitive concept that underlies them. The idea is to teach the computer what we know about the concepts that words refer to. In this way we can let the machine forget the words and remember the concepts that underlie them.

Once we have decided that a certain concept such as "possession-changing-action" is *primitive* enough—that is, it occurs frequently in what we say and write—we can begin to teach that concept to the computer. To begin with, the concept must be given a name. If we give it a common English word as a name, it would be difficult to keep it separate from all the extra baggage that the word normally carries with it. But the name we give to a concept hardly matters to a computer, since the computer starts out with no associations whatever.

ATRANS: A PRIMITIVE CONCEPTUAL REPRESENTATION

In our laboratory at Yale, we call the conceptual representation for "possession-changing-actions" ATRANS, for Abstract TRANSfer of possession. ATRANS is just an arbitrary name that doesn't mean anything special to the computer. We could have called it anything we like: CONCEPTUAL CATEGORY1, or GIVECON, or even DWEEP27. It would make no difference to the machine. What is important is that we tell the machine how to recognize this category, and what to expect when it recognizes it. The name ATRANS is just a convenient way for us to refer to that bundle of features and expectations. Just as the human brain doesn't care what we call its proteins and neurochemicals, the computer will not care what we call the primitive conceptual representations. What matters is what we teach the computer to *expect* when it reads sentences in which ATRANS is involved.

A conceptual representation such as ATRANS provides the computer with a set of expectations. When the computer reads a sentence and sees any words relating to transfer of possession it begins to look for the set of phenomena that are normally associated with any particular instance of ATRANS: an object being transferred, a receiver of that object, the original owner of that object, the method of transfer, and so on. In other words, it begins to know what it doesn't know, and this helps it figure out what the other words in the sentence it is reading might refer to.

This expectation-based approach to understanding is best understood in terms of SLOTS and SLOT-FILLERS. ATRANS tells the computer to open up a set of SLOTS. These slots need to be filled, sort of like an empty wine rack with room for 12 bottles. Each slot has requirements for what it will allow as a filler. That is, you cannot just put any old thing in any slot. ATRANS requires an actor slot, for example, that will allow only animate objects (it prefers humans) to fill that slot. If it cannot find a human in the sentence it is reading who could possibly fill the slot, it will have to start guessing. Once we know that some object has been transferred, we know that someone did the transferring regardless of whether that someone was explicitly mentioned in the sentence. Understanding what someone says, means being able to infer what objects and actors had to be involved in the action that the sentence describes, whether or not they were mentioned explicitly.

The basic idea in understanding, whether by computer or by people, is first to figure out what concepts are being communicated and then to use those concepts to help in figuring out what else might also be the case. Once we know there was a "giving" action we know that there was a "taking" and a "receiving;" we know that there was an object and that someone now has it and will probably use it for whatever it is normally used for. Ascertaining this kind of information is what understanding is all about. To see how this works, let's look at the notion of a primitive concept like ATRANS more closely.

Let's go back to the first of our example sentences involving trade and exchange:

1. John sold Mary a book.

What's really going on here? John is transferring possession of his book to Mary and Mary is transferring possession of her money to John. There are really *two* actions being performed in this event, and there are two actors. There are two objects, the book and the money; and two directions of each action, from John to Mary, and the reverse. How does the computer represent this event to itself? How can it use that representation to make paraphrases and inferences?

INPUT:	John sold Mary a book.			
INTERNAL REPRESENTATION:				
	ACTION:	ATRANS		
	ACTOR:	John		
	OBJECT:	book	ACTION:	ATRANS
	TO:	Mary -------	ACTOR:	Mary
	FROM:	John	OBJECT:	money
			TO:	John
			FROM:	Mary

OUTPUT— PARAPHRASES: Mary gave John some money and John gave her a book. Mary bought John's book. Mary paid John for a book.

OUTPUT— INFERENCES: Mary has a book. John has money. Mary wanted John's book. John didn't want the book anymore. John had already read the book. Mary will read the book. John needed the money.

In the schematic picture of the computer's internal representation of the event, we haven't shown all the elements that the computer would require in order to generate the above outputs.

The programming for this seemingly simple level of understanding is very complicated, but we can discuss its general features. Obviously, the computer must have the basic knowledge that the word *sell* involves *money* being ATRANSed in one direction and something else being ATRANSed in the opposite direction.

When the computer generates a two-part paraphrase of the event of *sell* using the verb *give*, it effectively splits the event into two component events, and treats them as two instances of *give* instead of as a two-part event of *sell*. If the sentence had been *John gave Mary a book*, the internal representation would simply have been:

ACTION: ATRANS
ACTOR: John
OBJECT: book
TO: Mary
FROM: John

The word *give* in this context would not suggest that another instance of ATRANS and another object (money) even entered into the picture at all.

The computer can paraphrase the event using different words, such as *paid* and *bought*, because it can determine that these paraphrases also fit its internal representation of the event in the original sentence. It would not have paraphrased *John sold Mary a book* by saying *Mary ate John's book* or *John beat Mary with a book*, because these events involve actions that have *different* primitive conceptual representations from actions involving giving and selling.

What then is the point of a primitive such as ATRANS? Computer understanding requires us to teach the computer some basic concepts (or units of meaning) and the rules for using those concepts. ATRANS is one such concept. It is of value to the computer in two ways. First, once the computer discovers that ATRANS is present it can begin to expect a set of related concepts (like possession, reciprocity, etc.) to be present. In essence, ATRANS means to the computer that there are a set of rules that it must fire off. These rules include the set of inferences associated with ATRANS. A typical rule might be that if someone gets something they want they may be happy about it and may use it. Another is that if someone relinquishes control of something it may be because they got something in return that they believed to be of greater value.

ATRANS, and any other primitive, also carries with it a set of language analysis rules. The inference rules above have nothing to do with any language per se; rather, they are culturally related. They reflect the kinds of things that people do. Any culture that has the concept of transfer of possession also is likely to have most of the same inference rules (but not all) associated with ATRANS. But language is a different story. English has a set of rules about what words express ATRANS, and how to find the objects and actors involved in an ATRANS that has been expressed in an English sentence. Another language would have a different set of such rules. In English, when you know you have an ATRANS and you want to find who received the object being transferred, you look for the word "to" followed by an entity that can have things. Obviously, this rule is not the same in French, Swahili, or Zoque.

The major value of concepts like ATRANS is to efficiently organize our world knowledge and our linguistic knowledge. If you get something you have it, if you receive something you have it, if you take something you have it, if you steal something you have it, if something is donated to you, you have it. Rather than write such rules over and over again for each verb that relates to transfer of possession, we write them only once for ATRANS.

Does the primitive action ATRANS work for all the sentences involving give and take? No, because not every use of give and take involves transfer of possession. As we have seen, sentence 7, *Burt gave Joe a black eye for calling him a name,* is absurd when read in terms of transfer of possession. Although the verb in sentence 7 is *gave,* the computer would have to be able to analyze the whole sentence and determine from context that the event in this sentence doesn't involve ATRANS. It would have to be given knowledge of what a black eye is that would enable it to figure out that the use of the verb *give* in this instance did not relate to transfer of possession but to *application of force.* Just as the computer has to know about cookie jars and robberies, it also has to know about black eyes, if it is to know what to expect in a situation where someone has been *given* a black eye.

PROPEL: ANOTHER PRIMITIVE ACTION

As a further example of the issues in representing actions, let's look at a possible internal representation for the action in the sentence *John hit Bill with a stick*. What is the basic action of hitting? There are a number of aspects common to the actions of beating, pounding, punching, striking, whacking, pummeling, and so on. The general action would seem to be *application of force*, so we can devise a conceptual representation which for the sake of simplicity we can call PROPEL. (Here again, this is just a symbol for the computer which in no way relates to the English word 'propel.')

When the computer sees an instance of PROPEL in a story, it will have expectations that relate to application of force. PROPEL on physical objects might involve damage or simple movement; PROPEL on animate objects might affect the HEALTH of the animal and be met with another instance of PROPEL. The internal representation of *John hit Bill with a stick* then would be:

ACTION: PROPEL
ACTOR: John
OBJECT: stick
TO: Bill $\longrightarrow$ HEALTH -3
FROM: John

Even though the only change in the representation seems to be the primitive PROPEL, instead of ATRANS, the computer makes a completely different set of inferences about this event. It would not infer that *Bill has the stick*. Whenever the computer comes across an instance of PROPEL, it can expect an actor, an object, and a direction, just as it does for ATRANS, but its expectations about the relationships that hold between these actors and objects are entirely different.

The computer would be told that whenever it sees an instance of PROPEL being carried out TO an animate object, it should expect a change in the HEALTH of that animate object, depending on the force of the PROPEL and the nature of the object being PROPELed. HEALTH might be a kind of primitive index for the *state* or *condition* of animate objects. The computer might read the input *John hit Bill with a stick* and infer that *Bill was hurt* or *Bill cried in pain*. But it probably would not infer that *John killed Bill*. The computer might be able to distinguish instances of PROPEL that involve certain objects that affect HEALTH more than others, so that it could read *John chopped Bill with an axe,* and infer that *Bill was bleeding* and that *Bill probably died.* The computer also would have to know that if John hit Bill with an egg, Bill might be annoyed more than hurt, but the egg would certainly have *its* physical state drastically changed (whereas the stick and the axe above are probably almost exactly the same as they were before).

Our examples are getting a little gory, but let's go one step further in discussing conceptual representations. The sentence *Burt gave Joe a black eye for calling him a name* is a little more complex in terms of the actions taking place and the expectations they should evoke. The internal representation might look like this:

```
ACTOR:    Joe
ACTION:   MTRANS (name)
FROM:     CP Joe
TO:       CP Burt ——→    ANGER -8
                            |
                            |
              ——→ ACTOR:    Burt
                  ACTION:   PROPEL
                  OBJECT:   fist
                  TO:       Joe's eye ——→ HEALTH -3
                  FROM:     Burt
```

The arrows symbolize the causal relationship that the computer would infer. ANGER is another index for the state or condition of an actor, like HEALTH. The primitive action MTRANS is a conceptual representation for Mental TRANSfer of information, in this case from one person's Conscious Processor (CP) to another person's. MTRANS is also used to represent transfer of information from one part of the mind to another. For example, the action in *remember* would be represented as MTRANS of information from long-term memory (LTM) to Conscious Processor.

Conceptual representations such as these give the computer a structural framework to use in reading stories. A person who read sentence 7 might respond *Burt must have said something insulting* or *Joe's eye probably hurts* or *Burt must have been angry*. Conceptual representation of meaning allows the computer to make appropriate responses, and to answer such questions as *What's a black eye? Why did Burt get angry?* and so on. The computer knows what it is talking about at the level of MAKING SENSE, in that it can make appropriate relationships and inferences.

A UNIVERSAL REPRESENTATION SYSTEM

Consider again the examples of PROPEL embodied in the sentences following:

1.	Mary socked John.	\	ACTOR:	Mary
2.	Mary punched John.	|	ACTION:	PROPEL
3.	Mary hit John with her fist.	\	OBJECT:	fist
4.	John was socked by Mary.	/	FROM:	Mary
5.	Marie a donne un coup de poing a Jean.	|	TO:	John
6.	Maria pego a Juan.	/		

The computer creates the same conceptual representation for *all* the above sentences, even the French and Spanish versions. The word *fist* doesn't appear in all the sentences but the computer could be told to assume *fist* for OBJECT when it sees the verbs *punch* or *sock* in such a context, which is what most people would assume. The computer uses the same conceptual representation for the event, regardless of what language was used. We can build language analyzers for French and Spanish, say, that decompose the sentences of those languages into the same conceptual representation that we were using for English sentences. In this way, the computer can effectively *translate* these languages into each other. Given the Spanish or French sentences, the computer can spout English paraphrases, but only by first decomposing the sentences into its conceptual representation and then recomposing the concepts into words in the target language.

The computer has been programmed to analyze sentences

using primitive conceptual structures, not words of any particular language. Computer understanding based on the representation of the underlying concepts involved in actions is independent of any language. ATRANS and PROPEL are not words in a particular language but elements of meaning that can be used to understand sentences in all languages.

There are several other primitive actions that the computer must use besides the three we have mentioned, but to belabor them here is beyond the scope of this book. The important point is that with very few of them (we actually use only 11 in the Yale programs) one can gain a great amount of representational power. The primitives combine somewhat as chemical elements combine to make compounds. They are versatile units of meaning. The juxtaposition of PROPEL and ATRANS, together with other primitives that describe grasping and ungrasping, can represent the underlying meaning of a word like "throw" in such a way as to describe that the receiver of what was thrown now has it, that a force was applied to the object that was thrown, that that object was released from the hand of the thrower, that it took a flight through the air and so on. Because of this combinational power, the set of primitives developed for the understanding programs at Yale has proven to be very useful. The theory is not that this or that set of primitives is "the one." The theory is that *some* kind of system of primitive conceptual representations is necessary for natural language processing. To get programs to analyze sentences, generate sentences, make inferences, apply rules of beliefs, track goals, create plans, and so on, it is imperative that all these parts of the understanding system be able to talk to each other. They must have common language, so to speak. The language they use in our programs is the conceptual representations we have been discussing. In this way, when the belief system wants to talk about what it knows about possession, it can use ATRANS and be understood by the planning system that knows how to achieve an ATRANS. The more powerful the primitives, the more powerful the understanding system.

The understanding systems developed at Yale usually have dealt with stories involving everyday interactions among people. More specialized systems now being built for business involve a different set of primitives. But the general idea is to find a set of concepts that can tie together all the various ways that one can express a thought. We don't worry about whether a particular set of primitives is the one "true" set, or the "right" set since there is no way of knowing what "right" would mean except with regard to a concrete understanding problem. All we can concern ourselves with is whether a certain set of primitives is useful to the extent that it allows a computer system to make appropriate inferences and to have useful expectations when it reads a story.

The important theoretical advance is that all the actions we can think of talking about can be broken up into a handful of primitive conceptual representations that enable a computer to understand our language. If this idea is right with respect to human understanding, then it says that people understand everything they encounter in terms of simpler, more basic things that they have encountered before. This is a very powerful principle which we shall encounter later when we discuss memory. The point is not exactly how many primitives there are, or exactly what they are. The point is that by giving the computer tools of this kind, we enable it to represent to itself the meaning of the sentences it reads. They allow the computer to have a dialogue with itself about what is happening in a story.

What is the meaning of a primitive concept such as ATRANS to the computer? The computer uses them as symbols with which it can cause other symbols to be used. But this also is the case with the symbols that people use. We can become excited by a series of numbers written on a piece of paper if that piece of paper is a check or a bank book. Computers also can react to symbols— not with excitement, but with actions. Each of the primitive elements we use in AI have very specific meanings to the machine. They indicate to the machine what actions it should take and what expectations it should have. These actions usually take the form of more symbol manipulations. Specifically, when the computer finds an instance of ATRANS, two important things happen. First, ATRANS tells us which slots have to be filled and what will fill them in completing the details of any event in which there is an ATRANS. Thus the first use of a primitive action is to make the other symbols that it organizes, and the actions organized under *those* symbols come into play. In this way,

ATRANS directs the analysis of the rest of the sentence; once the main action in a sentence is understood, the computer can determine more easily what else is going on.

ATRANS also tells the computer what set of inferences are fired off when the analysis of the initial sentence is complete. Once we know that Jill hit Mary for example, we also can assume that Jill was angry at Mary, that Mary might be hurt in some way, that she is very likely to be upset, that she might get angry at Jill, that she might hit her back, and so on. All these statements are possibly true inferences from the initial sentence. We cannot be sure that they are true, indeed if we heard that Jill hit a policeman, we might be more concerned about Jill's health than we would about the policeman's. But, nevertheless, some set of mental processes do cause us to think about all these things.

These processes are stored not under the word hit, but under the concept of *hitting*. If these processes were fired off every time the word hit were seen, then we would find ourselves inquiring about the state of the home run (or at least the ball) when we hear that Babe Ruth hit a home run, and we would wonder about what was going on at all when we heard that a Broadway play was a hit. Further, if these processes were stored under words, the duplication would be enormous. As understanders we care what word was used only insofar as it tells us what action occurred. The difference between beat and hit is one of nuance. The computer has to pay attention to these nuances, too, but explaining how we do that is more technical than is necessary here. Understanding a sentence involves more than just understanding the sentence per se; it also means understanding everything else that also might be true. And doing this requires a conceptual representation that conveniently organizes all the information we have about a concept under that concept.

Does the computer really understand what it is doing? When it understands a sentence, does it understand that it understands? When we complete a transaction in a bank, make a deposit, ask about the current interest rates, we do not care whether the bank official has *really* understood us or whether he was just manipulating symbols. What matters to us is that we accomplished our goals at the bank. So, if a computer understands us well enough to produce output that enables us to get what we want, we don't have to worry whether it has understood its own actions. We worry if a bank teller has counted our change and entered our deposit correctly. We do not worry whether he truly understands the economic basis of money.

AI is primarily thought of as a branch of computer science. Yet the theory of conceptual representation we have presented here is not a theory about computers as much as it is a theory about people. A primitive action such as ATRANS is extremely useful because it can represent the meaning underlying a large number of verbs and forms the basis for the representation of simple events.

The conceptual representation theory is by no means a complete theory of how to represent the kinds of knowledge that people use in understanding natural language. Primitive actions are the smallest units in the service of very complex knowledge structures we must develop for any understanding system.

CHAPTER
SIX

KNOWLEDGE
STRUCTURES

Getting computers to behave intelligently means giving them detailed knowledge about the world we live in. A person understands what you mean only if he shares a significant amount of knowledge with you. If you talk about baseball, he must know something about baseball. If you talk about business, he must know about business. The same is true of computers. No computer will ever *understand* anything you say about your business unless it has been provided with detailed knowledge about business in general, and at least some knowledge of your type of business in particular. The computer also must be told how to use this knowledge.

Sentences mean different things in different contexts. For a computer to know what we mean, it must know what we *could* mean. The computer should not treat every utterance as if it were the first time it had ever heard such a thing. If we walk into our house and say, *It's hot in here,* an intelligent voice-activated household computer should not respond with astonishment that humans have heat-sensing ability. Rather, the intelligent computer should adjust the thermostats it controls.

We want our computers to be able to do more than simply display a table labeled 'Bills Outstanding' when we type *List bills outstanding*. We want the computer to know why we are asking so that it can get at the heart of our question. We also want to be able to ask the computer *What are my debts?* or *How much do I owe the gas company?* We don't want to have to go through unnecessary steps either. We want to be able to come home and simply type in *Pay VISA and gas company* and have the computer infer that we mean those bills for this month.

A computer must know what it means to owe money, to pay money, and to need money. It may never know it in the way that an owner of a business knows it when it is time to meet the payroll. It would take COMPLETE EMPATHY, or something close to it, for a computer to feel the sense of panic that can be felt by someone who owes money. But it must know enough about owing to be able to respond to the many other possible ways one could have asked for information on outstanding bills, such as *Who owes us money?* or *Can we meet this month's payroll?* To do this means that we must provide computers with the same knowledge that people use to answer these questions. It's that simple. It's that difficult.

People have a great deal of knowledge about a great many subjects, from how to get to New York to how to start their cars in cold weather. It really isn't so amazing that people know so much. Rather it is amazing that people can find exactly the knowledge they need in a given situation so effortlessly. How do people know what is appropriate in a particular situation? How do we know that if we have been talking to them about our debts and we ask, *What about the phone company?* we are more likely to mean, *What about our debts to the phone company* and not *How many debts does the phone company have?*

How do you know that in a restaurant you can ask a waitress to get you some food and she will bring it to you, but if you meet the waitress on a bus or at the theatre and ask her to bring you some food she will respond, *Are you crazy?* When we go to the hospital, what keeps us from asking the doctor for an extra-dry martini with two olives? When we're in a restaurant, what prevents us from taking off our clothes and asking the waitress to give us a check-up? These questions underlie the problem of getting machines to apply knowledge the same way we do.

MAD LIBS

Some years back a very interesting game appeared called *Mad Libs*. Each *Mad Lib* was a one- or two-page story with a title like "Newspaper Article," "At the Dentist's Office," or "Going to a Restaurant." The stories were unexciting except for the fact that they were incomplete. Certain words were missing from each story, leaving 20 or so blanks labeled only with the part of speech— noun, verb, adjective, adverb, etc.—syntactically required to complete each sentence. To play the game, one or more people must think up words for the parts of speech requested by the person holding the game (henceforth known as the *caller*), who writes the words on the blanks to complete the story.

As an example, imagine a short Mad Lib called "John Eats at Eddie's Dinateria:"

As John was walking along the ____, he noticed a restaurant
_{noun}

called Eddie's Dinateria, and walked in. The ____ came over
_{noun}

to him and said "Hi! What would you like to ____?" John
_{verb}

looked at the ____ and said "I'll have the oven-broiled
_{noun}

____. It sounds ____." The waitress brought him his food.
_{noun}   _{adj.}

It is very easy to think of words that could go in the blank-spaces of this story: *street, waitress, eat, menu, steak, delicious*. But the players of this Mad Lib would not know what the context of the words they chose would be. They know only that they have to give the caller the parts of speech he asks for: two nouns, a verb, two more nouns, and an adjective. The players might give the following words: *hubcap, underwear, eradicate, umbrella, tractor, obvious*. The caller then would complete the following story:

JOHN EATS AT EDDIE'S DINATERIA

As John was walking along the hubcap, he noticed a restaurant called Eddie's Dinateria, and walked in. The underwear came over to him and said "Hi! What would you like to eradicate?" John looked at the umbrella and said "I'll have the oven-broiled tractor. It sounds obvious." The waitress brought him his food.

What makes this story so ridiculous? It hasn't violated the laws of grammar. The sentences in the story make perfect syntactical sense, yet the story as a whole doesn't satisfy any of our normal expectations. It doesn't conform to what we know about eating in a restaurant or what we know about the behavior of the things it mentions. The only sentence that *makes sense* at all is the last one—a nice, normal sentence that we easily can relate to the title of the story.

A Mad Lib is funny precisely because it violates our normal expectations, inferences, and knowledge of what should occur in a given context. The context of the above story leads one to expect certain meanings, but these meanings aren't there. In their place are totally unexpected meanings. The completed Mad Lib is a unique story. Although we can't understand the crazy sentences at a very deep level, we can MAKE SENSE of them, and it is important to examine the process by which we make sense of a story, even a crazy story.

Let's suppose the Mad Lib had been filled in with expected or "correct" words:

JOHN EATS AT EDDIE'S DINATERIA

As John was walking along the street, he noticed a restaurant called Eddie's Dinateria, and walked in. The waitress came over to him and said "Hi! What would you like to eat?" John looked at the menu and said "I'll have the oven-broiled steak. It sounds delicious." The waitress brought him his food.

This little story is so elementary that it becomes trite and boring. The story is loaded with familiar structures and clichés, and some of us may have said or written these sentences word for word at one time or another. The ease with which we comprehend most of what we see and hear makes it difficult to have any sense of the underlying processes involved. Determining the limits of our ability to comprehend, or to MAKE SENSE of a situation, can tell us a great deal about how we understand. The Mad Libs example helps to illustrate the process by which humans find meaning in stories. Certain scenarios and contexts are very familiar to us, and we can recognize them from a very small amount of information.

Now consider the following sketchy story:

> John was hungry. He ordered a cheeseburger. He spilled ketchup on his leg.

Even though much of what actually must have happened has been left out of this story, we have no trouble recognizing the fairly restricted story line involved here. Most Americans have been to a restaurant many times in their lives, and have developed a set of rules and expectations for what goes on in the restaurants with which they are familiar. We are equipped with *knowledge structures* that allow us to make sense of stories about going to restaurants. If a computer is going to understand stories about going to restaurants, we will have to give it knowledge structures that tell it what to expect in a restaurant. These knowledge structures will be similar to those that any human would develop in the course of his experience with restaurants.

SCRIPTS

We have called the knowledge structures used in such situations *scripts,* in part because they resemble a script for a play. Scripts are prepackaged sets of expectations, inferences, and knowledge that are applied in common situations, like a blueprint for action without the details filled in. In the same way that SLOTS and SLOT FILLERS were used in the conceptual representation of events, a script is a collection of SLOTS FOR EVENTS. A script, when used by an understander, helps the understander know what to expect. A script tells what is likely to come next in a chain of events that are stereotypes. Scripts tell us what might happen next and enable us to understand the relevance of what actually does happen next; they provide connectivity between events. Consider another story about John going to a restaurant:

> John went to a restaurant. He asked the waitress for coq au vin. He paid the check and left.

This story is understandable because it makes reference to a script. The three sentences are connected by our ability to reference a script we have formed based on our own experiences. We even can add some of the missing pieces of the story. We can infer that John looked at a menu, because we know that coq au vin is served only in places fancy enough to have a menu. We can expect that he *ate* the coq au vin. We can also assume that he sat at a table, and that the coq au vin was served on a plate. We can be pretty certain that these things took place. They are the main conceptual scenes required to make sense of the story.

WHAT ISN'T THERE: KNOWLEDGE OF THE POSSIBLE

The story doesn't contain any details about what the restaurant looked like, whether John liked the taste of the food, whether the meal satisfied his hunger, or whether he chatted with the waitress or busboy. We don't know whether he met someone he knew and stayed for an hour, or whether he ate in silence and rushed off to finish a day's work. But look at this list again. What I have just said is not simply a list of the things that might or might not have occurred. It is a complex structure of what I know to be possible in this particular situation. The fact that we consider these things as possibly connected to the situation is far more important than how we determine whether they actually took place.

Suppose I had pointed out that the story doesn't tell us what planet the scene takes place on, or whether aliens from planet X invaded the restaurant and vaporized the customers with proton disruptors? The story doesn't tell us whether John took off his clothes and asked the chef to give him an appendectomy. It doesn't tell us whether the waitress gave John a manicure while he was waiting for a shave and a haircut. These events are all possible, of course, but we wouldn't want to go about assuming them in this context. They simply aren't part of the restaurant script. We would be surprised and shocked if any of these things ever occurred while we were enjoying a nice meal in a restaurant.

The value of scripts is not only to tell us what to expect, but to know that something odd was not expected. They help us understand what is special and merits closer attention. Finally, the assumption that the people we talk to share our scripts allows us to be briefer in what we say. We need not spell out all the details to an informed listener. To make our computer well informed, we must provide it with the ability to fill in the details for itself.

Without a script, we can see no great connectivity between events. Consider the following story:

> John went to the park. He asked the midget for a mouse.
> He picked up the box and left.

This story is difficult to understand because we know of no standard situation in which midgets, parks, mice, and boxes relate. We have no script for what is happening here. If there existed a standard *mouse-buying script* in which mice typically were purchased from midgets in the park, who wrapped them in boxes, then we could connect the parts of the story. Otherwise, connectivity is at a minimum in this story, and it might as well be another Mad Lib. But notice that the structure of this story is superficially identical to our restaurant story. The sentences are syntactically identical and perfectly grammatical. Nevertheless the story is confusing. These stories are very different structurally: One references a known script; the other does not.

Scripts represent the knowledge that people use for daily activities. There are scripts for large and complex activities, such as going to a restaurant, and for small and simple activities, such as parking a car in a garage. Scripts involve *routine activities* that many people perform, and they are fairly *specific*. We might have a script for *looking for a job* or for *throwing a party*. The scripts for *going to the bathroom* and *sharpening a pencil* are among the simplest scripts we employ.

Some activities don't lend themselves to scripts. We don't have scripts for *living* or for *coping with your teenager*. We might think that we have rules for such things, but they are immense, constantly changing complex systems of rules that may or may not bear any relation to those rules that another person might have. The scripts we have developed for understanding systems are made up of the fairly universal rules we all use when dealing with stereotypical situations. These rules are in the form of expectations of what will happen next and why. Consequently, there are no scripts for *painting a picture, writing a poem, making a scientific discovery,* or *creating a philosophic system.* Painters, poets, scientists, and philosophers may employ certain principles or methods for what they do, but these are so complex and so difficult to describe that few people can understand them, much less duplicate them using such a simple structure.

Certainly, the long-term goal of AI is to model such creativity, but we will have to wait for the development of knowledge structures that are far more complex than scripts.

The restaurant script contains all the information necessary to understand the enormous variability of what can occur in a restaurant. All restaurants are not created equal, and the restaurant script has particular *tracks* for different kinds of restaurants— a fast-food track, a coffee-shop track, a fancy French restaurant track, etcetera. These tracks allow the computer to understand the various entering, ordering, and paying scenes that different restaurants have.

We don't expect to be seated by a hostess or maitre d' in a McDonald's restaurant; nor do we expect to be asked for our order over a microphone at Maxim's in Paris. We expect to see menus in both a diner and a fancy restaurant, but they would differ markedly. We wouldn't ask for a wine list in a diner. Consider the track of the restaurant script we use to understand the following story:

> John went into the restaurant. He ordered a bacon double-cheeseburger and a milkshake. He paid for it and found a nice spot to sit and eat in the park across the street.

The kind of food ordered above, and the fact that John could take his order out of the restaurant and eat in the park, clue the reader in to the fact that this story involves a *fast-food* restaurant of some kind, a place where you can order food to go and receive it in a very few minutes. If John had ordered coq au vin and a bottle of chablis, we would be surprised and confused that he ate in the park. We would wonder what kind of restaurant he had been to. We could understand the story even though we have no script that fully accounts for it. The very fact that we *would* be surprised shows that we would have to use our standard restaurant script in order to interpret the story. We can understand the unusual only by comparison to the usual.

Like a Mad Lib, a script is made up of slots and requirements of what can fill those slots. The structure is an interconnected whole, and what we put in one slot affects what can be put in another. Scripts handle stylized everyday activities. They are not subject to drastic change; nor do they provide for totally novel situations. A script must be written from one particular actor's point of view. A customer sees a restaurant one way, and a cook sees it another. All the scripts from the points of view of all the people who work or visit a restaurant constitute what we might call the "concept" of a restaurant. Such a whole view of a restaurant is rarely, if ever, called up during story understanding, but it is there, and can be used if necessary.

APPLYING SCRIPTS

The following is a sketch of one track of the restaurant script called the coffee-shop track, from the point of view of the customer. (The computer's version of this script would be written entirely in terms of conceptual representations using the primitive actions we discussed in Chapter 5. Here, for the sake of simplicity, English descriptions of the events are used.) A computer program can use a restaurant script to understand stories by relying on a set of expectations about restaurants formulated in terms of the *underlying events* that take place, represented conceptually. Because it does not rely on a particular wording or vocabulary in order to understand any given story, the program applying this script can understand all the possible ways that a restaurant story may be told. The script is broken up into several scenes that naturally suggest themselves: entering, ordering, eating, and paying. The core of each event in the chain of events taking place in the story is the primitive action involved. The ordering scene is given below with a little more detail than the other scenes. Actually, all the scenes shown here are much sketchier than those used by the computer.

Script:	RESTAURANT
Track:	Coffee Shop
Props:	Tables
	Menu
	Food
	Check
	Money
Roles:	Customer
	Waitress
	Cook

Entry conditions:	Customer is hungry.
	Customer has money.
Results:	Customer has less money
	Owner has more money.
	Customer is not hungry.
	Customer is pleased. (optional)

Scene 1: Entering

Go into restaurant.
Look at the tables.
Decide where to sit.
Go to table.
Sit.

Scene 2: Ordering

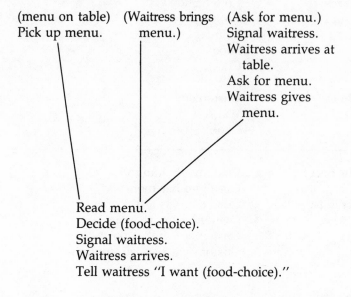

(menu on table) (Waitress brings (Ask for menu.)
Pick up menu.   menu.)   Signal waitress.
                                  Waitress arrives at
                                      table.
                                  Ask for menu.
                                  Waitress gives
                                      menu.

Read menu.
Decide (food-choice).
Signal waitress.
Waitress arrives.
Tell waitress "I want (food-choice)."

Waitress goes to cook.
Waitress tells cook to cook (food-choice).

Cook tells waitress there is   Cook prepares (food-
    no (food-choice).   choice).
Waitress arrives at table.   To Scene 3.
Waitress says "there is no
    (food-choice)."
(Go back to *) or
(Go to Scene 4 at no pay
    Path.)

Scene 3: Eating

Cook gives (food-choice) to
    waitress.
Waitress gives (food-choice)
    to you.
Eat (food-choice).
(Optionally return to Scene 2
    to order more; otherwise
    go to Scene 4.)

Scene 4: Exiting

Waitress arrives.   Signal to waitress.
Waitress arrives at table.
Ask for check.
Waitress writes check.

Waitress gives check to you.
Leave tip on table.
Go to cashier.
Give money to cashier.
(no pay path): Leave restaurant.

In order to schematically represent just one track of the restaurant script we have left out considerable detail and many possible options in each of the scenes. We have excluded entire scenes such as the *wait to be seated* scene. Anyone who has been to a few restaurants is aware of many more details; certainly there is room for a *seeing someone you know* scene, for example, as well as a *meeting someone new* scene. Some of the sideline events at a restaurant also can be scripts in their own right. For example, a *paying by credit card* script is a fairly simple script that is called up in many places besides restaurants.

People also possess a wealth of sensory or otherwise nonverbal information when they go to a restaurant. In the above sketch we do not systematically represent descriptive visual information such as the decor inside the restaurant. We also have left out what the customer smelled in the restaurant, what the food tasted like, why certain noises might have been bothersome, whether there was good music playing, whether the eating of the food resulted in pleasure, and so on. We have represented that the customer eats the food, but we haven't represented that eating normally results in an increase in pleasure, or even in satisfaction of hunger. The restaurant script can be expanded to understand and make sense of stories that include these details. The versatility and capacity for understanding of a script is limited only by the care and patience that we take in its design. The more we incorporate in the design, the greater the level of understanding that can be achieved.

The restaurant script is a giant chain of events, connected to each other by the causal relationships between them. New information in a story is understood by place in the causal chain in a script. The value of scripts to the computer can be illustrated rather simply. Consider again the story

> John went to a restaurant. He asked the waitress for coq au vin. He paid the check and left.

This story leaves out some of the main scenes that almost certainly would have to take place. Nowhere does it say that John *ate* the coq au vin, or that he had to look at a menu. The restaurant script would fill out the story by adding the scenes that were left out, such as eating. Thus a computer equipped with a restaurant script would understand the previous story as if it had been

> John went to a French restaurant. He sat down at a table. He read a menu. He ordered coq au vin. He ate the coq au vin. He paid the check. He left a tip. He left the restaurant.

Some stories involve situations that depart from the standard script or that cause the script to be interrupted or halted. Consider the following story:

> John went to a restaurant. He ordered a hamburger. It was cold when the waitress brought it. He left her a very small tip.

The first two sentences above describe scenes 1 and 2 in the sketch of the restaurant script. The third sentence involves scene 3 of the sketch, where the waitress brings the food, but also includes the information that the food is cold. The fourth sentence is a modification of the ATRANS of the tip in scene 4, stipulating that the tip was *very small*. The understander has to relate the small size of the tip to the fact that the hamburger was served cold. A script-applying mechanism would check the story against a standard script and relate the two deviations by inferring from the cold hamburger that the eating action of scene 3 did not lead the actor to experience pleasure upon eating. The concept of a very small tip can be stored within the restaurant script as a reaction to the absence of pleasure. A program that could work backwards from the news of the small tip to discover the source of dissatisfaction would have to understand a great deal of the complexities of eating at a coffee shop.

A crucial feature of any understanding system is that it not use inappropriate conceptual tools to deal with a situation. We already have seen the consequences of assuming you are in a restaurant when you recognize a waitress in a doctor's office. Misapplication of a given script in the wrong context can make a program wrong. The restaurant script should not be called up simply because a sentence refers to *eating*, or to *restaurant*, or because the sentence reads *Heating oil was delivered to the restaurant*. We need to know what a restaurant is, that it is a building requiring a heating system, and so on. Still, if the driver of the oil truck decides to come in and eat, the restaurant script should not refuse to serve him.

BEYOND SCRIPTS

It would be nice if the only knowledge structures required to understand stories were the scripts that dealt with the subject matter. However, aside from the fact that it is almost impossible to write down scripts for all the things stories and texts can be about, we know that human understanding has many other elements besides scripts. We can imagine scripts such as *what to do when the professor says he's giving you an F*, and *how to react when a state trooper pulls you over*. These scripts might work perfectly well, but since scripts are acquired (by people) by repeated experience with an event, the only people we could expect to have scripts like these would be chronic goof-offs or speeders. But even they would have had to plan their method out initially. Most of us improvise when we find ourselves in these situations because we are planning them for the first time. Scripts will work well enough in mundane situations. But for computers to be really intelligent, we need more.

People can deal with situations they have never encountered before. They can see what needs to be done in a new situation and can plan in order to achieve whatever goals they might set. Most of us can construct useful and relevant plans for whatever we desire, and intelligent computers also will have to do this. Computers must be able to plan things out in a new situation, without having to resort to a script.

Any computer-understanding system must be able to understand new or unexpected situations. Real understanding requires the ability to establish connections between pieces of information for which no prescribed set of rules, or scripts, exist. We must be able to recognize general elements of connectivity between events when specifics are unavailable. We must have general principles for organizing seemingly disparate events in meaningful ways. We are able to estimate what to do in a certain situation, even a rarely encountered one. We have general knowledge structures that tell us the kinds of things other people want and how they might think of getting what they want. If we want a computer to connect together novel actions that people do, we must give it a mechanism for understanding *why* people do the things they do.

In simple terms, computers have to know what people need and desire. A computer that reads a story about a man lost in the forest has to know that a person needs to eat food and drink water every few hours or he will die. A computer that reads stories about the Middle East must know that people harbor nationalist prejudices and religious beliefs for which they are willing to kill each other. A computer that reads newspapers will have to be told that two big nations might build nuclear bombs as part of a plan to keep their relations peaceful, if it is to understand stories about international relations.

This simple observation opens up what may be the single most important problem in getting computers to understand natural language in particular, and to behave intelligently in general. If we don't want the computer to be lost at the most crucial moments, namely when events don't proceed according to plan, then computers must know about the kinds of goals people have and the plans they make for achieving them.

People have many desires, and spend the better part of their lives trying to satisfy these desires. Some people desire only a slice of bread. Some desire power and vast riches. Some desire (perhaps paradoxically) to sacrifice their own desires for others.

Some people want to own three cars, even though they can drive only one of them at a time. It is no surprise, then, that most of what we write about and talk about in our thousands of languages has to do with people and their desires. Whether we are trying to predict stock market fluctuations, assess political risks, or find a good dentist, we must understand the desires, goals, and hopes of the people involved.

When we read a story, we try to evaluate the reasoning processes of the main character. We try to determine why he does what he does and what he will do next. We examine what we would do in a similar situation, and we try to make the same connections that the main character seems to be making. We ask ourselves, *What is he trying to do? What's his plan? Why did he do what he just did?* Any understanding system has to be able to decipher the reasoning processes that actors in stories go through. Computer understanding means computers understanding people, which requires that they understand how people formulate goals and plans to achieve those goals. Sometimes people achieve their goals by resorting to a script. When a script is unavailable, that is, when the situation is in some way novel, people are able to make up new plans.

For a computer to be able to do this we have to supply it with general information about what kinds of goals the actors in a story might want to achieve, and what steps they might take in pursuit of their goals. The computer should be able to explain how an event or action can be seen as part of an overall plan. No computer can possibly claim to have expertise or intelligence without this ability.

Consider the following story:

> John knew that his wife's surgery would be very expensive. There was always Uncle Harry. He reached for the phone book.

How are we to make sense of such a story? None of the sentences relate directly to scripts that could be applied here. Most people don't have a *paying for expensive medical treatments* script, and such a script would be of little use, anyway. After all, the understanding problem presented by this story isn't changed much if we replace *wife's surgery* with *son's education* or *mortgage downpayment.* In each case, the general goal is something like *raising a lot of money for an important family expense.*

We need general understanding mechanisms that can connect this goal to a set of possible actions that might be taken to realize it. Even though the second two sentences above may seem remote from the first sentence, they are somehow less remote than *There was always the helicopter pilot. He went out and mowed the lawn.* Knowing why Uncle Harry is more relevant than the helicopter pilot is the job of an understanding system that incorporates plans and goals.

Plans are formulated to achieve one or more goals. Certain goals may be more far-reaching than others and may require more planning to achieve. Consider the far-reaching goal in the following sentence:

> The Jackal was hired to assassinate President Charles De Gaulle. He went to the library and began reading French history.

and the less far-reaching goal in,

> Fred couldn't get the jar lid off. He went down to the basement and got a pair of pliers.

We can see real connectivity between the parts of these little stories. In each case, the first sentence suggests the goal involved, and the second sentence somehow clues us in to the plan. Suppose we exchanged the second sentences of these examples. We might believe that the Jackal really intends to use a pair of pliers in his plan to kill De Gaulle, but would we say that Fred plans to get the jar lid off by reading French history in the library? No. We know what can be used for what, and how one might go about doing certain things.

KNOWLEDGE STRUCTURES FOR GOALS AND PLANS

In much the same way that we formulated primitive conceptual representations for the actions in events, we have developed representations that the computer can use to understand how events fit together with respect to the plans and goals that actors might be using in stories. It is not important here to give the details of these representations. Rather, let's just look at some of the concepts that we must give a program in order to enable it to understand what goals and plans people make.

One type of goal that is quite useful are goals for changing the state of something. There are at least five important goals of this type:

CHANGE-PROXIMITY	desire for a change in location or proximity
CHANGE-CONTROL	desire for achieving possession or control over something
CHANGE-KNOWLEDGE	desire for acquisition of knowledge
CHANGE-SOCIAL CONTROL	desire for power or authority to do something
CHANGE-AGENCY	desire for getting someone else to pursue a goal on your behalf

The next question is how to satisfy such desires.

PLANS FOR GOALS

While there are occasions when human planning is so wildly novel that it seems impossible to figure out how anyone could have come up with such an idea, planning usually is not particularly difficult to explain. We have found that there is a standard set of methods that one can use in planning to change the state of something, and that these methods usually are the first things tried by a planner.

All CHANGE-GOALs have standard plans associated with them. For example, the standard plans for achieving a CHANGE-PROXIMITY goal are:

USE PRIVATE VEHICLE

USE PUBLIC TRANSPORTATION
USE ANIMAL
USE SELF

These plans are pretty much self-explanatory. They account for all the modes of getting somewhere that we might choose, from elephants to bicycles, to airplanes, to windsurfers, to our own two feet. Suppose we read the following story:

> Frank wanted to go to the Bahamas. He picked up a newspaper.

The plan READ NEWSPAPER obviously doesn't apply directly to Frank's CHANGE-PROXIMITY goal. READ NEWSPAPER is a standard plan for CHANGE-KNOWLEDGE, a subgoal Frank might have in the service of his larger CHANGE-PROXIMITY goal. Our hero might be trying to learn about cheap flights or good hotels in the travel section of the newspaper. What else should we assume? That the newspaper is irrelevant and the writer threw in the reference to it just to confuse us? No. We usually depend on context being helpful to our understanding of a story. We would be surprised if the story went like this:

> Frank wanted to go to the Bahamas. He picked up a newspaper. He began reading the fashion section.

Nevertheless, we still would expect some link to be made between fashion and the Bahamas. As understanders, we must fit people's actions into our model of the world. Maybe Frank is looking for a place to buy light clothing for the tropics. Maybe there's a fashion show in the Bahamas that Frank wants to attend.

THE ART OF PERSUASION

Notice that the goals represented by the four CHANGE-GOALs after CHANGE-PROXIMITY all involve desire for power, control, acquisition of knowledge, and influence over others. Much of what we desire has to do with getting others to do what we want, enlisting their help, convincing and cajoling them into giving us a hand or at least not harming us. Influencing others is perhaps the most important planning we can do for achieving whatever goals we may set. An individual's survival often is determined by his mastery of persuasion. It is no coincidence that one of the most important sets of plans we will need to understand human planning (and to explain it to the computer) is the PERSUADE package.

If you want something and someone else has it, you have a number of choices. You can ask for it. You can suggest an indirect reason why the person you are asking should do it based on your relationship (*I am the one who fed and clothed you when you were a baby, you know.*). You can give a good reason (*I need it to save your fortune, you fool.*). You can bargain by offering an object (*I'll give you five dollars*) or a favor (*Do it for me and I'll make it up to you.*). Or, you can just threaten (*You want to see your children again?*).

AI involves the science of the obvious. Everyone knows, at least implicitly, about how to get what they want. We don't teach persuasion in school, and children are probably not born knowing such things. But they learn how to persuade others over time, by imitation, by trial and error, and so on. Computers don't inherently know such things either, and we have yet to create computers that can grow up in a normal home environment. We first must find out specifically what it is that people know about how to get things, and then put this information in the machine so that when the computer needs something it will have some idea how to get it, so that it can understand what a robber is doing when he says, *Your money or your life!*

Our plan understanding programs make use of the following six plans for persuasion (corresponding to the ideas we have just expressed above):

ASK
INVOKE THEME
INFORM REASON
BARGAIN OBJECT
BARGAIN FAVOR
THREATEN

The computer treats this package of plans for persuasion as the set of strategies it can expect when any of the CHANGE-

GOALs appear. What better way to achieve a CHANGE-CON-TROL goal or a CHANGE-SOCIAL CONTROL goal than to PER-SUADE another person to give you what you want or help you achieve it? If you want control or possession of an object, such as the car, you may have to PERSUADE the person who already has control over it to give it to you or let you borrow it. In addition to the six plans in the PERSUADE package, there are two other plans for CHANGE-CONTROL: You can STEAL (CHANGE-CONTROL without the knowledge or permission of the other person) and you can OVERPOWER (CHANGE-CONTROL with that person's knowledge but without his/her permission).

Let's take another look at the story of John and his financial problems:

John knew that his wife's surgery would be very expensive. There was always Uncle Harry. He reached for the phone book.

Understanding this story requires realizing that John needs money. To CHANGE-CONTROL of money often entails per-suading someone who has money to give it to you. To persuade someone you must be able to communicate with him/her and one such method is the telephone. Thus the computer must understand "picking up the phone book" as an attempt to fulfill all the conditions that must be satisfied to enable communication which then will enable persuasion. Figuring out that John needs money and that John intends to talk to Harry are rather different from inferring the plan. We can use the mechanisms outlined in Chapter 5 to take care of these issues. The problem now is to connect these observations. How can calling Uncle Harry be part of a plan for getting money? Telephoning Uncle Harry must be understood as a subplan in the service of the bigger plan to PERSUADE Uncle Harry to give John the money he needs.

So, to program computers for *understanding*, there are really two distinct problems. First, the machine must understand what has been said. On the surface, any sentence conveys a meaning, but understanding what meanings are being conveyed is a complex problem. The computer must be given an understanding of how words carry meaning and how these meanings allow inferences to be made which allow additional meanings to be understood.

Second, people do not *say* everything they *mean*. They are intentionally telegraphic (as if they were paying by the word). They do not say every single idea that is in their minds. People expect the understander to add, from their own knowledge, all the implicit ideas inherent in their sentences. As intelligent actors in the real world, we must know why people do what they do if we are to anticipate correctly their actions and not see every single event as novel and wondrous. If we must know how to do this, then so must computers. In order to develop an understanding system we have had to develop conceptual tools for recognizing a great many more specific goal states and desires.

OTHER GOALS

Any smart understanding system needs to know that a character in a story who goes without sleep or food for more than 12 hours or so will be tired and hungry. It also must assume that the characters it hears about will have standard needs and desires, such as the need for companionship, respect, love, a warm place to rest, and so on.

The system must know that the blocking or frustration of any of these goals may, depending upon their importance to the character, cause him to make new plans to achieve these goals. An understander must be prepared to recognize that when certain goals have been frustrated, a planner may get more and more distraught.

For example, a story about a man lost in the woods should imply immediately that the actions of the character will begin to reflect his plans for eating, even if eating is never mentioned. If the story we are reading never mentions how he ate, we might begin to get upset and soon disbelieve the story itself. Understanders demand that what they hear make sense. A computer must have the ability to get frustrated when it "hears" something that makes no sense. People might walk out of a movie complaining that the hero would never have treated the heroine that way in real life. A computer movie reviewer would have to be able to assess what people want, what they value over what, and under what circumstances they are likely to abandon certain goals or work harder to achieve them.

The computer needs to know that people pursue many goals for enjoyment. People go out of their way to be entertained, to travel, to play sports, or to meet people because they believe they will enjoy these activities. Frustration of these goals usually results in mild or moderate disappointment. Predictions about alternative routes of satisfaction sometimes can be made from context, as when a character finds a movie theatre closed and notices an ad for a jazz festival nearby. Frustrated enjoyment goals do not have the predictable urgency of goals like hunger or rest. If you cannot eat in one way, you must find another. If you are thwarted from playing basketball, you may get somewhat upset, but your frustration is not likely to make you violent because there are probably other goals that you can substitute for the original one.

The computer must understand which goals are critical and time dependent and which can be approached in a more leisurely fashion. People must act quickly in a crisis, and the computer must know, as we know, when there is a crisis. The computer has to understand that a fire or a sudden illness can put all the plans that currently were being pursued "on hold." The computer would have to know that frustration of a crisis goal would not normally result in substituting one goal for another. We might expect that someone who couldn't go sailing when he wanted to might settle for a fancy dinner instead because substituting pleasure goals is a common phenomenon. But the story, *John couldn't get Mary to the hospital in time so he helped put out a neighbor's grass fire* would seem odd. The machine needs to know that crisis goals generally take precedence over all other goals, even those that must be satisfied on a daily basis.

An intelligent understanding system must model the reasons the actors in the world behave the way they do. The system also must know what knowledge structures are available to the actors to help them achieve their goals, from very stylized ones such as scripts to more general planning mechanisms.

Plan and goal structures serve to equip an understanding system with a comprehensive picture of what humans do and why they do it. People, unlike computers, are driven to do a great many things, from eating Twinkies to building nuclear missiles. If the computer is to see anything but sheer nonsense in these activities, we have to set the context for them.

Of course, in order to tell them all about our experiences, we really have to understand our own world first.

CHAPTER SEVEN

A LOOK
AT SOME
AI PROGRAMS

My colleagues and I at the Yale Artificial Intelligence laboratory
write programs in order to crystallize our theories. Ordinarily,
our theories encompass such a complex range of processes that
we cannot tell if they will do what we thought they would without actually writing the program and finding out. The early versions of programs rarely do fulfill our expectations completely,
not unlike a first set of plans by an architect. The finished product, after having undergone numerous revisions, including perhaps a complete recasting of the problem, may bear little relation
to the original idea. Every program we have written at the Yale
laboratory has been an attempt to get a handle on a particular
problem during our progress in solving some other problem. We
may stop briefly and jump for joy at what a completed program
does, but soon enough we are thinking about fixing its problems
and moving along to the next program.

The real excitement in AI comes when we realize what we
have left out of our previous attempt, which then tells us what
to try next. Why we wrote these programs is more important
than any of the programs themselves. With this in mind, let me

offer a look at some of the programs we have produced over the last decade.

FALSE STARTS

Work on natural language processing began in the 1950s, but those initial attempts bear almost no resemblance to our approach today. These researchers, whether they happened to be in computer science or linguistics, started out by attempting to find the formal rules that might underlie language itself. This may not seem wrong in principle, but the question, *What is language?* is not quite the same as the question, *How do humans understand one another?* Early research concentrated on the outer *form* of language rather than on the *content* of communication, and focused on getting a computer to break a sentence down into its parts of speech rather than into its elements of meaning.

These early researchers first attempted to build a *parser*. They wanted the computer to *parse* or convert sentences into grammatical structures according to standard grade-school rules. These programs told the computer how to find the noun phrases, verb phrases, prepositional phrases, etc., in a sentence by using the rules of how sentences are constructed. These investigators hadn't really given any thought to what would come after that. They never succeeded in writing down all the grammar rules, and found themselves with a lot of unanswered questions about how to get the computer to use language effectively.

On the surface, at least, language is composed of vocabulary, grammar, syntax, and semantics (whatever that is). But this kind of definition doesn't tell us much about what language has to do with understanding. Language is, above all, a medium for communication between people. It cannot be correctly analyzed without considering what kinds of ideas people want to express. Language must be treated as a *vehicle* rather than an entity in and of itself.

The statement *I want ice cream* isn't effectively analyzed if all we do is break it up into its subject and predicate. If a child came out with this sentence we wouldn't reply to him *all right subject, I'll bring you some direct object.* But this is what programs that rely primarily upon syntactic rules, as well as some of the commercial systems now available, actually do. They match words in certain syntactic slots (the head noun, for instance) to field names in data bases. This allows them to find the information about "employees" under "employees" in the data base. But since these programs have no idea what "employee" means, heaven help them if the user of the system should mistakenly refer to them as "wage earners," or worse yet ask about the "money people make" instead of using the correct field name, "salary."

PLAYING DOCTOR

Other early programs searched for key words or phrases in sentences without regard for the role of those words in the sentence, or their meaning. This yielded programs that at most demonstrated people's gullibility. The most frequently cited examples of this approach are programs that simulated some of the questions and answers that a Rogerian psychiatrist might offer.

It isn't difficult to see how one could create a very simple program that appears to mimic a psychiatrist. In key-word systems, the computer can print messages that previously were composed by people, when the program tells it to do so. A machine that prints "HELLO" when you type "Hello" might seem to be communicating even though such behavior proves nothing about understanding. This method of printing certain messages in response to certain inputs works well enough if your goal is to achieve not understanding but simply the *appearance* of understanding. One rule you might give such a program would be that whenever the program sees the words *mother, father,* or *parents* in the user's input, the program should print *Tell me about your relationship with your* _____, tacking on whichever word had appeared in the user's input. This will work well enough when the input is *My mother made me come here.* But the user might type in *My ring is made of mother of pearl,* or *Do you read* Mother Jones *magazine?* The computer would use the same rule in each case and reply, *Tell me about your relationship with your mother.* This ridiculously simple rule may indeed convince the user that he is talking to a psychiatrist who wants to bring the discussion around to the user's parental relationship. It also may convince the user that he is talking to an idiot. (When I showed one of the more sophisticated of these programs to a psychiatrist, he concluded that a computer program that was supposed to model paranoia instead had *brain damage,* a diagnosis that may have been more accurate than he realized.)

When this program failed to see any of the "parents" words in the user's first few statements, it would print, *You haven't talked about your family very much.* This gives the user the impression that the computer thinks he is avoiding the subject; however, the computer isn't thinking anything. Instead, it has been programmed to count the number of statements until it has to print that message. Another very simple, yet highly deceptive, print rule would be to tell the computer to print what the patient has said, changing only the personal pronouns and perhaps a few other words. This can have the effect of encouraging the user to think about what he has said and to elaborate on it. A conversation like the following might take place:

```
COMPUTER:   You haven't talked about your family very much.
USER:       Yes, well, I didn't get along with my family very well.
COMPUTER:   You didn't get along with your family.
USER:       Well no, not for most of my childhood.
COMPUTER:   Not for most of your childhood.
USER:       That's right. My parents were always criticizing me.
COMPUTER:   Your parents were always criticizing you.
USER:       Yes. They never thought I was a good person.
COMPUTER:   What does your father do?
USER:       He's a professor.
COMPUTER:   How do you feel about professors?
```

The computer can't miss with the last question. The computer has been given a simple rule telling it to let the user make two or three statements after the family question, replying to them only by repeating them, and then ask, *What does your father do?* Of course, as happened in one instance when these type of programs were being taken rather seriously, if a user responds *He's dead,* the computer's response, *How do you feel about deads?* can be fairly irritating. Such a program obviously doesn't exhibit much true understanding.

The point here is that the program anticipates certain key words and responds to them with certain canned responses. A computer programmed to convert the statement *I hate you* to *Why do you hate me?* doesn't understand anything, doesn't have any expectations or knowledge structures for what it says, and, most importantly, doesn't tell us anything about the nature of human understanding. (It does serve to test a hypothesis that I assume no one ever had, namely, that people respond to sentences by parroting back what they heard. Some people may well do this—they may even get paid to do it—but as a theory of understanding it falls apart rather quickly.) If the user said, instead, *The very sight of you makes me want to throw up,* the computer wouldn't understand. A tricky programmer might have told it to print, *Are you feeling ill?* whenever it saw the words *throw up.* This program would be no more than a set of tricks. It might initially look convincing, but it wouldn't take long to get exasperated with it.

In the late sixties, researchers—myself included—began to consider problems of meaning as central to the development of natural language processing by humans or computers. We began to look at the underlying problems of language—the nature and representation of meaning—in the hope of developing a completely new approach to natural language processing. The previous chapters have introduced some of the most important elements of this new approach. The best way to appreciate how far we have come is to look at various programs and see how we progressed from one to the other.

The programs I have chosen to discuss were all done under my direction, since it seems most sensible to discuss the work I know best.

THE PROGRAMS

My students and I decided that it would be better to try to extract meanings from sentences than to extract grammatical units from sentences. Where the old objective of a parser was to make a grammatical analysis of a sentence, we decided that the new objective should be a *meaning analysis* of the sentence. In other words, rather than concentrate on how a sentence was constructed, we worried about how to *represent what was happening* in the event that the sentence describes. Our aim was to write programs that would concentrate on crucial differences in meaning, not on issues of grammatical structure.

This view redefined the parsing problem. We used whatever grammatical rules were necessary in our quest to extract meanings from sentences but, to our surprise, little grammar proved to be relevant for translating sentences into a system of conceptual representations. While I was at Stanford in the late sixties and early seventies, we began work on a program that could parse English sentences into conceptual representations. At the same time we began to build a *generator*, that is, a program that could take conceptual representations and make English out of them. We realized that if you could extract the meaning from a sentence by representing it conceptually, you had better be able to retrieve the English, or you would have lost information in the process.

If early work on parsing was overly concerned with syntax, the work on generation of sentences by computer was even worse. Early efforts on the generation of English sentences had concentrated on the problem of generating random sentences. Since the computer had nothing to say, generating sentences only could serve as an exercise in the grammatical construction of a sentence. But the moment we had achieved even the crudest levels of language understanding—the most primitive form of meaning representation—we realized that we needed a generator right away. Like the parser, the generator had to be constructed from new principles.

From the very beginning, the theories of language generation that evolved in AI looked considerably different from those developed in fields that were concerned with language per se rather than with understanding. An AI generator has to express what the computer wants to say. However, getting a computer to have something to say poses a problem. In this first stage, the computer just "wanted" to express what it had just parsed, so we could start with a meaning and then find a form to express it, rather than the other way around. In linguistics, for example, rules for the generation of sentences started with the idea that since a sentence consisted of a noun phrase and a verb phrase, then the generation of a sentence required the selection of a noun phrase and hence a noun. Thus, generating a sentence meant just finding its form and then finding a meaning to fit that form. Clearly this method would not work for either computers or people.

The basic intent of our work was to provide unique representations for ideas that could be expressed in many ways. Because of this, our programs could understand an event to be the same one as one seen previously, even if the previous expression of that event had been quite different. The conceptual representations that we devised (like those shown in Chapter 5) were intended to facilitate the automatic *paraphrasing* of a sentence that the program read, and even the translation of that sentence into other languages. We connected the generator to the parser to get a paraphrasing program. We found some graduate students who knew German and Chinese, so they went to work on building generators for those languages, which gave us the ability to develop translations of a sentence. Translation followed rather naturally from what we were doing. Once the parser represented the meaning, encoding that meaning into a language again was just as complex a task whether the language was English or Chinese. As long as the representation had no language-specific parts, that is, if it were truly conceptual, translation and paraphrase were essentially the same task. By 1973 we could parse, generate, paraphrase, and even translate sentences. We did not yet have an understanding system, but we had a new view on the problem and a cascade of solutions and new ideas.

MARGIE

Where did we go from there? Clearly, paraphrasing is not all we can do when we read a sentence. We can extrapolate from the smallest amount of information. The full meaning of a sentence is more than the sum of its parts. People speak in a kind of shorthand, expecting that their listeners will fill in assumptions as needed. We needed to program the computer to understand not only by extracting meanings from sentences, but also by making *inferences*. We began to develop a theory of inferencing, and built an inferencer.

Then someone suggested that we should put the parser, inferencer, and generator together in one big program, so we did and called it MARGIE. (Computer scientists constantly are giving birth to new programs, and with birth comes the right to name the baby. Computer scientists love to use acronyms for names.

MARGIE stood for *M*emory, *A*nalysis, *R*esponse *G*eneration *I*n *E*nglish. MARGIE also is the name of my mother.) This was the first time anyone had created a system that could paraphrase meanings, translate, and draw inferences from sentences.

MARGIE was our first attempt to parse English into conceptual representations. It consisted of three separate programs: a parser, which we called a Conceptual Analyzer to distinguish it from other syntactic parsers (the parser was written by Christopher Riesbeck as part of his Ph.D. work at Stanford); an inferencer (written by Chuck Rieger as part of his Ph.D. work at Stanford); and a generator (written by Neil Goldman as part of his Ph.D. work at Stanford). The output in Figure 1 shows MARGIE in two different modes of operation. In the INFERENCE mode all three programs were linked together. The parser sent its output to the inferencer which then made inferences and sent them to the generator to be expressed in English. In the PARAPHRASE mode, the parser decomposed the sentences into conceptual representations and then the generator expressed those representations in a number of different ways that showed the power of the representations.

No sooner did we gain some success than we began to see trouble ahead, or new problems to work on. MARGIE showed us that inferencing required careful control. We had 16 basic rules of inference, each of which was used every time the computer read a sentence. These rules were fairly simple, but the goal was merely to *test* some ideas about inferencing. Since people also make inferences from inferences, the program subjected the new conceptual representations that it had derived from the inference process to the 16 rules of inference and generated inferences from each of them. A combinatorial explosion of inferences quickly resulted. Some of the new inferences were valid and sensible, but many were ridiculous and irrelevant. Our new problem involved getting the computer to know the difference.

Two important theoretical issues emerged from the work on MARGIE. First, we had to find a way to focus the inferencing process in such a way as to pursue only reasonable paths at reasonable levels of detail. The second problem, related to the inference explosion problem, had to do with the initial restrictions placed on MARGIE. MARGIE handled individual sentences that were unrelated to one another. We began to concern ourselves

```
INFERENCE MODE
INPUT:     John told Mary that Bill wants a book.
OUTPUT1:   A book about what?
OUTPUT2:   Mary knows that Bill wants a book.
OUTPUT3:   Bill wants to come to have a book.
OUTPUT4:   Bill wants someone to cease to have a book.
OUTPUT5:   Bill wants to read a book.

INPUT:     John gave Mary a beating with a stick.
OUTPUT1:   A stick touched Mary.
OUTPUT2:   Mary became hurt.
OUTPUT3:   John wanted Mary to become hurt.
OUTPUT4:   Why was John angry?

INPUT:     John gave Mary an aspirin.
OUTPUT1:   John believes that Mary wants an aspirin.
OUTPUT2:   Mary is sick.
OUTPUT3:   Mary wants to feel better.
OUTPUT4:   Mary will ingest the aspirin.

INPUT:     John is going to go to the store.
OUTPUT1:   John wants to be at the store.
OUTPUT2:   What does John want to buy?
OUTPUT3:   John will trade money to the store for something.

PARAPHRASE MODE

INPUT:     John advised Mary to drink the wine.
OUTPUT:    John told Mary that drinking the wine would benefit her.

INPUT:     John killed Mary by choking Mary.
OUTPUT1:   John strangled Mary.
OUTPUT2:   John choked Mary and she died because she could not
           breathe.
OUTPUT3:   Mary died because she was unable to inhale some air and
           she was unable to inhale some air because John grabbed
           her neck.

INPUT:     Reading the book reminded Rita to loan the book to Bill.
OUTPUT:    Rita remembered to give the book to Bill and she expects
           him to return it to her because someone read the book.

INPUT:     John prevented Bill from giving a banana to Mary by
           selling a banana to Rita.
OUTPUT1:   Bill was unable to give a banana to Mary because Rita
           traded John some money for a banana.
OUTPUT2:   Mary could not get a banana from Bill because Rita
           bought a banana from John.
```

FIGURE 1
THE MARGIE PROGRAM, 1973

with the differences between understanding sentences by themselves, out of context, and understanding cohesive paragraphs which themselves were part of a larger context. We could parse sentences individually, but we had no idea what it would mean to relate them to one another. If we wanted a computer to process and understand text, then a program would have to be able to connect one sentence to the next.

Fortunately, these two problems were related. Inference explosions aren't as likely to occur in context since we have a sense of what a paragraph is really about. Understanding in context, therefore, poses a fundamentally different problem than the one presented to MARGIE. Serendipitously, the same basic parsing and generation techniques did apply.

SAM

I sat in a villa by a lake for a year working on these two problems. (An AI researcher doesn't need a computer most of the time. All he needs to begin with are a pencil and paper.) Both problems, inference explosion and connected text, were intimately related and could be solved with similar mechanisms. We developed a system of causal chaining, principles that allowed the computer to tie the meaning of one sentence to that of the next sentence by attempting to infer the connections between them. For example, one of the results of the first sentence might have to do with enabling an action in other sentences in the paragraph.

At Yale in 1974 we began to try to program rules for causal chaining to limit inferences during the reading of stories. But some connections between sentences couldn't be figured out as if they were "logical." It isn't "logical" to think that looking at a menu naturally precedes eating, in the context of a restaurant. People don't attempt to figure out the connection between those two events each time as if it were the first time they had encountered such a situation.

Scripts were invented by Robert Abelson (a psychology professor at Yale) and myself to solve this problem. They enabled the computer to process stories by providing rules for understanding the connectivity in a stereotypical situation. We wrote

SAM (Script Applier Mechanism), a program that could read stories that were scriptlike or script based.

SAM could read a variety of stories, including actual newspaper stories on specific subjects. Since we already had the translation ability that the conceptual parsers and generators from MARGIE provided, we could translate the stories that we read into other languages. We concentrated on car accident stories because they were both scriptlike and plentiful. We built programs to translate car accident stories from the *New Haven Register* into Russian and Spanish. A few people who knew both languages would look at the Russian and Spanish versions of a story and say, *Hey, these aren't exact translations of each other.* We told them no, they weren't exact translations of each other. The student who had written the Russian generator wrote it differently from the one that the Spanish-speaking student had written. Each system was independent, and the meaning representations used reflected not only linguistic but also cultural differences. (The Russian-speaking student reported, for example, that Russian newspapers never report car accidents, so he had a fair amount of difficulty just deciding what vocabulary to use.) The translation modules converted the conceptual representations that SAM produced into an appropriate expression in the target language.

SAM had four basic modules. It used the parser and generators from MARGIE, although they were in a somewhat modified form. The center of the program was the Script Applier which also contained a memory and inference part. The Script Applier was written by Richard Cullingford as part of his Ph.D. thesis at Yale. He also put all the other pieces together to make it all work. A question-answering module attempted to figure out the intention of a question and give the memory a clue as to where the answer might be found in the conceptual representation of the story that had been produced by the Script Applier. The question-answerer was written by Wendy Lehnert as part of her Ph.D. thesis at Yale. The Russian generator was written by Anatole Gershman, and the Spanish one by Jaime Carbonell.

Once again, what SAM could not do made it obvious what to do next. We had been dealing with highly restricted scripts, but real stories contain interesting complications and unusual consequences. Stories have characters who find novel ways to get what they want, characters who act without resorting to a

A LOOK AT SOME AI PROGRAMS

```
Input:

Friday  evening   a   car  swerved off  Route 69.   The  vehicle struck a tree.
The passenger, a New Jersey  man,  was  killed.    David  Hall,  27,  was
pronounced dead  at  the  scene by Dr. Dana Blanchard, medical examiner.
Frank Miller, 32, of 593 Foxon Rd., the driver,  was  taken  to  Milford
Hospital  by  Flanagan Ambulance.   He  was  treated and released.  No
charges were made.  Patrolman Robert Onofrio investigated the  accident.

English Summary:

AN AUTOMOBILE HIT A TREE NEAR HIGHWAY 69 FOUR  DAYS  AGO.    DAVID  HALL,
AGE 27,  RESIDENCE  IN  NEW  JERSEY, THE PASSENGER, DIED.  FRANK MILLER,
AGE 32, RESIDENCE AT 593 FOXON  ROAD  IN  NEW  HAVEN,  CONNECTICUT,  THE
DRIVER,  WAS  SLIGHTLY  INJURED.    THE  POLICE  DEPARTMENT  DID NOT FILE
CHARGES.

Spanish Summary:

UN AUTO CHOCO CONTRA UN ARBOL CERCA DE LA CARRETERA  69  EL  VIERNES  AL
ANOCHECER.   DAVID  HALL,  DE  27 ANOS,  QUE  VIVIA  EN  NEW JERSEY, EL
PASAGERO, SE MURIO.  FRANK MILLER, DE 32 ANOS, QUE VIVIA  EN  593  CALLE
FOXON  EN  NEW  HAVEN,  CONNECTICUT, EL CHOFER, QUEDO UN POCO HERIDO.  EL
DEPARTAMENTO DE POLICIA NO ACUSO A NADIE.

Question-Answering Output:

Q1: Was anyone killed?
A1: YES, DAVID HALL DIED.

Q2: Was anyone hurt?
A2: YES, FRANK MILLER WAS SLIGHTLY INJURED.

Q3: Why was Miller hurt?
A3: BECAUSE THE AUTOMOBILE HIT THE TREE.

Q4: Did Miller go to the hospital?
A4: YES, HE WAS IN THE MILFORD HOSPITAL.

Q5: How did Miller get to the hospital?
A5: THE FLANAGAN AMBULANCE COMPANY TOOK HIM TO THE MILFORD HOSPITAL.
```

FIGURE 2
THE SAM PROGRAM, 1975

```
INPUT TEXT:

    John wanted money.
    He got a gun and walked into a liquor store.
    He told the owner he wanted some money.
    The owner gave John the money and John left.

INPUT:    Why did John get a gun?
OUTPUT:   Because John wanted to rob the liquor store.

INPUT:    Why did John threaten the shopkeeper?
OUTPUT:   Because John needed to get some money.

INPUT:    Why did the shopkeeper give John the money?
OUTPUT:   Because the shopkeeper didn't want to get hurt.

INPUT:    Why did John leave?
OUTPUT:   Because John didn't want to get caught.

OUTPUT:

STORY FROM JOHN'S POINT OF VIEW:

    I needed to get some dough.  So I got myself this gun, and
    I walked down to the liquor store.  I told the shopkeeper
    that if he didn't let me have the money then I would shoot
    him.  So he handed it over.  Then I left.

OUTPUT:

STORY FROM THE OWNER'S POINT OF VIEW:

    I was minding the store when a man entered.  He threatened
    me with a gun and demanded all the cash receipts.  Well, I
    didn't want to get hurt, so I gave him the money.  Then he
    escaped.
```

FIGURE 3
THE PAM PROGRAM, 1977

script. We had to start developing structures that allowed the computer to understand a character's *plans* and *goals*. In order to understand a story about a liquor store robbery we could have created a *liquor store robbery* script. But most people don't have such a script, having neither observed nor participated in a liquor

```
INPUT TEXT:

    John wanted to win the stockcar race.
    Bill also wanted to win the stockcar race.
    Before the race John cut Bill's ignition wire.

INPUT:   Why did John break an ignition wire?
OUTPUT:  Because he was trying to prevent Bill from racing.
INPUT:

    JOHN WANTED BILL'S BICYCLE.
    HE WENT OVER TO BILL
      AND ASKED HIM IF HE WOULD GIVE IT TO HIM.
    BILL REFUSED.
    JOHN TOLD BILL HE WOULD GIVE HIM FIVE DOLLARS FOR IT,
    BUT BILL WOULD NOT AGREE.
    THEN JOHN TOLD BILL HE WOULD BREAK HIS ARM
    IF HE DIDN'T LET HIM HAVE IT.
    BILL GAVE HIM THE BICYCLE.

    QUESTION: Q1
        Why did John walk over to Bill?
        Because he wanted to get his bicycle.

    QUESTION: Q2
        Why did Bill give his bicycle to John?
        Because he didn't want to get hurt.

    QUESTION: Q3
        What were the consequences of John's walking over to Bill?
        This enabled him to ask him to give him Bill's bicycle.

    QUESTION: Q4
        What were the consequences of John's asking Bill to give him
        Bill's bicycle?
        Bill told him that Bill wouldn't give him Bill's bicycle.
```

FIGURE 3
THE PAM PROGRAM, 1977 (continued)

store robbery. We could have given the computer a large range of understanding by giving it an endless number of scripts, but when it found itself without a script it would have been stymied. We had to give the computer methods for dealing with the world when it did not have an applicable script.

PAM

As a way of exercising our ability to program plan and goal structures, we were building TALE-SPIN at the same time as we were building SAM. This was the first program to *make up* its own stories using just some principles of storytelling and rules for planning in an imaginary world. We then used these ideas of how people plan to achieve goals to help in getting computers to understand stories by building PAM (*Plan Applier Mechanism*), a program that attempted to understand the world in terms of the rules we have for resolving goal conflicts, achieving temporarily blocked goals, and so on.

PAM was written by Robert Wilensky as part of his Ph.D. thesis at Yale. The generator used by PAM was different from our MARGIE generator. The generator for PAM was written by Richard Granger. Because PAM used goals to track its characters, it was possible to tell stories from the viewpoint of those characters. We also added some vocabulary typical of different types of people to make the output seem realistic. The vocabulary trick was showy but involved little theory.

POLITICS

Once we built a program that used plans to understand stories, we opened up a set of new problems. For example, once we create a plan, someone else can come up with a counterplan. When we read stories, we aren't just aware of plans, we can recognize counterplans and counter-counterplans. With this in mind, we wrote POLITICS (we never did think up an acronym for this one), a model of a U.S. senator's position on foreign policy questions, complete with separate belief systems that held the beliefs of a conservative and those of a liberal. POLITICS was intended to sound like a U.S. senator by reflecting some of the reasoning processes that a senator might use in answering questions that were asked of him.

POLITICS was written by Jaime Carbonell as part of his Ph.D. thesis at Yale. It differed from our other programs in that it was an integrated system. Rather than have a separate parser as we

```
The US Congress is expected to approve the Panama Canal Treaty.

CONSERVATIVE MODE:

INTERPRETATION COMPLETED, READY TO ACCEPT QUESTIONS.

Q1:  Should the US approve the treaty?
A1:  NO, THE TREATY IS BAD FOR THE UNITED STATES.

Q2:  Why is the treaty bad for the US?
A2:  THE UNITED STATES WOULD LOSE THE CANAL TO PANAMA
     AND THE UNITED STATES WILL BE WEAKER.

Q3:  What might happen if the United States loses the Canal?
A3:  RUSSIA WILL TRY TO CONTROL THE CANAL.

Q4:  Why would Russia try to take over the Canal?
A4:  RUSSIA WANTS TO EXPAND ITS MILITARY CONTROL.  THE
     PANAMA CANAL HAS HIGH MILITARY VALUE.

Q5:  How might this happen?
A5:  THE UNITED STATES MAY NOT BE ABLE TO STOP ANYONE
     TAKING OVER THE PANAMA CANAL.  TORRIJOS IS A COMMUNIST.
     TORRIJOS WILL LET RUSSIA CONTROL PANAMA.

Q6:  Why should the US worry about Russia taking over the Canal?
A6:  BECAUSE RUSSIA WANTS TO CONTROL THE WORLD.

Q7:  What should the US do to stop Russia from taking over the Canal?
A7:  CONGRESS SHOULD VOTE AGAINST THE PANAMA CANAL TREATY.

LIBERAL MODE:


INTERPRETATION COMPLETED, READY TO ACCEPT QUESTIONS.

Q1:  Should the US approve the treaty?
A1:  YES, THE PANAMA CANAL TREATY IS GOOD FOR THE
     UNITED STATES.

Q2:  Why is the treaty good?
A2:  THE PANAMA CANAL TREATY IMPROVES RELATIONS WITH LATIN
     AMERICAN COUNTRIES.

Q3:  What happens if the US keeps the Canal?
A3:  THIS WILL CAUSE DISCONTENT AND CONFLICT IN
     PANAMA AND LATIN AMERICA.
```

FIGURE 4
THE POLITICS PROGRAM, 1978

THE COGNITIVE COMPUTER

```
Q4:  Why would this lead to conflict?
A4:  THE CANAL ZONE IS A UNITED STATES COLONY.  LATIN
     AMERICA DOES NOT LIKE COLONIALISM. THE UNITED
     STATES WOULD MAINTAIN COLONIALISM.

Q5:  What if Russia tries to take over the canal?
A5:  RUSSIA DOES NOT WANT CONFLICT WITH THE US.  RUSSIA
     WILL STAY OUT OF THE CANAL IF THE UNITED STATES
     DEFENDS IT.  THE UNITED STATES DEFENDING THE CANAL
     IS PART OF THE TREATY.

Russia is massing troops on the Czech border.

CONSERVATIVE MODE:

INTERPRETATION COMPLETED, READY TO ACCEPT QUESTIONS.

Q1:  Why did Russia do this?
A1:  BECAUSE RUSSIA THOUGHT THAT IT COULD TAKE POLITICAL
     CONTROL OF CZECHOSLOVAKIA BY SENDING TROOPS.

Q2:  What will Russia do next?
A2:  RUSSIA MAY TELL ITS TROOPS TO START THE INVASION.

Q3:  What else can Russia do?
A3:  RUSSIA MAY WAIT FOR CZECHOSLOVAKIA TO GIVE IN TO
     RUSSIAN DEMANDS.

Q4:  What happens if Czechoslovakia does not give in?
A4:  RUSSIA MAY DECIDE TO START THE INVASION.

Q5:  What should the United States do?
A5:  THE UNITED STATES SHOULD INTERVENE MILITARILY.

Q6:  What else can the United States do?
A6:  THE UNITED STATES CAN DO NOTHING, OR IT CAN INTERVENE
     DIPLOMATICALLY BY CONFERRING WITH RUSSIA ABOUT
     CZECHOSLOVAKIA.  THESE ALTERNATIVES ARE BAD FOR THE
     UNITED STATES.
```

FIGURE 4
THE POLITICS PROGRAM, 1978 (continued)

had done before, POLITICS used its knowledge of the situation to help it understand sentences.

POLITICS demonstrated that one must interpret any new item of information using all the mental processes available. Beliefs, inferences, plans, goals, scripts, prior memories—all were relevant to the understanding of international events. In POLITICS they all were there in one place.

FRUMP

Success in these programs led us to begin to attack our old problems in different ways. First we tried to speed up what we had done already. Next we tried to fully integrate all the processes we knew about into one grand story understanding system. SAM had been slow—it made inferences for every single aspect of a script-based story as it read through, and it took the computer a very long time to process each story. Although we believed that the processes SAM went through were part of language understanding, not all those processes were used all the time. We decided to work on turning off some of SAM's processes at appropriate times. Another problem with SAM was that it was modular. It first put a sentence through a parser, then through the inferencer, script applier, and generator. But real human understanding is more likely to be integrated. We start parsing, making inferences, and generally interpreting a sentence even before we have heard the end of it. We do not wait to see how a sentence will turn out before we begin to understand it.

We decided to integrate everything and speed everything up by not wasting time on spurious inferencing. We wrote FRUMP (*Fast Reading, Understanding, and Memory Program*). We hooked this program up to the United Press International news wire, and the program zipped through it, summarizing the stories that it understood in several languages.

FRUMP was written by Jerry De Jong as part of his Ph.D. thesis at Yale. FRUMP was a complex program and Jerry had many assistants to help build various parts of the program. These included Kris Hammond, Jim Hendler, and Bill Ferguson. FRUMP was our first attempt to build a product-directed program. We wanted to see how hard it would be to make the story-understanding process fast. As a result we sacrificed careful understanding for speed. Nevertheless, theoretical advances did come from FRUMP, the most notable being the fusing of the parsing and inference process into one basic process.

```
INPUT:

     WASHINGTON, MARCH 15 - THE STATE DEPARTMENT ANNOUNCED TODAY
THE SUSPENSION OF DIPLOMATIC RELATIONS WITH EQUATORIAL GUINEA.  THE
ANNOUNCEMENT CAME FIVE DAYS AFTER THE DEPARTMENT RECEIVED A MESSAGE
FROM THE FOREIGN MINISTER OF THE WEST AFRICAN COUNTRY SAYING THAT HIS
GOVERNMENT HAD DECLARED TWO UNITED STATES DIPLOMATS PERSONA NON GRATA.

     THE TWO ARE AMBASSADOR HERBERT J. SPIRO AND CONSUL WILLIAM C.
MITHOEFER JR., BOTH STATIONED IN NEIGHBORING CAMEROON BUT ALSO
ACCREDITED TO EQUATORIAL GUINEA.

     ROBERT L. FUNSETH, STATE DEPARTMENT SPOKESMAN, SAID MR. SPIRO AND
MR. MITHOEFER SPENT FIVE DAYS IN EQUATORIAL GUINEA EARLIER THIS MONTH
AND WERE GIVEN "A WARM RECEPTION."

     BUT AT THE CONCLUSION OF THEIR VISIT, MR. FUNSETH SAID, EQUATORIAL
GUINEA'S ACTING CHIEF OF PROTOCOL HANDED THEM A FIVE-PAGE LETTER THAT
CAST "UNWARRANTED AND INSULTING SLURS" ON BOTH DIPLOMATS.

SELECTED SKETCHY SCRIPT $BREAK-RELATIONS

CPU TIME FOR UNDERSTANDING = 2515 MILLISECONDS

ENGLISH SUMMARY:
    THE US STATE DEPARTMENT AND GUINEA HAVE BROKEN DIPLOMATIC RELATIONS.

FRENCH SUMMARY:
    LE DEPARTMENT D'ETAT DES ETATS-UNIS ET LA GUINEE ONT COUPE
    LEURS RELATIONS DIPLOMATIQUES.

CHINESE SUMMARY:
    MEEIGWO GWOWUHYUANN GEN JIINAHYAH DUANNJYUELE WAYJIAU GUANSHIH.

SPANISH SUMMARY:
    EL DEPARTAMENTO DE RELACIONES EXTERIORES DE LOS EE UU Y GUINEA
    CORTATON SUS RELACIONES DIPLOMATICAS.

INPUT

        MOUNT VERNON, ILL, (UPI) - A SMALL EARTHQUAKE SHOOK SEVERAL
SOUTHERN ILLINOIS COUNTIES MONDAY NIGHT, THE NATIONAL EARTHQUAKE
INFORMATION SERVICE IN GOLDEN, COLO., REPORTED

        SPOKESMAN DON FINLEY SAID THE QUAKE MEASURED 3.2 ON THE RICHTER
SCALE, "PROBABLY NOT ENOUGH TO DO ANY DAMAGE OR CAUSE ANY INJURIES." THE
QUAKE OCCURRED ABOUT 7:48 P.M.  CST AND WAS CENTERED ABOUT 30 MILES EAST
OF MOUNT VERNON, FINLEY SAID.  IT WAS FELT IN RICHLAND, CLAY, JASPER,
EFFINGTON AND MARION COUNTIES.
```

FIGURE 5
THE FRUMP PROGRAM, 1979

```
      SMALL EARTHQUAKES ARE COMMON IN THE AREA, FINLEY SAID.

 SELECTED SKETCHY SCRIPT $EARTHQUAKE

 CPU TIME FOR UNDERSTANDING = 3040 MILLISECONDS

 ENGLISH SUMMARY:
      THERE WAS AN EARTHQUAKE IN ILLINOIS WITH A 3.1999 RICHTER
      SCALE READING.

 INPUT:
           THE CHILEAN GOVERNMENT HAS SEIZED OPERATIONAL AND FINANCIAL
 CONTROL OF THE U.S.   INTEREST IN THE EL TENIENTE MINING COMPANY, ONE
 OF THE THREE BIG COPPER ENTERPRISES HERE.  WHEN THE KENNECOTT COPPER
 COMPANY, THE OWNERS, SOLD A 51 PER CENT INTEREST IN THE COMPANY TO THE
 CHILEAN STATE COPPER CORPORATION IN 1967 IT RETAINED A CONTRACT TO MANAGE
 THE MINE.  ROBERT HALDEMAN, EXECUTIVE VICE PRESIDENT OF EL TENIENTE, SAID
 THE CONTRACT HAD BEEN "IMPAIRED" BY THE LATEST GOVERNMENT ACTION.  AFTER
 A MEETING WITH COMPANY OFFICIALS AT THE MINE SITE NEAR HERE, HOWEVER, HE
 SAID THAT HE HAD INSTRUCTED THEM TO COOPERATE WITH EIGHT ADMINISTRATORS
 THAT THE CHILEAN GOVERNMENT HAD APPOINTED TO CONTROL ALL ASPECTS OF THE
 COMPANY'S OPERATIONS.

 SELECTED SKETCHY SCRIPT $NATIONALIZE

 CPU TIME FOR UNDERSTANDING = 3457 MILLISECONDS

 ENGLISH SUMMARY:
      CHILE HAS NATIONALIZED AN AMERICAN MINE.
```

FIGURE 5
THE FRUMP PROGRAM, 1979 (continued)

FRUMP worked so well that people were calling up to ask us to create a program that could read and keep track of massive texts such as the Congressional Record, and to build systems that could analyze foreign publications. We had to point out that FRUMP only contained a few scripts to read restricted kinds of news stories, and that any kind of general understanding system would require *thousands* of scripts.

IPP

We next wrote a program called IPP (Integrated Partial Parser). IPP was essentially like FRUMP except that it had detailed knowledge of one domain—terrorism—and it could add to that knowledge by absorbing information from what it read into its memory. We were attempting to address two different problems in IPP. First, if we ever are to automate the reading of news wires, we will have to build in detailed knowledge of the subject matter to be read. IPP concentrated on only one domain of knowledge so that it could attempt to build up its knowledge in that domain. Our goal was to get IPP to build up that knowledge automatically, by learning from what it read. The second goal in IPP was to put all the knowledge structures we had devised in the same program. FRUMP used only scripts. IPP used plans, goals, scripts, and also had a memory.

IPP was written by Michael Lebowitz as part of his Ph.D. thesis at Yale. The major intention of IPP was to add to its knowledge structures by forming new structures as a result of what it read. The program makes a new generalization about Basque terrorist attacks which it constructed for itself after reading the following three stories. Often the generalizations that IPP made were a bit spurious. Nevertheless, it was beginning to update and expand its own memory structures, and that was of critical importance.

BORIS

After spending a fair amount of effort on news stories, we began to be concerned that there was a range of phenomena in understanding that did not come across on the news wire but nevertheless posed significant problems. We wanted also to see how we could improve our general story understanding capabilities by using a new set of memory structures we were devising, ones more suited to facilitate learning by cross-contextual understanding. We created a more fully integrated program that relied on a model of human beliefs and interactions that we could use in understanding little melodramas. This program was called BORIS. (We were feeling a bit whimsical in naming this one. In fact, we named it long before we wrote it. The name expresses our frustration with some of our previous programs: *Better Organized Reasoning and Inference System*.)

As our lab grew, we started to add new faculty and projects which often were not run directly by me. The BORIS project was supervised by Wendy Lehnert, who by this time was a professor

```
*(PARSE S1-7)

          (10 9 79) SPAIN

(STEPPING UP EFFORTS TO DERAIL A BASQUE HOME RULE STATUTE
THAT WILL BE PUT TO A REFERENDUM THIS MONTH BASQUE GUNMEN
IN SAN SEBASTIAN SPRAYED A BAR FREQUENTED BY POLICEMEN WITH
GUNFIRE WOUNDING 11 PERSONS)

(IN PAMPLONA AOTHER BASQUE CITY TERRORISTS MURDERED A
POLICE INSPECTOR *COMMA* KILLING HIM AS HE DREW HIS OWN
WEAPON IN SELF-DEFENSE)

>>> Beginning final memory incorporation . . .

Feature analysis:  EV1 (S-DESTRUCTIVE-ATTACK)
     RESULTS        HEALTH       -10
                    AU           HURT-PERSON
                    HEALTH       -5
     VICTIM         NUMBER       MANY
                    ROLE         AUTHORITY
     TARGET         PLACE        BAR
     ACTOR          NATIONALITY  BASQUE
     METHODS        AU           $SHOOT-ATTACK
     LOCATION       AREA         WESTERN-EUROPE
                    NATION       SPAIN

Indexing EV1 (S1-7) as variant of S-DESTRUCTIVE-ATTACK

>>> Memory incorporation complete


          (5 15 80) SPAIN

(A BASQUE SEPARATIST GUERRILLA SHOT TO DEATH THREE
YOUNG NATIONAL POLICEMEN AT POINT BLANK RANGE THURSDAY
AS THEY DRANK THEIR MORNING COFFEE IN A BAR)

>>> Beginning final memory incorporation . . .

Feature analysis:  EV5  (S-DESTRUCTIVE-ATTACK)
     TARGET         PLACE        BAR
     VICTIM         GENDER       MALE
                    ROLE         AUTHORITY
     ACTOR          NATIONALITY  BASQUE
                    DEMAND-TYPE  SEPARATISM
     METHODS        AU           $SHOOT-ATTACK
```

FIGURE 6
THE IPP PROGRAM, 1980

```
          LOCATION        AREA          WESTERN-EUROPE
                          NATION        SPAIN

    Creating more specific S-DESTRUCTIVE-ATTACK
        (G1-1 : BASQUE-GEN) from events EV1 (S1-7)
        EV5 (S1-6) with features:

    VICTIM        (1)     GENDER        MALE
                          ROLE          AUTHORITY
    ACTOR         (1)     NATIONALITY   BASQUE
    METHODS       (1)     AU            $SHOOT-ATTACK
    LOCATION      (1)     AREA          WESTERN-EUROPE
                          NATION        SPAIN
    TARGET        (1)     PLACE         BAR

    >>>Memory incorporation complete

    "Terrorist attacks in Spain are often shootings
     of policemen in bars by Basques"
```

FIGURE 6
THE IPP PROGRAM, 1980 (continued)

at Yale. BORIS was written by Michael Dyer as part of his Ph.D. thesis. Tom Wolf and Pete Johnson also worked on the project. BORIS was a rather complicated program that employed new parsing techniques, new inference techniques, and used different memory structures than we had been using.

The language understanding programs we had built so far were satisfying in that they showed us we could do what we set out to do. But they also were frustrating because each showed us a new set of problems that were unsolved and lay as obstacles on the road to automating the understanding process. These programs became more and more complicated to write as they encompassed ever more processes and greater and greater knowledge.

CYRUS

Perhaps the program that we have written that best illustrates just where we are going is CYRUS. CYRUS stands for Computerized Yale Reasoning and Understanding System. (In this case, we knew the name had to be CYRUS—it was just a question of

```
PROCESSING PARAGRAPH 1:

    Richard hadn't heard from his college
    roommate Paul for years.
    Richard had borrowed money from Paul
    which was never paid back.
    But now he had no idea where to find his old friend.
    When a letter finally arrived from San Francisco,
    Richard was anxious to find out how Paul was.

READY TO ACCEPT Q/A :

    >What happened to Richard at home? <
    RICHARD GOT A LETTER FROM PAUL.

    >Who is Paul? <
    RICHARD'S FRIEND.

    >Did Richard want to see Paul? <
    YES, RICHARD WANTED TO KNOW HOW PAUL WAS.

    >Had Paul helped Richard? <
    YES, PAUL LENT MONEY TO RICHARD.

    >Why didn't Richard pay Paul back? <
    RICHARD DID NOT KNOW WHERE PAUL WAS.

    >How did Richard feel when the letter appeared? <
    RICHARD FELT GLAD BECAUSE PAUL AND HE WERE FRIENDS.


PROCESSING PARAGRAPH 2:

    Unfortunately, the news was not good.
    Paul's wife Sarah wanted a divorce.
    She also wanted the car, the house,
    the children, and alimony.
    Paul wanted the divorce, but he didn't want to
    see Sarah walk off with everything he had.
    His salary from the state school
    system was very small.
    Not knowing who to turn to, he was hoping
    for a favor from the only lawyer he knew.
    Paul gave his home phone number in case
    Richard felt he could help.

READY TO ACCEPT Q/A :

    >What was the letter about? <
    PAUL AND SARAH WERE GETTING A DIVORCE.
```

FIGURE 7
THE BORIS PROGRAM, 1981

```
>Did Paul write Sarah? <
NO, IT WASN'T SARAH, IT WAS RICHARD WHO GOT THE LETTER.

>Why was Paul upset about the divorce? <
PAUL AND SARAH WERE FIGHTING OVER THE FAMILY POSSESSIONS.

>What did Paul do for a living? <
PAUL WAS A TEACHER.

>What did Sarah want? <
SARAH WANTED TO HAVE THE CAR AND THE HOUSE AND THE KIDS AND
THE ALIMONY.

>Why did Paul write to Richard? <
PAUL WANTED RICHARD TO BE HIS LAWYER.

> go <
```

PROCESSING PARAGRAPH 3:

```
Richard eagerly picked up the phone and dialed.
After a brief conversation,
Paul agreed to have lunch with him the next day.
He sounded extremely relieved and grateful.
```

READY TO ACCEPT Q/A :

```
>Why did Richard call Paul? <
RICHARD WANTED TO ARRANGE A MEETING WITH PAUL.

>Did Richard contact Paul? <
YES.  RICHARD CALLED PAUL.

>How did Richard contact Paul? <
BY PHONE.

>How did Paul feel when Richard called? <
PAUL WAS HAPPY BECAUSE RICHARD AGREED TO BE PAUL'S LAWYER.

> go <
```

PROCESSING PARAGRAPH 4:

```
The next day, as Richard was driving into the restaurant,
he barely avoided hitting an old man on the street.
He felt extremely upset by the incident,
and had three drinks at the restaurant.
When Paul arrived Richard was fairly drunk.
After the food came, Richard spilled a cup of coffee on Paul.
```

FIGURE 7
THE BORIS PROGRAM, 1981 (continued)

A LOOK AT SOME AI PROGRAMS

```
        Paul seemed very annoyed by this so Richard
        offered to drive him home for a change of clothes.

READY TO ACCEPT Q/A :

    >Why did Richard eat out with Paul? <
    RICHARD WANTED TO DISCUSS THE DIVORCE CASE WITH PAUL.

    >What happened to Richard on the way to the restaurant? <
    RICHARD ALMOST RAN OVER AN OLD MAN.

    >Why did Richard get drunk? <
    RICHARD WAS UPSET ABOUT ALMOST RUNNING OVER THE OLD MAN.

    >What happened at the restaurant? <
    RICHARD SPILLED COFFEE ON PAUL.

    >How did Richard feel when the coffee spilled? <
    RICHARD WAS UNHAPPY.

    >Why did Richard spill the coffee? <
    RICHARD WAS DRUNK.

    >When did Richard almost hit the old man? <
    WHILE RICHARD WAS DRIVING TO THE RESTAURANT.

    >Where did Richard have lunch with Paul? <
    AT A RESTAURANT.

PROCESSING PARAGRAPH 5:

    When Paul walked into the bedroom and found
    Sarah with another man he nearly had a heart attack.
    Then he realized what a blessing it was.
    With Richard there as a witness,
    Sarah's divorce case was shot.
    Richard congratulated Paul and
    suggested that they celebrate at dinner.
    Paul was eager to comply.


READY TO ACCEPT Q/A :

    >Why did Richard drive Paul home? <
    SO PAUL COULD CHANGE HIS CLOTHES.

    >What happened to Paul at home? <
    PAUL CAUGHT SARAH COMMITTING ADULTERY.

    >How did Paul feel? <
```

FIGURE 7
THE BORIS PROGRAM, 1981 (continued)

```
PAUL WAS SURPRISED.

>Why did Sarah lose her divorce case? <
SARAH COMMITTED ADULTERY.

>Why did Richard congratulate Paul? <
PAUL WON HIS DIVORCE CASE.

> go <

TEXT PROCESSING COMPLETE ON:  DIVORCE-STORY
```

FIGURE 7
THE BORIS PROGRAM, 1981 (continued)

figuring out what CYRUS could be an acronym for.) CYRUS was a memory program that received from FRUMP all the stories it could find about Cyrus Vance, who was Secretary of State at the time. (The program later switched to Muskie.) CYRUS compiled a professional and personal history of Cyrus Vance. This was an attempt to begin to model the memory of a particular individual. In some sense, the program thought of itself as Cyrus Vance. (Well, we wrote it that way. It is hard to say that this program thought anything about itself.) We wanted the program to constantly change on the basis of its new experiences. It succeeded to some degree, but its success is not quite the point.

In a sense, CYRUS, or programs that will succeed CYRUS, will replace the large data base programs we have today. The problem with today's data bases is that they don't know what they know. CYRUS reorganized itself continually so as to best reflect what it knew. And, although it was only an experiment, it taught us a great deal about what it means to remember.

CYRUS was written by Janet Kolodner as part of her Ph.D. thesis at Yale. Perhaps CYRUS's most interesting highlight was its ability to answer questions about which it had no direct information. When CYRUS responded (see p. 161) that Mrs. Begin had met Mrs. Vance, the program actually was just guessing. It figured that if it could find a situation when both women were likely to be present, then it could assume that they had met. The program thus searched for social situations (to which wives might have been invited) that occurred on trips that either one of the men might have made with his wife to the home of the other.

```
@CYRUS

ARE YOU INTERESTED IN MUSKIE OR VANCE?  (M OR V) : *VANCE

*(DIALOG2)

>When was the last time you were in Egypt?

     inferring a diplomatic trip
     answering question using time context

ON DEC 10 1978.

>Why did you go there?

     answering question using previous context

TO NEGOTIATE THE CAMP DAVID ACCORDS.

>Who did you talk to there?

     inferring undifferentiated political meeting
     answering question using previous context

WITH ANWAR SADAT.

>Has your wife ever met Mrs Begin?

     inferring a social political occasion

YES, MOST RECENTLY AT A STATE DINNER IN ISRAEL IN JAN 1980.

>What heads of state have you met?

     inferring a diplomatic meeting
     searching directly for $MEET
      .  .  .

     applying strategies to search memory
      .  .  .

       searching for sM-CONFERENCE
        .  .  .
       searching for sM-VIPVISIT
        searching sM-VIPVISIT instance for $MEET
        .  .  .
       searching for I-NEGOTIATE
        .  .  .
```

FIGURE 8
THE CYRUS PROGRAM, 1980

THE COGNITIVE COMPUTER

```
KING HASSAN, MENACHEM BEGIN, MUSTAFA KHALIL, IAN SMITH,
PRESIDENT ASSAD, KING HUSSEIN, AND ANWAR SADAT.

>Last time you went to Saudi Arabia, where did you stay?

    inferring a diplomatic trip
    answering question using time context

IN  A PALACE IN SAUDI ARABIA ON SEP 23 1978.

>Did you go sightseeing there?

    answering question using previous context

YES, AT AN OILFIELD IN DHARAN ON SEP 23 1978.


**************************

@CYRUS

ARE YOU INTERESTED IN MUSKIE OR VANCE?  (M OR V) : *MUSKIE

*(DIALOG2)

>Where are you today?

     inferring a diplomatic trip

  PROBABLY IN THE UNITED STATES ON JUN 14 1980.

>Where were you three weeks ago?

     inferring a diplomatic trip

  IN EUROPE.

>Why did you go?

    answering question using previous context:

  TO TALK TO ANDREI GROMYKO.

>Who did you talk to?

    inferring undifferentiated political meeting
    answering question using previous context

  TO NATO IN BRUSSELS ON MAY 14 AND TO ANDREI GROMYKO IN
  VIENNA.
```

FIGURE 8
THE CYRUS PROGRAM, 1980 (continued)

```
>Did you give a speech?

    answering question using previous context

    YES, ONE TO A GROUP OF REPORTERS AND ONE TO NATO.

>Are you going to Asia?

    inferring a diplomatic trip

    YES, THIS MONTH.

>Who will you talk to?

    inferring undifferentiated political meeting
    answering question using previous context

    TO NATO IN ANKARA, TURKEY.
***************************
```

FIGURE 8
THE CYRUS PROGRAM, 1980 (continued)

Finding a state dinner in Israel that occurred during a trip where Mrs. Vance did accompany her husband, it assumed the rest.

THE ROAD AHEAD

On a crude level, both CYRUS and IPP could be reminded of a previous story, and compare the two in search of some general characteristics. For example, IPP researched some generalizations on its own derived from what it read. The program decided that every terrorist attack in Ireland was by the IRA; in every terrorist attack in New Zealand the weapon was a boomerang; and that every time there was a hijacking in Lebanon it was in protest of the disappearance of a Shiite Moslem leader. But more and more, we came to realize that scripts, plans, goals, and cross-textual referencing weren't the only crucial elements of an understanding system. Understanding a story can involve everything a person has ever known. We began to realize the importance of a *dynamic* memory, one that changes every time it understands a story.

A dynamic memory program would be able to find experiences from its past to help it understand a new event. A program equipped with such a memory would read a story differently each time it saw it, since it would be updating memory the first time, but be bored the second time. Or, alternatively, it might learn more from it the second time, if it had gathered many new experiences that related to the subject of that story in the interim. Our early programs never changed their processing structures as a result of reading a new story. They served to lead us into what may be the most complicated elements of any understanding system—the memory problem and the learning problem. CYRUS and IPP were our first attempts at getting programs to learn, a problem in which we now are engrossed in our laboratory at Yale.

We are trying to develop a system that is capable of building up an increasing number of memories about different situations it has experienced, which it then can use in understanding even more stories and experiences. We don't all have the same knowledge of earthquakes or even of driving a car because we don't all have the same experiences with earthquakes and cars. We don't just want to have to *put in* everything we have ever known about earthquakes; we want to enable the machine to *generate* its own knowledge of earthquakes derived from *its* experiences. An understanding system should expand its knowledge with experiences.

Reading a story should change the way we read a later story on the same subject. Creating a belief system with some knowledge structures about what humans might do in certain situations depends upon the development of good representational methods. Getting a system that can use all its beliefs at any given time and modify them on the basis of what it reads, one that can learn from its experiences, requires an even more flexible representation than the kind we had been using.

How do people expand their knowledge so that it helps them with everything, so that it changes even the way they parse sentences? Children are constantly dreaming up generalizations, seeing when they fail, and modifying them on the basis of their experiences. Intelligent readers learn from what they read—that is *why* they read.

It is clear, then, what we must do next. We must develop systems with flexible, changeable knowledge structures that can learn while doing.

CHAPTER EIGHT

THE LEARNING BARRIER

The ability to use scripts and to employ planning mechanisms constitutes a large part of intelligence. Yet there is far more to the human mind than is suggested by these knowledge structures. If all the types of knowledge structures we have mentioned in this book, covering a full range of human experiences, were available to a computer, we would have quite a powerful machine. But the machine would not have yet achieved COGNITIVE UNDERSTANDING. We would have given the computer a great many conceptual representations for some of what people do in stereotyped and stylized circumstances. The model of the world embodied in such programming enables the machine to MAKE SENSE of some simple stories about people going to restaurants, getting money from their relatives, escaping burning buildings, and the like. These advances are encouraging, but we must admit that the machine still is not very intelligent. Why not?

We have developed only the beginnings of an understanding system. Today's AI programs can understand some simple things, but how will it learn to understand at a deeper level? It cannot make high-level analogies; nor can it change its knowledge structures when appropriate. The computer only can deal with what we have taught it to deal with. It has no general understanding ability. If it encounters a truly novel situation, it will not even be able to MAKE SENSE of what it reads.

To achieve the level of intelligence we are looking for, we have to provide the computer with more general structures, the same ones that allow people to make connections at a very high level of abstraction. We want the computer to learn something when it reads. We want it to thoroughly integrate a story into its knowledge structures. We want it to be able to distinguish what is important from what is trivial in a story, and remember things it read in the past just when they are most applicable to a situation it is processing currently. We want computers to have flexible, *dynamic* memories that will enable them to be reminded of past experiences and to profit from those experiences.

Learning something new might involve seeing something familiar in a new light; recalling something that we previously thought was unrelated; or remembering a crucial detail that never seemed to be important until some new experience caused us to appreciate its significance. If the computer is going to learn, it has to be able to bring its prior relevant knowledge to bear at just the right moment in order to understand what is happening. The computer must be able to carry on a dialogue with itself about what it already knows and what it is in the process of trying to understand. It has to be able to relate new knowledge to old knowledge in important and useful ways. The computer must learn to know what it knows.

People can make analogies and comparisons between seemingly unrelated events, and can formulate new generalizations from them. For example, we tend to see events in Iran or Afghanistan in terms of previous acts of intolerance or aggression in history. The ability to see new or unlikely connections between events is another facet of human intelligence. The bright kids in a class tend to be the ones who get reminded of something they have seen previously or have heard at every turn. They continually perplex the teacher by going off on a tangent during a math class, or digressing to what happened during show-and-tell in the middle of reading period. Being excited by the relationships between things is part of what compels us to learn more. Learning is related to the connecting of seemingly disparate events.

SCRIPTS, MINDS AND REMINDING

Our research using scripts, plans, and goals has convinced us that knowledge structures are absolutely vital to any understanding system. In a nutshell, we learn in terms of what we already know. If we want a system to know more, then it must have a basis on which to build. To provide this basis the system must be told all the intimate details about the *connectivity* that humans see in the world. If we want it to make connections, we have to tell it how to do so.

Scripts, developed as a structure for stereotypical world knowledge, direct the inference process that is so vital to understanding, and help tie together events in an input. Input sentences are connected by relating them to the overall structure of the script to which they refer. Scripts are knowledge structures that supply background information and an organized inference structure during the understanding process.

But scripts don't just appear out of thin air. They are built up, over time, as a result of experience. How exactly that takes place is critical in the construction of an understanding system. The scripts that people use are changed by their use. We know more about restaurants in general with each new visit to a restaurant.

We can make new knowledge structures when necessary. We can learn. Knowledge structures cannot be rigid, static entities that never change. As we become older and wiser, our memories grow larger. What we know to be true changes over time. Thus, scripts, plans and goals in computer programs must be *dynamic* memory structures. They must change by relating experiences that are currently being processed to ones that have already been processed. In that way they provide the mechanism for seeing new things in terms of the old.

DYNAMIC MEMORY

Both FRUMP and SAM had the same, serious flaw: They could each read the same story a hundred times and never get bored. They were not being *changed* by what they read. People are intolerant of such boredom because they hope to profit in some way from their reading efforts. Any understanding system has to change, in at least a small way, when it encounters a new story, whether it is human or electronic. To do this, an understanding system must be capable of being reminded of something it has stored in its long-term memory. But memory mechanisms are not random. Sometimes it is the "remindings" that we are least aware of that are the most useful. We get reminded of prior experiences in order to connect what we know to help us to find out more. How can we bring in exactly the right script at the right moment? If there are thousands of scripts available to us, this can be a very complex problem. But if we see every experience we have as a knowledge structure in its own right, then thousands of structures quickly become millions of structures. We search our minds constantly for the structure that is most closely related to our current experience. This ability reveals itself to us in the form of remindings.

When we go to a McDonald's restaurant for the first time, we might be reminded of an earlier trip to Burger King. In fact we should be, because what we have learned about Burger King will help us to function more easily in McDonald's. If someone *failed* to notice the connection between Burger King and McDonald's after a trip to each we would wonder about that person's reasoning ability. Similarly, it requires considerable power of abstraction to make the connection between *Romeo and Juliet* and *West Side Story*, but most intelligent high schoolers can make such a connection fairly easily. Seeing a connection between these two stories doesn't require a genius, but it does require someone who has been paying attention at more than a superficial level.

If we cast these two examples of remindings in terms of relative similarity, the two fast-food restaurants are very similar (although some people swear there is a world of difference between a Big Mac and a Whopper). The story line of Shakespeare's play about rival families, however, differs widely from that of the musical about racist gang warfare. There is a great deal of obvious detail that could discourage us from connecting *Romeo and Juliet* to *West Side Story*. Yet there is something similar about the two stories. It might only be the theme: *Two young lovers are denied happiness because of the conflicts of the groups to which they belong.* We could phrase it a thousand ways: *Love striving against evil; Individuality vs. social obligation; Mutual understanding trampled by mass hate*. There are quite a number of ways to characterize the connectivity between the two stories.

It is doubtful that we are born with such high-level thematic structures in our heads, or even with a special sensitivity for assessing the quality of others' relationships. We have learned certain things about the world that are of use in seeing connections between very different stories. What are the mechanisms we use in making such connections? How can we connect stories with similar underlying themes but containing radically different contexts? How does memory change as a result of new stories and information? These aren't peripheral questions. The process of reminding is critical to the nature of how we learn. It seems clear that we need to begin answering all these questions before we will be able to build machines that can learn from what they read.

People really aren't equipped to examine the mechanisms of their remindings. Most of our remindings pass in and out of our consciousness without the slightest effort on our part. They are relationships that literally suggest themselves, as if a little man was sitting on our shoulder saying, *Hey, look at that, that's just like the time you did such-and-such.* The processing we do to find remindings is completely unconscious.

Freud tried to trace the connections that people make to their past experiences, consciously and unconsciously, throughout their daily lives. He was able to discover many things about his patients just by asking them to say what something *reminded* them of. He helped them analyze their own remindings and associations in light of their past experiences. He developed theories of the connections that people make most frequently. Unfortunately, these relationships have been made into clichés to be sprinkled into conversation: phallic symbol, Oedipus complex, anal retentive. In AI terms, Freud's most important discovery was that people drew many connections between their memories and experiences, and that some of these connections are based on the most abstract and oblique relationships.

The simple fact is that we rarely examine the process of our own memory, and even when we try, it is very difficult to do. Consciousness does not extend to an awareness of how we encode or retrieve experiences. Even when we are asked to remember something actively and consciously, it is hard to describe what we do. When we try to recall something, we can be aware of having it *on the tip of our tongue*. We may not remember what we are looking for until after the conversation has moved on, when, at some completely inappropriate time, we suddenly turn around and say to whomever is present, "I've got it! The *Jets!* You remember, don't you? The name of the gang in *West Side Story!*"

THE IMPORTANCE OF FAILURE

Although we have only recently begun to look into the problems of memory, a few observations can be made. At least one principal type of reminding is driven by *expectation failure*. Many remindings appear to be linked to the *failure* of one's expectations in situations where a knowledge structure has embodied in it very clear expectations about an event that is about to happen, and that expectation turns out to be wrong. This does not mean we only are reminded of our failures; rather, events that stick out in the past tend to be somehow anomalous or extraordinary. We tend to remember the times when the stereotypical script in a situation *wasn't* followed; when people turned out not to move toward the expected goals, or when they had unusual plans for achieving their goals. And, most importantly, when an expectation fails we want to know why. We attempt to *explain* the expectation failure. This explanation, in turn, helps us change our knowledge structures so that we can do better next time.

Although we think of scripts as fairly rigid and canonical, they provide a handy way of thinking about *failure-driven* reminding. When a script is followed very closely, we don't remember much. We tend to remember only unusual events since we can always reconstruct the usual ones. Taking a plane is a script-based activity, from buying the ticket, to boarding, to the lifejacket demonstration, to deplaning. The airline industry is in fact based on strict regulations and standardized procedures. A person who flies very often forgets all or most of the details of most of the flights he takes. What he does remember, however, is the time he was seated in first-class, even though he had an economy ticket. He remembers an enjoyable flight when, by coincidence, he was seated next to an old college buddy. And he remembers the flight where the pilot had to abort a takeoff because of a tire blowout.

Memory and reminding enable us to avoid thinking about irrelevant things in the hope that they may someday be useful. Our memory finds what we want when the information is needed. This is an amazing feat that computers cannot imitate yet.

In terms of the restaurant script, we don't tend to remember all the instances of eating in a stereotypical diner. But we savor the memory of that little place with good food we discovered off the highway, when we walked in tired and hungry and the waitress gave us free ice cream with our meal. We would tend to be unconscious of this memory most of the time. We might be reminded of this special roadside diner only when passing the same exit sign again two years later. And this reminding might require a highly circuitous process. We might think, *Hey, we've been on this highway before!* and *Yeah, but where were we going? Oh, that's right, we were driving up to Aunt Jean's place.* We might talk about Aunt Jean's cooking for ten minutes. Finally, someone would blurt out *Hey! There was that little place along here where we had a super steak dinner, and the lady gave us free ice cream!* From here, a cascade of other memorable details might come forth, regarding the trip, the meal, what people said, jokes, and so on.

Even with a full-blown memory of the diner, we still might have difficulty *finding* the place again. We wouldn't have remembered the exact route we took, if only because we all were tired and hungry at the time, and nothing memorable was happening. We first might have to look for the gas station where we stopped two years ago, just before finding the diner. The gas station might have been as uneventful and true to the script as ever, but we might only be able to remember the location of the diner in relation to the gas station. To search effectively we must *remind* ourselves of what we are looking for. We have to locate the memory/processing structure that was used to understand the material in the first place. It often helps to put yourself in the *original processing situation.* It may require seeing the same exit sign and finding the same gas station. It even might require that someone be *hungry* when they looked at the exit sign, or be thinking of ice cream.

We remember particular experiences because they somehow thwarted our dull, normal expectations of what should happen and how people should behave. A large part of understanding a story involves predicting people's behavior. We want to understand why someone does something and what he will do next. When we fail in our predictions, we remember our failure for the next time that we find ourselves in similar circumstances. Failure-driven reminding is based on failures in our predictions of other people's actions, or of the actions of physical events. We didn't expect the waitress in *Eddie's Dinateria* to give us free ice cream; nor did we expect the waitress in the *Knute Rockne Truckstop* to be so crabby when we asked for real milk instead of non-dairy creamer in our coffee. These failed expectations enable our memories to tell us to speed past the *Knute Rockne* and look for *Eddie's* next time we're on the highway.

To take this one step further, suppose we end up at the *Walt Whitman Truckstop* and get non-dairy creamer for our coffee. We might remember what happened the last time we were at a turnpike truckstop and asked for real milk. In this case, our expectation is based on a reminding of a *failure* of a previous expectation, not on a standard script. If the waitress were courteous to us, we might remember the *Walt Whitman* as a very congenial place, even though we would have thought nothing special about it if we hadn't stopped at the *Knute Rockne* first.

We know that any understanding system that is going to do more than just MAKE SENSE of an isolated story will have to be able to recall related stories and to see complex connections between them. An understanding system must have expectations in certain contexts and these expectations, on occasion, will be wrong. When they are, the system has to be able to take note of the important and relevant details, and store the experience in such a way that it can make use of it at a later time. When things fail consistently, for the same reasons, we must build new structures that accommodate the new facts.

QWERTY AND THE NEWLYWEDS' HAM

Human memory is full of what seem to be random associations. In fact, "random" memories are not random at all. Our minds attempt to process everything we see and hear in any way that can help us learn from what we have experienced. From these remindings we gain new insights about the world around us.

When we first discovered the significance of the reminding phenomenon in our laboratory at Yale, we spent a fair amount of time collecting "reminding experiences" of the various people who worked in the lab. We did this in order to get a better insight into what the reminding process was for and how it worked. Below are some of remindings we collected, together with some comments on their significance.

QWERTY AND THE NEWLYWEDS' HAM

IN:

One student was reading a book that described how the standard QWERTY keyboard [This is the name of the standard typewriter keyboard now in use. Its name comes from the first six letters of the keyboard.] was originally designed. The intent was to make typing as SLOW as possible in order to keep the keys from jamming. The author was complaining that now people were trying to make arguments about how the QWERTY keyboard was a great benefit to typers in that it made typing easier. The author's point was people can find rationalizations why the way things are is the way they are supposed to be, regardless of the facts.

REMINDING:

This student was reminded of a story about newlyweds who were having the mother of the bride over for dinner and were making ham. The wife took the ham out of the refrigerator, cut off one end, and put the rest in a baking pan and then into the oven. At first her husband assumed there must have been something wrong with the end she discarded, but he checked and there wasn't, so he asked her why she cut it off. Her answer was that that's just the way you make ham, and that her mother ALWAYS cut off the end before sticking it in the baking pan. So when the mother arrived, he asked HER why she cut off the end of hams, and she replied

> that that's just the way you make ham and that HER mother always did it that way. So he called the grandmother and asked her, and she explained that in all these many years, she never got around to buying herself a big enough pan.

Many remindings are actually examples of how people attempt to understand unusual circumstances. The student in the above story was attempting to understand, at the COGNITIVE UNDERSTANDING level, the argument of the author. Often the best way to understand what someone has said is to cast it in light of other things that you already have understood. This student must have had a class of events in her mind that we could label *times when people do things without understanding why*. This story about the QWERTY keyboard was understood by this student in terms of conclusions she previously had drawn from the story about the ham.

When we understand something one way, it is often difficult to see it in any other way. Having seen the QWERTY story as an instance of people being too foolish to realize why something was the way it was, this student might now be unlikely to think about why QWERTY worked as a method of slowing people down, for example. Of course, the author intended her to think of exactly the aspect of the QWERTY issue that she did. Her reminding exemplifies *how* she understood the story.

For a computer to "get reminded," the computer must be able to categorize its prior experiences effectively. To understand we must be able to *contrast and compare* the first story with the second so as to be able to speculate on what each has to say about the other. The advantage of getting a machine to do this seems clear; this kind of contrasting and comparing is critical to understanding.

WARRANTED SKEPTICISM

IN: A person saw an ad for video games. The woman in the ad was bubbling about the free video game one got when one bought two at the normal price.

REMINDING: The observation that the flip side of a hit record usually has an awful and unheard-of song on it;

REMINDING: a theater's "free play for subscribers" which is usually one they can't sell out;

REMINDING: movie and book excerpts that are often the only part worth seeing or reading;

REMINDING: the strawberries on the top of a basket always are the best.

Here we see an example of how we attempt to understand by using what we know, with new information to confirm our beliefs. This person obviously believes that *Anything that is free is worthless.* We have adages that conform to such beliefs and we are reminded of these adages when they apply. *You only get what you pay for,* or *There is no such thing as a free lunch* come to mind here. To create and maintain beliefs such as this, we constantly must be on the lookout for new "facts" to add to our collection that will confirm what we know. Doing this requires that we be able to see new events as instances of a general category of events that we have constructed for ourselves. Getting a machine to build up its own set of beliefs, therefore, requires giving it the ability to categorize new events in a fashion that makes this possible.

THE OPTICIAN AND *THE WINDS OF WAR*

IN: After several years without ever having had any bad encounters waiting for the bus at night, a student had a bad scare. She was in a bad neighborhood and was nervous about being mugged. Instead, she was hit in the face by a snowball, which had the result of breaking her glasses. The next day, she went to an optician in another bad neighborhood to have her glasses fixed, but while there she began to feel uneasy. She was the only one there other than the young man and young woman who worked there, and they were acting strangely. She was still jittery from the night before, and so she decided that she wanted to leave. The problem was that the very people she was afraid of had her glasses. This meant she was going to have to ask them to give her her glasses back, and she was afraid of them. Nevertheless she asked for them and, of course, got them back.

REMINDING: In Wouk's *Winds of War*, Natalie, trying to get out of Nazi-threatened Europe, goes to the Lufthansa office to pick up tickets. She has to give them her passport (her major protection as a Jew and an American), but feels reasonably safe until the Lufthansa employees give her a form to fill out that asks her religion. This shakes her, and she decides that flying Lufthansa is even more dangerous than its alternatives. She wants to get out of the ticket office and abort the whole transaction, but the Germans still have her passport! She asks for it back, and they refuse to give it to her at first, but she finally manages to get out of the Lufthansa office, safely and with her passport.

The similarity between these two stories is striking, down to the details of the feelings and attitudes on the parts of the participants. We must have very complex and detailed memories indeed to be able to store and retrieve such intricate stories on the basis of a set of rather subtle details. The value of the reminding in this case is fairly clear. By storing information about the problems of others, even if they are fictional characters, we can learn from their actions. When our own circumstances match those of people we have heard about, we can conclude that there is cause to modify our behavior so as to learn from the commonality of experience. Here the student presumably learned a new fact: *Hold on to your valuable possessions when you are frightened. Without them you may not be able to get away.*

Learning and reminding are strongly related. When we experience something twice, either ourselves or vicariously, we want to be able to profit from the experiences. We cannot do this if we fail to recall one experience while processing the other.

Reminding is the basis of much of our conversation and of our thought. Therefore, it is quite naturally found in all kinds of literature. As an example, here is a quote from Mrs. Nickleby (from Dickens' *Nicholas Nickleby*):

> "Kate, my dear," said Mrs. Nickleby, "I don't know how it is, but a fine warm summer day like this, with the birds singing in every direction, always puts me in mind of roast pig, with sage and onion sauce, and made gravy."
>
> "That's a curious association of ideas, is it not, Mama?"
>
> "Upon my word, my dear. I don't know," replied Mrs. Nickleby. "Roast pig; let me see. On the day five weeks before you were christened, we had a roast—no, that couldn't have been a pig, either, because I recollect there were a pair of them, and your poor papa and I could never have thought of sitting down to two pigs—they must have been two partridges. Roast pig! I hardly think we ever could have had one, now I come to remember, for your papa could never bear the sight of them in the shops, and used to say that they always put him in mind of very little babies, only the pigs had much fairer complexions; and he had a horror of little babies, too, because he couldn't very well afford any increase to his family, and had a natural dislike of the subject. It's very odd now, what can have put that in my head? I recollect dining now once at Mrs. Bevan's, in that broad street round the corner by the coachmaker's, where the tipsy man fell through the cellar-flap of an empty house nearly a week before the quarter-day and wasn't found till the new tenant went in—and we had roast pig there. It must be that. I think that reminds me of it, especially as there was a little bird in the room that would keep on singing all the time of dinner—at least not a little bird, for it was a parrot, and he didn't sing exactly, for he talked and swore dreadfully, but I think it must be that. Indeed I am sure it must. Shouldn't you say so, my dear?"

We don't always know why we are thinking of whatever happens to be on our minds at the time. Reminding goes on whether we take advantage of it or not.

We only recently have begun to develop programs that have some reminding capability, in an attempt to get closer to the solution to the learning problem. We are slowly but steadily developing the knowledge structures that understanding systems require in order to process stories in much the same way we do. We are by no means close to fully modeling human intelligence or understanding, but we have made very exciting progress. Research at AI laboratories has to concentrate on the learning process. Any successes that come from attempts at learning programs in the next decade will be only the beginning, pointing out where to look next.

The world of AI in the next decades can concern itself with two different issues. First, it must solve the learning problem in order to create truly intelligent systems. And, if past history is any indication, there are likely to be numerous problems beyond learning that will show up on the road to very intelligent machines. The second issue is: What we can do in the meantime? Theory-directed AI researchers can continue working in the hopes of developing the numerous breakthroughs they will need in order to evolve the systems that we imagine. Product-directed AI, on the other hand, can and will begin to make its presence felt. There are many systems that we can build now that, although they cannot rightly be called intelligent, may still prove to be very nice to have around.

THE DOMAIN PROBLEM

I have talked about the possibilities for applications of AI: computer chefs, stockbrokers, insurance brokers, bankers, and drivers. I also have discussed the impossibilities, at least in the very near future, of the all-knowing experts, or programs that change themselves over time. But what is the difference between the possible and the impossible? The real possibilities for the near future all have one thing in common: They all require knowledge and understanding of one not extremely complex but highly specific *domain*.

The first applications of AI will begin to emerge in the next few years. These will not require learning or vast knowledge. Rather, they will be applications within restricted domains of knowledge. Any programs that we develop in the near future that are capable of learning will also be specialists in one domain only. In today's technology, just being able to capture all the knowledge necessary to automate one domain of expertise is difficult enough. The difficulty in getting knowledge into the computer, and in representing that knowledge, for some time will prevent us from making computers any more than specialists within one field.

The difference between representing information in one field or another will make certain kinds of specialists much more difficult to create than others. Because the knowledge required for certain aspects of banking or other areas of finance is representable, it is possible to build systems that dispense that knowledge through simple natural language interaction. As long as it is clear what knowledge belongs in such a system, as long as we know how to represent that knowledge, as long as the vocabulary needed to interact with that knowledge is not inordinately large, and as long as we do not expect the system we build to be able to learn very much, it is possible today to build computer models that can be rather useful. Such systems will be able to dispense advice to consumers, for example. By telling the machine what we know about various types of bank accounts, it is possible to build a program that converses with a bank customer in simple typewritten English, answering his questions about what banking services are right for him. This same capability can be applied to areas such as insurance, or certain forms of investment where the knowledge required, while complex, is not so abstract as to be impossible to represent.

RETIREMENT BY COMPUTER

As an example of the kind of thing that we are capable of doing now, consider the problem of an automated retirement counselor. Not every bank has the time or personnel to devote to the problem of giving good advice to people who want to have enough money put away when they reach retirement age. By using the techniques we have developed over the years we can create a computer program that functions as a human financial planner would—asking and answering questions in conversational English, gathering all the necessary information about the client's existing financial situation, and offering advice about the best investments to make to ensure a comfortable retirement. We soon may see such systems in the branch offices of financial institutions.

There are two types of knowledge needed to offer helpful and accurate advice about financial planning. The first is basic factual information about finances and investments, including an understanding of the various types of bonds, savings plans, tax shelters, retirement plans, etc. available to an investor. In addition to this factual knowledge, the program also must have some set of decision-making rules that enable it to make judgments about a situation.

A client would be able to communicate with the system in conversational English and the system would ask questions, offer advice, and ask for clarifications in order to gather all the information necessary to offer sound investment advice. In addition, the user would be able to type questions and get answers at any point in a dialogue with the machine.

The following is a hypothetical user session with such an Automated Retirement Counseling Service. The system first queries the user, in an interactive session, about his financial situation and his retirement plans. Once the system has an understanding of who the client is and what his desires are, it would then be able to offer advice about the most advantageous investment opportunities available.

In the following example, the system has already learned that John Smith is 43, married, his wife Mary does not work, and he has two kids in school.

HOW MUCH ARE YOU EARNING RIGHT NOW?
> *I make $40,000 a year as a senior research scientist.*

DOES YOUR COMPANY HAVE A PENSION PLAN?
> *Not at the moment.*

ARE YOU INVOLVED IN ANY TAX-SHELTERED SAVINGS PLANS (SUCH AS AN IRA)?
> *What's an IRA?*

SINCE YOU DO NOT HAVE A PENSION PLAN WHERE YOU WORK, YOU QUALIFY FOR AN IRA (INDIVIDUAL RETIREMENT ACCOUNT). AN IRA ACCOUNT WORKS AS FOLLOWS:

YOU ARE ALLOWED TO DEPOSIT A LIMITED AMOUNT OF MONEY INTO YOUR IRA ACCOUNT EACH YEAR. NEITHER THESE FUNDS (NOR THE INTEREST THEY ACCRUE) WILL BE TAXED UNTIL THE FUNDS ARE WITHDRAWN.

SINCE YOUR WIFE DOES NOT WORK, YOU CAN DE-POSIT AS MUCH AS $3,000 ANNUALLY INTO YOUR IRA ACCOUNT.

YOU MAY WITHDRAW IT ONCE YOU REACH THE AGE OF 59. AT THIS TIME YOU MUST PAY AN ORDINARY INCOME TAX ON EACH AMOUNT WITHDRAWN. BY THEN, HOWEVER, YOU WILL BE IN A LOWER TAX BRACKET.

> *What if I need the money before I reach 59?*

THE FUNDS YOU WITHDRAW EARLY ARE SUBJECT TO AN ORDINARY INCOME TAX PLUS A 10% INTEREST PENALTY ON THE AMOUNT DRAWN. HOWEVER, THERE IS NO PENALTY IF THE FUNDS ARE WITHDRAWN IN THE CASE OF A DEATH OR DISABILITY.

> *What if I change jobs?*

YOUR IRA ACCOUNT IS YOURS. IT "GOES WITH YOU" WHEN YOU CHANGE JOBS. FURTHERMORE, YOUR EM-PLOYER MAY WANT TO SET UP A SIMPLIFIED EM-PLOYEE PENSION (SEP-IRA). YOUR EMPLOYER CAN CONTRIBUTE UP TO 15% OF YOUR EARNINGS ($7,500 MAXIMUM) TO YOUR IRA AND DEDUCT IT AS A BUSI-NESS EXPENSE.

DO YOU HAVE ANY SAVINGS?

> *Yes. I have around $9000 in a savings account and also some common stock.*

WHAT TYPE OF SAVINGS ACCOUNT IS IT? (A NOW-AC-COUNT, REGULAR SAVINGS, SAVINGS LINKED TO CHECKING, ETC.)

> *It's just a regular savings account.*

A SAVINGS ACCOUNT IS A VERY POOR PLACE TO IN-VEST THAT MUCH MONEY BECAUSE THE INTEREST PAID IS SO LOW. SINCE YOU HAVE $9000 SAVED, YOU OUGHT TO CONSIDER PURCHASING 91-DAY SAVINGS CERTIF-ICATES. THE MINIMUM DEPOSIT FOR THESE CERTIFI-CATES IS $7,500. THESE GIVE A MUCH BETTER YIELD AND YOUR MONEY IS ONLY TIED UP FOR SHORT PE-RIODS OF TIME.

> *What if I need the money before the 90 day period is up?*

THE MONEY CAN BE REMOVED EARLIER, BUT THERE IS A PENALTY FOR EARLY WITHDRAWAL.

> *What about Money Market Funds?*

THESE FUNDS ARE ACTUALLY A TYPE OF MUTUAL FUND, SO THEY DO NOT POSSESS ABSOLUTE SECURITY ON INVESTMENT (UNLIKE THE VARIOUS SAVINGS CER-TIFICATES THAT ARE AVAILABLE AT A FEDERALLY-IN-SURED BANK). THE RATE OF INTEREST ON A MONEY MARKET FUND FLUCTUATES ON A DAILY BASIS.

ASSUMING THE CURRENT PURCHASING POWER OF THE DOLLAR, HOW MUCH PER MONTH WOULD YOU LIKE TO RETIRE ON WHEN YOU REACH 65?

> *At least 75% of what I'm earning now.*

THEN, TO ACHIEVE SUCH RETIREMENT-LEVEL EARN-INGS, I SUGGEST THE FOLLOWING INVESTMENT STRATEGY:

PER ANNUM SAVINGS INVESTMENTS:

IRA ACCOUNT	—	XXX
91-DAY CERTIFICATES	—	XXX
MUTUAL FUNDS	—	XXX
TOTAL YOU MUST SAVE (PER MONTH) =		YYYY

> *How much will I have per month when I'm 65 if I follow your advice?*

$XXX PER MONTH.

The value of such a system is significant, but only if it can answer *any* question that a user asks. As we have said, this issue relates directly to the domain problem. As long as the user stays within the domain of financial planning and keeps questions fairly simple, we can do this kind of thing today.

BEYOND A DOMAIN

It is easy to make the assumption that one kind of information is like another. For example, we might think that if we can make a retirement counselor, why not an expert that can advise us on matters of foreign policy with respect to Russia? Certainly, if machines can read English, then it would be a good idea to have them read all there is to read about Russia so that they could become helpful and informed foreign policy advisors. But there is a big difference between reading simple stories and reading large texts. The latter requires the ability to know what to store and what to forget, and to understand how prior knowledge can be modified by new information. In short, although it isn't obvious, reading effectively requires the ability to learn from what you have read. We are back at the learning problem again.

In order for computers to really understand any complex situation, they must, just as people do, be able to understand all the surrounding pieces of knowledge that have bearing on the subject matter at hand. Understanding Russia demands an understanding of the nature of people and society in general, before one can even get into the details of Russian history. It is an unbelievably complicated task just to get a human to integrate such a broad domain of knowledge. The Russian policy computer would have to have knowledge spanning many domains, from armaments to the Middle East situation, to dissident ballet dancers and the economics of grain exports. Just entering into the computer all the knowledge that a Russian foreign policy expert might have about Russia is a formidable task. We won't accomplish it until we solve the basic problems of learning, memory, and planning with which all of AI now is struggling. For this reason, the Russian policy advisory system is much farther down the road than the automated insurance advisor or automated stock broker.

Insurance and investment *are* highly restricted domains of knowledge. The principles and concepts they involve don't require general world knowledge across many domains, although they do require some. (For example, it may be possible that a good investment advisor ought to know the details of each industry he deals with. To the extent that that is true, a truly expert investment advisor system may be quite far off. To the extent that only principles of finance and basic information about how to judge the success of a company are required, however, such a system might be possible today. The more restricted the knowledge needed by the computer, the sooner we will see systems that automate such knowledge. We should see systems that are practical, fun, and fairly easy to use in the very near future.

PEOPLE AS GENERAL LEARNING SYSTEMS

The domain problem is critical to understanding how we are to assess the possibilities of what we can build today. But the domain problem is also related to the learning problem. Creating a system with a less domain-restricted understanding implies giving it a general learning ability, the ability to learn within other domains. People seem to be general learning systems. They can learn an entirely new domain with little trouble. But that is because they know so many domains so well in the first place. Small children overgeneralize as they learn, as would a computer that started from scratch. In reality, people are severely domain restricted, even though they are technically able to learn anything they might need to learn. People actually learn new things in terms of the ones they already know. We see the world in terms of specialized knowledge.

We often label people according to their domain restrictions, or specialties. As youngsters we are bombarded with cute stories of all the different occupations one can have: firefighter, engineer, police officer, lawyer, doctor, postal carrier, construction worker, welder, and so on. Later in life we learn about even more specialized occupations: account representative, assistant vice-president for employee relations, senior programmer/analyst, and human resource specialist. We always are interested in people who defy such domain restrictions, such as the banker who paints or the shoe salesman who loves to play polo. The point is that while people are often very domain-restricted, computers will be even *more* domain restricted. They will be great medical advisors but know nothing whatsoever about cooking; they may be terrific French chefs but never have heard of François Mitterrand.

The domain problem is one of the most difficult problems facing AI. While the domain problem doesn't prevent us from creating a computer chef or computer engine mechanic, it prevents us from getting a computer to read all the bills in the Congressional Record and analyze them in depth. The domain of knowledge required for cooking or for auto mechanics is fairly small, and more or less clearly defined. But the domain of knowledge required to read all the bills that might ever be voted on in Congress is massive. We have to do much more than merely getting the computer to know all the words the Congressional Record might contain. It requires much more than getting the computer to read and paraphrase a text.

Congressional bills can pertain to almost anything, from laws protecting snail darters to laws governing importation of sweatshirts from Mexico, and from nuclear energy regulations to equal rights amendments. Congress itself has had to confront the domain problem because not even humans are equipped to understand such a wide range of subjects in any detail. Congress has been forced to form committees—small study groups whose members become well-versed in specific areas and inform the rest of Congress on their findings. Congressmen simply don't have the time, much less the mental ability, to become experts on everything from freshwater conservation to the economics of sweatshirt importation. Programming a computer to understand all the laws that might pass through Congress would require putting into the computer, in gory detail, every bit of information about human ethics and morals, special interest groups, and the nature of politics, in addition to details about snail darters. In fact, getting a machine to understand even one bill in depth could be a monumental task, since most bills relate in one way or another to the history of the United States, including such issues as the Bill of Rights, the attitudes of Americans, and so on.

LEARNING: A PRACTICAL APPROACH TO AN IMPOSSIBLE SITUATION

It is practically impossible for a congressional representative or senator to know everything he needs to know in order to vote intelligently on the issues. Yet these elected officials have a perfectly well-developed system for adding new knowledge, requiring mostly that he read or listen to advisors. Imagine how much less likely it is that we can put even a fragment of the knowledge available to people into the computer. As long as our programs are incapable of simply reading and learning, each individual piece of knowledge must be added by someone trained in AI, who must painstakingly consider how to represent it so that no detail is ignored. Remember that the computer cannot "read between the lines" unless it has sufficient knowledge in the first place. It would take several generations of thousands of workers in different areas just to obtain all the information and determine how it should be represented. In the meantime, knowledge would be changing and new discoveries being made. It is simply unrealistic to contemplate doing this, even if we had built a system that could organize and store all the material properly.

One cannot solve the problem of information storage on a massive scale without having some sense of the place where new knowledge might fit eventually. New things may fit neatly into established structures, but much learning is about radically new information. People have a deep understanding of domains, and can effectively draw useful analogies between them. Computers also will have to be able to characterize what they know in ways that are abstract enough so that connections can be made across domains.

We will have to search for more efficient ways of designing an understanding system. We have to figure out how to enable a program to pick up new information on its own, whenever it needs it. What kind of an expert, after all, fails to continually add to his store of knowledge within a specific domain? A doctor is an expert not because he has memorized all the medical knowledge in existence while he was in medical school and can spit it back out, but because he can decide in a given situation where to get the very detailed information he needs and how to apply it. If he reads about a new therapy or drug, he can integrate it into his old knowledge. He knows enough to know what he doesn't know. He knows how to find the information he needs. When confronted with an unusual case, he can narrow down his search for information to the three or four diseases or problems his patient might have. I would rather have a doctor who knows how to use a library very well than one who merely has memorized every book in an entire medical library.

We will have to look for ways to enable an intelligent machine to learn an entirely new domain of knowledge whenever it encounters one. Such a computer will have to have the crucial feature of being able to *know that it doesn't know* something, so that it could seek an answer. Socrates' guiding principle of learning was that all he knew was that he knew nothing. We can imagine a computer that can recognize its own lack of knowledge, and know where to locate the information it needs.

Although such a system is possible theoretically, we are still very far from developing one. AI research is a continuous discovery of what we don't yet know how to do, an evolution of thought. AI research is dynamic and full of life. With this persistent knowledge of what we don't know, we might be able to follow the Socratic path toward self-knowledge and our thought processes.

PART

THREE

PART

THREE

CHAPTER
NINE

LEARNING
FROM
COMPUTERS,
NOT
ABOUT THEM

Sometime in the late seventies the computer industry discovered that you can sell a small computer. Suddenly a great many people wanted to possess their very own computers. A few fledgling companies popped up to meet the demands of this untapped market. Apple Computer, for example, was born in a garage and in four years the company was grossing millions. All of this occurred despite the fact that most people who buy computers have no idea what they're buying or why. Should one buy a personal computer? What can personal computers be made to do?

People who wonder how useful a home computer will be shouldn't have to work themselves into near paranoia about their lack of computer skills. The issue is not how much one knows *about* computers, but what we can learn *from* them. The first thing to learn about today's computers is what they can do for us.

If we want to know what the home computer can be made to do for us, we need to learn enough about AI to develop a sense for what AI products are likely to surface soon and which may come in the years ahead. We don't want to waste our time learning skills that soon will be out of date.

Finally, we should learn what the long-term effects of a successful computer revolution are likely to be. AI won't arrive until we solve many difficult problems. However, most technological achievements seemed impossible at one time. I do believe that these problems will be solved. We should be thinking *now* about the implications of something so radical as the possibility of intelligent machines, even though they are only a remote possibility.

Anyone who is considering buying a personal computer should keep in mind that the home computers of four years from now will be far more powerful than those we can buy today, just as today's computers are much more powerful than those of four years ago. Computers will become faster, more efficient, more compact and, most importantly, cheaper. Whenever a better system is developed, no one will want the older, less powerful systems. Despite these improvements, one big question always will remain: What can we do with them? This question is already starting to nag the average owner of one of today's tin lizzie computers, and its answer will become even more important as time passes.

Personal computers have applications in three areas: business, personal or household tasks, and education. But what do we get to do with all this computer power? This question has one answer, and it isn't *hardware*. The answer is *software*.

SOFTWARE FOR BUSINESS

Many people suffer from the illusion that the business world knows what to do with computers. It is true that large businesses have been using computers for years, but not in any interesting way. The computer industry claims that business can be automated, but what does that mean?

Mostly, big businesses use computers for payroll or to keep records of customers. The advantage of having corporate records on a computer is enormous. It is a great deal easier to find what you want by using a computer data file than by looking through huge files of paper or ledgers. By typing a few simple commands, you can find what you want to know from the computer's files as long as the information you seek has been given a name or number that you can recall easily. Typing "John Jones" will call up what is in the computer about John Jones, and typing 6250 322 98745 will bring up the information about the business transactions you have labeled with that number. These kinds of systems are of great use to credit card companies who can find out about you by typing in your name or card number and by airlines who can find out about the status of a flight by typing its number. Because so many businesses do find such systems to be useful, and in some cases vital (like airline reservations), the use of computers has become more and more widespread.

Unfortunately a number of problems arise as a result of this kind of computer use. First, this information is not accessible in any other way than by its unique name or number. If you want to know something about a transaction and you don't have the sales number, you may have great difficulty finding what you want. You may think that a company is simply being annoying when it fails to give you the information you want, but it is likely that the company can't find the information in the first place. The more complex the information stored by the computer, the more likely you are to have difficulty securing some of the information you need. It may seem a simple question to ask for the names of all the people who live in New York and own Buicks, but unless the programmer knew you were going to ask such a question, even if that information is already stored in the machine, it may not be possible to get it.

Computers store data effectively, but since no one has written intelligent software to organize the data, getting useful information back out is sometimes no easier than the old way of going through the files with a good file clerk. The business world needs software with a new, more efficient approach. Business today needs programs that the computer industry is just not yet prepared to create.

This is the reason why so many businesses are exasperated by their data processing departments. Software developers currently must anticipate all the uses of that software ahead of time. If the airline fails to tell its software developers that it will want to know how many people fly on discount fares in December, the machine, which may well have all flights and all fares listed in its data base, will answer; *What?* The problem is that today's computers don't know what they know. The *content* of data means nothing to the machine. Without an AI capability, the machine has a great deal of information, but no knowledge.

A second major problem with the use of computers in business is that there often exists too much data, too much information. Once all the records of a company are automated, it is only a matter of time until a senior vice-president of a company lands face-to-face with a 3" thick printout from the computer that contains every single number he could possibly want to know about the company's business. Too much information, obviously, can be worse than not enough. It can take hours to read through such data; one easily can feel overwhelmed by hundreds of pages of statistics. Here again, AI would help. The computer should know how to summarize the data and draw some conclusions.

The intelligence necessary to draw conclusions from hundreds of pages of data is not as great as the intelligence involved in "real AI." Nevertheless, some intelligence is needed to decide when a statistic is relevant and to sort data by considering the content of that data. Computers have become invaluable to large companies, but these companies will need AI to keep them from becoming encumbered by those very same computers.

AI MEETS THE SMALL BUSINESSMAN

Today, hundreds of small businesses seek "automation" because they hear it will save them time and worry. But a small business cannot afford to hire an army of programmers to write software especially tuned to that particular business. So they buy standardized application packages that don't do things exactly as they want. When the hardware or software breaks down they all are at the mercy of the vendors' repair teams. This may not be of such special concern when your copier breaks down, but computers have a way of "taking over" one's business to the point where businesses have great difficulty functioning without them. If all your data are stored in the machine, a computer breakdown can be disastrous.

AI-based software offers tremendous potential for small business. Such businesses need software that is suited to their specific business needs. A business person should be able to ask, *Who owes me money?* or *Is Jones selling his share of widgets?* He wants to have someone at his side who is up to date on all the details of his business from inventory control to accounts payable. You don't need a learning, thinking, AI-type machine to do this. But you do need AI's techniques to process English commands and to define this businessman's fuzzy questions.

There is an important intermediate stage between today's small computers and HAL of *2001: A Space Odyssey* or C3PO of *Star Wars*. This stage is a modern-day computer with sophisticated software. We are starting to see better and better software each year, and it is only a matter of time until software gets good enough to allow someone with no training to get what he or she needs from a computer.

Innovations in the software industry are starting to emerge that take away the need to learn how to do more than turn the system on. This is why Visi-Calc© (a program that does accounting spreadsheets, changing all numbers before your eyes as you change any one number upon which the other numbers depend) was so successful. This is why business software that has an English language parser attached to the front, so that you can type the commands you want in English instead of command language, also will be successful. AI's true effectiveness, in the short run, will be to make business software usable by businessmen.

AT HOME

The home computer situation currently is in much worse shape than in the business computer world. Software designers at least have some sense of what software business applications are possible. After all, business people care about inventory, accounts receivable, employees, and so on. The "every business needs the same software" approach will go away as specialist software programs (software for autoparts stores, for example) become the norm. Right now, unfortunately, there is very little comparable value in home application software. But there soon will be discovered a number of important uses for computers in the home.

The home is the province of AI's most valuable potential contribution to our lives. We cannot yet create the brilliant machines that every magazine promises. But we can make the not-so-brilliant machines of today more usable. Putting computers in the hands of those who need them is a battle of great significance which can be won, not only in business but at home and in school as well.

We really have no idea what people will do with computers in their homes. How much do they care about their home finances? Enough to buy software and carefully log in all the relevant data? Do they want to plan a game? Do they want to write? The reason there is so little good software available for home use is that no one really knows what home users want.

People who aren't computer buffs don't need sheer computer power; they need access to useful information, and useful information exists on computers in all sorts of institutions around the world. Time-sharing networks that can be addressed in everyday English will enable a person to hook up his home computer to any data base that interests him without having to decipher the internal structure or system of whatever computer has the information he needs. This possibility is quickly approaching, thanks to AI research. It effectively will allow the user to make use of the full potential of any machine to which he/she has access.

Since the key to the value of the home computer is *information*, breakthroughs in the home computer industry will happen through hardware innovations. Hardware inevitably will become more or less standardized, just like cars, in order to avoid complete chaos. When information networks and time-sharing services can offer useful programs to the average person, no one will buy a machine that isn't more or less universal.

The ultimate value of the home computer will be its function as a library and a purveyor of services. An *automated library* will be able to tell us what we need to know without our having to leave our homes or learn a complex cataloging system. When everyone has a home computer that can be hooked up to networks and computer centers, *intelligent* information networks may develop. You will just call up the automotive advisory system and type in, *I've got a problem with my car* and the system will respond, *What's wrong?* You describe the problem, and the system teaches you how to fix it, or tells you that you can't fix it yourself.

How many arguments have you had in which a simple fact would have made a great deal of acrimony disappear? How many times have you needed to find some information to help you make an investment decision, a choice of schools, a choice of cars, or perhaps information that would be useful in business or life decisions? We usually don't have the time or opportunity to do the research we need in order to make informed decisions. It may surprise you to know that computer data bases contain much of the information you seek. But you would need *access* to them, and you would need to know how to program your computer to communicate with a data base.

Companies are eager to sell services directly to the home via computer. Home banking, home shopping, home travel agents, and such should be the first services made available. The right networks of computers will need to become accessible by telephone or cable hook-up to your home computer. But you will not want to learn how to use the computer services of each company you use. When you can ask for what you want in everyday English, such home services will be a serious possibility.

New computer software applications are continually suggesting themselves as their use increases. When the byproducts of AI research become available, a whole new world of additional possible applications will arise. The AI software that will be issued in the next few years has the potential to change our perception of the computer. This isn't going to happen overnight. AI software currently is very expensive to develop. Home computers and minicomputers are still too slow and have too little memory to run complex AI programs. But the hardware industry constantly is improving the speed and the memory capacity of its computers. Computer programs that take advantage of the early progress in natural language processing will be useful for the average person just as soon as the hardware needed to run such programs becomes cheap enough. Such programs have just started to appear, and will become more generally available and cheaper soon.

Hundreds of software companies are peddling programs in ads that promise, *Our program speaks your language, Talk to our software in English,* and *The computer that understands you.* These companies have realized that such claims will sell software, no matter how unsophisticated the programs are. Once the ad has fooled someone into buying their product, it takes only a little common sense to see that the claims were misleading, at best.

The software may indeed use a few dozen common English words as commands, instead of symbols or computer jargon. But these programs usually function *only* when certain English words are used, and only in certain ways; they may even make the software *more* time-consuming to use.

THE HOME FINANCE PROGRAM

As an example of the striking difference in usability that AI techniques can make, let's take a look at one of the most touted pieces of home software, the home finance program. Imagine that you buy a piece of software for your home computer that is advertised as being able to understand English. When you start the program, the computer prints out *Welcome to the home finance program!* In the lower left hand corner it reads *Hit return.* You hit Return and the screen displays a menu with the choice of five or six things you can make at this point. A small note tells you to move the cursor (position indicator, or arrow) to the number of the task you want and then hit Return. You might choose *Balance checkbook.* The screen then displays a formatted spreadsheet with columns for all the data about whom you wrote the checks to, for how much, what number, whether they were tax deductible, and so on.

This program gives you little more convenience than a normal check ledger and a hand calculator. It probably has a very limited search ability. If you needed to know something about a check you wrote three months ago, you would have to find the right spreadsheet and look through all the entries until you found it. The program might automatically calculate your balance for you, and give you a statement of income and expenditure every month, but it will only do this if you ask it the right way. If it's programmed to do this when you type in *Show balance,* it won't be able to respond to another phrasing of this question, such as *How much money do I have left?*

Unless you want to sit down with a user's manual and menorize the pseudo-English that the computer understands, don't buy this kind of software. Hang on to that worn-out hand calculator and ledger for another three years or so. They're as user-friendly as you could wish for the speed and convenience they provide.

Now imagine a home finance system where you simply sit down and type in *check #344 to Village Hardware for $34.56*. The computer responds simply, *OK*. It has understood this phrase exactly as you would expect your personal accountant to understand it, and has stored the information in the right place. It isn't going to bombard you with a menu of 20 choices so that you can tell it which spreadsheet to display. It isn't going to ask you if you want to balance your checkbook. It is perfectly capable of determining that you want to balance your checkbook from the meaning and context of what you type in.

You could type in *Lost number 345, and 346 is void*. The computer would understand this exactly as a human would. It would know to tell the bank to cancel the lost check. You could say *$12.23 to paperboy, $22.50 to a bookstore on 4th ave, mortgage payment $377.51, check for around $30, I forget where*. The program would have no more of a problem dealing with all this information than your personal secretary might. It assumes that the check numbers progressed in order, and even will remember to go back and correct the amount of the unknown check when it comes back. If you had told the computer all the details of your mortgage agreement, it would automatically keep track of it just by hearing that you made a payment. At any time, you could ask it, *What's my equity?* and it would estimate it using its most recent information.

The program would have a general understanding of all financial affairs and what they involve. If you came back from a business trip and simply wanted to add up all your receipts, you could type in *I want to add up the following amounts:* You would type in the numbers, leaving a space in between them, and get the total. If you were responsible for 25 percent of the cost over $65 per day, and spent three days, you could simply type in *I spent this in three days. I have to pay 25% of anything over $65 per day. What do I owe?* You would get your answer immediately. The computer would print the equation it used to solve the problem, so you could check it for errors. You might take a vacation with three friends and want to split up all the costs. You wouldn't buy a piece of software called *Sharing Vacation Expenses*. Even an expert programmer wouldn't bother writing a program in BASIC for this specialized instance; he would dig out his hand calculator instead. But a good home finance system could handle the problem for you, and break it down into beer fund, cabana rental, suntan lotion, boat charter, and so on.

If you ask the program, *What's my balance* or *What's left in the checking acct?*, it might respond, *Around $1,223.* It would know that this balance wouldn't be exact until it knew the amounts of any missing checks. Needless to say, if you asked the program, *What's my shoe size?* it would reply, *I can't answer that question.* If you asked, *Tell me a good recipe for moussaka,* it would have to reply, *I can't. I only know about home finance.*

This home finance program is entirely possible using current AI methods. It requires far more space than is available currently on a personal computer, but if it were installed in a larger computer at a bank, anyone with a personal computer at home could hook up to it.

Home finance is just one of many areas where current AI research could be applied for home use in the next few years. But until we start to see programs that approach some level of understanding, we have to learn how to distinguish between software that is touted as *knowing English,* and software that really has some understanding ability. Like the old days of the traveling medicine show, we have to beware of snake oil salesmen who have learned merely the words the consumers want to hear.

COMPUTERS AT SCHOOL

One of the most significant applications that can be made of today's personal computers is in the field of education. This use wouldn't necessarily require the latest AI research. Today's personal computers have enough computing power and graphics capabilities to enable clever programmers who know something about education to build some very exciting software. Let's explore the phenomenon of computers at school in greater depth.

The nation's schools have begun to panic about computer literacy. Educators suddenly have become fearful that they are not training people for tomorrow's world, and that they should teach children about computers. The computer industry is taking advantage of this panic and offering incentive discounts so that schools can buy hundreds of personal computers.

LEARNING FROM COMPUTERS, NOT
ABOUT THEM

What should schools be *doing* with all of these computers?
We could teach children word-processing, but that couldn't be
what we mean by training them for tomorrow's world, could it?
We could teach kids to play video games, but is that what we
mean by computer literacy? Do we teach them keypunch operation? Data entry?

Schools don't really know *why* they need these computers.
They haven't really come to grips with the fact that the only
valuable computer skill you can teach is *programming*. Serious
problems occur with programming instruction. You have to have
a programming *teacher*, and a very good one. Most good programming teachers are working for big companies, attracted by
large salaries. There has been an attempt, however, to train
schoolteachers to handle programming classes. But training a
teacher who has little or no previous experience with programming to teach a programming class is likely to cause us to end
up with a whole lot of kids learning very little about programming, and learning it in the wrong way. Most of the personal
computers that big companies have been unloading on the school
systems understand only BASIC. But BASIC, although it is simple, is not a very good language for teaching programming concepts to anyone, let alone children.

But *what is the value of learning to program?* There are two
possible answers:

1. To get a job
2. To train the mind, to sharpen thinking

The child who has been taught programming in BASIC by
a history teacher who has been trained to teach only BASIC *isn't*
going to land a programming job. Nor has he/she been given a
head start toward learning programming later on in college. There
aren't going to be all that many jobs for programmers if computers get smarter than they are today, anyway. Programmers
today are like auto mechanics 80 years ago. They are specialists
in something very few people can do, and there aren't enough
of them. But in 20 years, programmers might be like auto mechanics are today—they no longer work in a sought-after profession. Finally, a child isn't going to get *any* good jobs or be trained

for *any* world unless he can read and write. If we could be absolutely positive that kids could read and write well by the end of high school, it wouldn't matter what else we taught them beyond arithmetic. They would have the tools to learn anything they might need on their own.

As for teaching programming as a training exercise for the mind, the schools simply are not doing it with that aim in mind. It is very demanding to teach programming in such a way that it can sharpen a child's thinking ability. Programming instructors in the schools haven't learned to teach programming that way.

The ideal programming teacher has to really understand, in a fundamental sense, how to write or create algorithms and what a process-based system is all about. Most importantly, he must teach these things in a lively, relevant, and interactive manner. If children are to learn something worthwhile from programming, learning how to write algorithms is critical. Programming therefore can—and should—teach logical reasoning. It is an important way to exercise the mind, but only if taught as such.

Unfortunately, it really isn't feasible to teach schoolteachers how to think algorithmically. This takes time and effort over a period of years. It is much easier to teach teachers to teach BASIC, since that takes weeks. But it is a generally poor idea to have the teachers of a subject be people who are not trained in the fundamentals of this subject. Children can live easily without computer skills, and they are better off without poorly taught computer skills. Despite the clamor from parents to teach their children about computers, it simply isn't realistic to advocate a programming or computer technology curriculum for school-age children.

THE TRAGIC STATE OF EDUCATION

We currently have a whole world of interconnected problems in our schools. At a time when we can't even teach kids how to read and write properly, we are worrying about whether or not we should teach them second-rate programming. What better illustration of the problems in our school system could we think of? There are many other problems, of course:

1. Children are bored in school.
2. Many teachers are not interested in teaching.
3. Schools treat children as a mass instead of as individuals.
4. Children don't get enough attention from their teachers.
5. Teachers get bored and frustrated, and stop caring.

We allow children to reach high school without ensuring that they can read and comprehend a short story. A child who gets a few weeks or months behind in reading at age 6 or 7 has only limited opportunity to catch up. He typically is allowed to slide for three or four years, often labeled a discipline problem or a slow learner. The rude awakening comes in junior high or high school, when he is asked to pass reading tests to matriculate. Bad grades start to mean something to this troubled student as well as to the schools. Unfortunately, such students generally are so far behind that only careful one-to-one tutoring will bring them up to their proper level, and this extra, intensive tutoring is almost certainly unavailable to any large degree in many school districts. The child becomes an adolescent, and must face the additional emotional difficulties of that period. Any instability at home complicates this further. He feels inferior to his peers, even though their reading ability many times is only slightly better.

Instead of receiving the care he needs at this stage, the student becomes the target of teacher scorn and contempt. He is a threat to them now. They cannot and will not take the extra time to help him. By age 16 or 17, he will have been *taught* only that school is a frustrating, pointless, punitive system that cannot help him. He certainly will not go to college, and may drop out of high school after 16. The ability to read at the eighth grade level and to write a decent résumé and cover letter for a job application would make a tremendous difference in his life, even as a dropout, but he can't even do this.

Most of today's inner-city schools and even suburban schools function as little more than day-care centers for older children. If we are lucky, they keep the kids out of their parents' hair and off the streets for a few hours each day. Some schools don't even do this well. These are tragic problems for the society, and we should be worried about them.

LEARNING FROM COMPUTERS AT SCHOOL

We are worrying about education and about computers, but we are not worrying about them together. The computer can enable us to carry out a revolution in education. Almost every one of the problems I've just mentioned could conceivably be remedied by the computer. How?

1. Computers are fun.
2. Computers can be programmed to teach far more thoroughly and interactively than textbooks.
3. They can be individual—a child can have his own computer teacher who keeps track of progress.
4. Computers can be used by almost anyone, no matter how hyperactive or lazy.
5. Computers don't get bored or frustrated with students or with teaching. They won't punish the student or single him out for contempt.

Computers can serve as *excellent individualized teachers*. If we can create very intelligent knowledge systems, one of the first valuable tasks would be to have them know everything about a certain subject, and thus be available to teach a child patiently. A computer teacher could have a fundamental understanding of a student's errors, good work, and general progress.

Computers can begin to be the patient teacher you never had. Today's education tends to be a passive experience. Children are supposed to listen, read, and follow instructions. But the best educational environment for children is *interactive*. Children like to be challenged and be rewarded for their accomplishments. They like to see results from their actions and thoughts. Workbooks can't give results, but a computer can. AI research will allow us to create interesting interactive educational software. Fortunately, however, we needn't wait for AI to materialize quality educational programs. AI researchers already have developed programs that can transform the computer, even a small personal computer, into a powerful teaching tool. An interactive reading program or math game can provide an interesting learning environment.

We can build terrific educational software for today's public schools. Why isn't this happening? Because computer scientists and educators haven't understood each other's needs. Nor have they understood correctly the power of the computer as it applies to education. This situation, however, is slowly changing.

Automated, intelligent, individual instructors are one of the most interesting and socially significant possible applications of AI. Computer teachers could take much of the pressure off human teachers. Human teachers then could function as they really should, namely as leaders and counselors, encouraging the children and providing a friendly, warm, and open atmosphere. Teachers could be free to concentrate on providing children with those elements of a good education that do not directly involve the acquisition of abstract knowledge. They could provide direction to children in building their social skills, their self-confidence, and their creative drive.

Individualized knowledge systems can treat children as individuals at precisely the age when our current school systems develop curricula and tests that tend to treat them as a bunch of robots who must all do the same exercises. Children are incredibly diverse—some like drawing but hate geometry; some like creative writing but refuse to complete grammar exercises. Some cannot work on a particular idea for more than 15 minutes. There undoubtedly would be some students who could not interact with a computer at all, but the teacher would have a little more time to accommodate the incredible diversity of students. Children need to develop all their abilities to the fullest in a stimulating environment.

The watchwords of AI applications in the classroom have to be individuality, freedom, and above all, fun. A sweatshop approach is not our goal. We wouldn't strap all the kids in front of a terminal and make them hit keys for 40 minutes each day for each subject. The kids could go up to the knowledge system anytime and start a geometry game, then switch to a reading program, then play a logical reasoning game that also teaches beginning algebra. Children learn quickly when their interest is aroused. If the knowledge system became aware that little Billy hadn't done any math games for a long while, it could alert the teacher, who then could give him more personal attention. The system could even remind Billy by printing *What about the math game we were playing last week?*

The vision of such a computerized classroom may seem very radical. But we are just seeing the tip of the iceberg in AI's involvement in education. One example of AI is the programming language LOGO, a valuable tool for teaching children how to program and how to think. LOGO is a spin-off of AI research, developed specifically for children by Seymour Papert and his students at the AI laboratory at MIT. It is the first programming language to be developed for teaching programming and logical reasoning. LOGO's value is that it teaches children to reason without overtly trying to do so. LOGO challenges the children to draw a picture or solve a fun problem, and compels them to think carefully about what is going on. The kids get to do something they want to do in a logical way that ends up helping the child accomplish more than he had intended. The painful and tedious task of learning a new principle in the abstract is bypassed. The child has to form the principle himself to finish a game or get through a fun situation.

One of the most valuable aspects of computers is their ability to teach by presenting children with tasks that they like to do (witness the current video-game craze). This aspect can be coupled with a simple trick. Instead of the dubious skill of mastering fast hand-eye coordination in order to shoot down enemy planes, we can have the child master a useful skill like logical reasoning, or even simple mathematics or the ability to read. Imagine learning to read in order to win a game!

WORKBOOKS: THE PRISONHOUSE OF THE MIND

One reason why schools are in such trouble is that school is often quite boring. A major cause of boredom in schools is the *workbook method of teaching*. Schools traditionally teach basic subjects by giving every child the same book and making her go through it at classroom pace from page 1 to page 200, doing every single exercise in the book. This is the way he is taught spelling, reading, writing, geometry, math, and science, and this is the way he becomes bored to death. What is a classroom pace? Is it appropriate for every child? No. Children should learn at their own pace. Some children need twice as much work than others in some areas; some cannot stand workbooks of any kind, and need a more interactive learning environment. The student who says he hates math class but loves shop class might really mean that he hates the math workbook and loves moving things around, cutting them in half, measuring them with a tape measure, and then putting them together. He loves it when all his calculations work correctly—in shop class, that is. He might appreciate shop class because shop teachers have to look out for and be involved in their students' work in ways that English and math teachers do not. He just might appreciate the shop teacher because he gets encouragement from him even when his work is flawed. There is nothing a child loves more than to be congratulated on work well done. The interactive world this child loves is exactly what math could become if it were taught by an intelligent teaching system and a much less pressured teacher who could monitor progress carefully.

If today's teachers were watching each child carefully, they could vary the complexity and amount of the examples in the books so that each child could maintain interest according to his progress. If workbooks were *smart* enough they could do this by themselves. But workbooks don't know whether or not a child is doing the exercises correctly, or how far he has gone. A workbook isn't able to stop him in the middle of page 54, exercise D, problem 13, and say, *No, you've missed something, let's go back to that tricky problem on page 50.* Nor can it say *Great! You've got the hang of it. Let's go on to something else.* Think of how alienating and dehumanizing the grade-school textbooks and the instruction that is coordinated with them really are: Textbooks come complete with a teacher's edition that makes the perfunctory duty of marking the student's wrong answers easier. Teachers are alienated by this method of learning as well. It is deadly boring to grade 25 workbooks. A page of exercises filled in with doodles and swear words, from a kid with a healthy contempt for workbooks, infuriates the teacher and makes him think the student doesn't care. The student *does* care, very much, about the material and how it is presented: He hates it.

READING: FAR MORE BASIC
THAN *BASIC*

One of the most valuable results to come indirectly out of AI is our knowledge of how humans learn to read. In order to ascertain how *machines* might be able to read, we have spent a great deal of time trying to figure out how *people* read.

Today's textbooks are as alienating and dehumanizing as computers ever could be. The books teach the rules for getting the right answer without having to think or, worse yet, by thinking in entirely wrong ways. Some boast a snappy design and appear to offer a totally new approach to workbook and textbook learning. Some are even written in computerlike type, or with pseudocomputer program exercises. But the fact remains that a workbook is essentially passive, while real teaching and learning must be an active process. Computers can be interactive in ways that keep teaching from being boring and make learning fun. A workbook can't tell when a student has mastered an idea; it just tells him to do 50 examples of the same thing.

As if this weren't bad enough, the material in these books often is just plain wrong. Many textbooks are based on useless or spurious ways of looking at words and language. As an example, my son came home with his third-grade grammar book, and showed me a page with an exercise about "Words beginning with dis-." One would think that there must be some meaning for the "dis-." It happened to be parents week at the school so I went to his teacher and asked her what the meaning of the prefix dis- was. She said it means anti- or against or un- or not, or something like that. I asked her, "Do you know what the words he had to learn in this section were? They were *display* and *disgusting*. Does display mean *un-play*? Does disgusting mean *antigusting*?" (Historically it does, but that is little help to a child.) She agreed and said that she actually hated teaching that section of the workbook, but that she had no choice.

It isn't computers that will dehumanize or devalue teachers. That job has already been done by workbooks.

Some sample questions, typical of the type of questions found in many fourth-grade readers illustrate the problems with workbooks:

Circle the word synonymous with the italicized word.

1. Mrs. Smith went to the *pharmacist* to buy aspirin and vitamins.
doctor   druggist   gift shop

2. Joan wanted to be a *secretary* for a doctor in a small office.
helper   secret   plumber

3. The glass was so *fragile* that Mary's mother wouldn't let her hold it.
old   breakable   faded

These examples are supposed to teach vocabulary. But isolated sentences do not really provide enough context. It is very difficult to learn new words from reading them in sentences when the sole purpose in reading those sentences is to circle a correct answer. In that case, the child needs to know not the meaning of the word, but just enough about the meaning of the surrounding words to discern the correct answer. The child is being asked to make the best guess about the right answer. He need not even look at "pharmacist" to know that the right answer is "druggist." In fact, the association of pharmacist-druggist need never be made at all by the child. In example 2, the vocabulary item in question, "secretary" is likely to be known by the average fourth grader. One thing that is being shown (probably inadvertently) is that the suffix "-ary" has no meaning in English in general. This is illustrated in the test itself by the use of "secret" as one of the possible answers. (This example appeared in a section of the reading text labeled 'words ending in "-ary".') The child's task, after discarding the premise that Joan wished to grow up to be a secret, is to determine whether a secretary is a helper or a plumber. The choice is obvious if you know the meaning of the word and impossible if you do not. Furthermore, the correct choice is virtually absurd. Is the meaning of "secretary" really "helper?" What does the child learn from a task such as this?

What's the point of such books and how do these books end up being used by the schools? All sorts of forces contribute to this. People who do reading research know that these books don't teach in the right ways at all. But as long as schools buy these books there is little incentive for change. School districts are loyal to certain publishers, and don't have the kind of money needed to make new purchases (perhaps because they're spending it on second-rate programming classes). An additional problem is that teachers who complain about curricula, whether in private or public school, are looked upon as troublemakers.

COMPUTER LIBERATION

Computers allow us to realize new innovations in teaching while bypassing the bureaucracy. Computers can design software to teach reading and all the other things that students currently agonize over in workbooks: arithmetic, geometry, algebra, physics, chemistry, biology, and even music. I am not proposing that we simply make electronic books out of these subjects. That is equally pointless, although unfortunately plenty of people are doing exactly that. If the only difference between a computer and workbook is looking at a screen and pressing a button for the next alienating page of exercises, nothing will have changed.

We are able to do much more on the computer than simply make electronic workbooks. Computers can make learning fun. We can teach geometry with computer graphic presentations of rotating triangles. We can demonstrate axioms graphically by letting kids create a triangle, bisect it, and build congruent or complementary angles in the format of a game. These games take the drudgery and distraction out of geometry. When the student masters one game, another one comes along. If at some point he forgets an earlier idea, it returns for him. The student would feel challenged to finish a concept and use it to develop another, not abandon it as if it were a workbook exercise with 30 practice problems. The computer could keep track of his progress and manage his learning environment within a given subject far more closely than a teacher who has 25 or 30 students on his mind.

If intelligent teaching software were to be developed for chemistry, physics, and biology, these laboratory science classes would be much easier to learn and could be introduced at an earlier age. Instead of having to memorize the immense amount of abstract knowledge involved in basic chemistry, for example, a student could create reactions and manipulate different chemicals graphically on the computer. The program would teach the

student why certain things combine in certain ways, and allow
him to learn from his mistakes. The student could form his own
concepts, rather than having them drummed into him. He would
learn, rather than merely *repeat*, the principles of chemistry. Most
children want desperately to make something blow up in a chemistry lab or with their own chemistry sets. There are good reasons
for prohibiting them from doing this. But a computer-graphics
experiment that taught a student all the principles involved in an
explosive reaction and then allowed him to set one off would
harm nobody if it blew up. Computer simulations are used to
train airline pilots. Why not children, too? Laboratory experiments could relate directly to the student's conceptual knowledge
and offer exciting and challenging learning.

Teachers, in turn, would feel better able to cope with the
real problems that kids bring to school—worries, feelings of in-
feriority, loneliness, lack of self-confidence, problems in social
situations, and so on. A child with genuine learning problems
could receive extra attention at the necessary higher level, and
not just be forced to muddle through remedial or special workbooks. Freeing teachers and students from the workbooks and
textbooks of today's school system would be a liberation of great
significance. It would be a liberation of the mind.

AI research has already taught us enough about reading and
understanding to make a great impact on the current state of
education. The tools are already in place to create computer software that will educate children in a challenging way. The software will improve as AI makes progress in the next two decades,
but we needn't wait. Programs that make the child behave intelligently need not be intelligent themselves. We simply need to
start writing and using worthwhile good educational software
now.

Educators must watch out for a number of pitfalls however.
Very little of the educational software that will be coming out in
the next few years will achieve an interactive goal. There is nothing easier than entering all the exercises from a current workbook
on a floppy disk and peddling it to the school systems in a box
printed "Educational Knowledge System." Textbook publishers
will want to supplement their already out-of-date texts with has-
tily conceived educational software. Can we allow computer programmers who know nothing about children, reading, AI, or ed-

ucation to write this software just because they know how to program? We have an opportunity now to launch a teaching revolution. We must seize the educational opportunity that AI research affords. There are hundreds of ways to misapply computers in the schools, but only a few ways to apply them properly.

Of all the computer applications that are possible today, education seems to me to be the most important and potentially beneficial. We can and must take the opportunity presented by advances in AI and our increased knowledge of reading. If we get computers into the schools we must get good educational software into the schools as well.

Schools *should* pay attention to computers, but not because they are going to take over our lives unless we control them, and not because everyone has to prepare for a job as a programmer. The schools should pay attention to computers because computers are part of the solution to our problems in education. Schools needn't teach children about computers—educators should program computers to teach children.

CHAPTER
TEN

THE
EFFECTS OF AI

AI is a science of the future. AI researchers always are talking about what they could build if, and what they might build when. Whenever AI researchers build a new system or write an interesting program, people tend to denigrate it because it isn't as futuristic or intelligent as what they see in their imaginative fantasy of machine intelligence. Someone can always say *Well, the program doesn't do X and Y, and it will never be able to do Z.* AI is always defined by what we can't do at a given time. The moment we succeed on some AI project, it no longer seems to be AI. When we succeed in creating an intelligent program at some level we end up having to admit that it is not, after all, very intelligent. We go back to the drawing board. AI is the study of the impossible.

THE BAD CHILD OF ACADEMIA

Because of this unique posture, AI is the bad child of the sciences, the half-breed of academic research in psychology, philosophy, linguistics, and computer science. Many researcher in other scientific disciplines don't respect AI, and people in the humanities frequently lump AI research and computer technology together as dehumanizing and dangerous. The progress of AI research is steady and plodding, compared to the pace in disciplines such as physics and molecular biology, where progress can speed along overnight. When an AI person gets an inspiration of some kind, no one can tell what its value is until several major projects have been completed using the new ideas. Each program teaches us what to try to accomplish in the next program. When a new system or project is completed, an AI person comes up with new approaches and ideas almost intuitively. But he never really knows what shape a new idea will finally take until it has been incorporated into a new system, at which point he may see refinements and new angles that effectively change the original idea.

We could say simply that we succeed whenever we get an AI program to do what we set out to make it do. By this definition, every AI program is a success. By another definition, *every* AI program is a failure, if only because it is never a complete embodiment of human intelligence, but only one aspect of intelligence, with respect to one domain or subject. The real climax comes when we look at our finished projects and say, *Now I see exactly where we need to go from here. It's obvious what's missing.*

These are strange attributes for a science. I have called AI the science of the obvious, the science of the impossible, and the science of the future. I have pointed out that AI disappears at each point in its progress, that AI is always somewhere in between two projects or ideas. AI is clearly a misfit.

AI projects exist in only a few computer science departments across the country. Many refuse to set up AI laboratories, and have virtually outlawed AI research. AI is flaky, crackpot, and futuristic. But AI is looking less and less crackpot all the time, because we have started to come out with some very interesting programs that can be turned into useful products. AI has *just* started to produce software that is new and different, and people are noticing. A mere ten years ago, people would have ridiculed the idea that a computer could read stories about auto accidents on a news wire and summarize them in ten languages just as fast as the wire service could spit them out. They would have laughed even harder if they had been told that such systems were going to be on the *market*, and not merely singular systems installed in the research facilities of a few universities. They're not laughing any more.

Once an AI project is established in a university, everyone settles down and finds that their world hasn't fallen apart after all. In those computer science departments with strong AI projects, AI researchers coexist fairly happily with the rest of computer science. But AI doesn't really belong in computer science. Computer science departments supply computers upon which AI people build their understanding systems, but an AI person doesn't find much in common with other computer scientists. Computer scientists think like engineers and mathematicians more than philosophers and linguists. They are primarily concerned with speed and memory capacity, with numerical analysis, and with the design of operating systems. An AI person is more interested in talking with anthropologists, English professors, linguists, and psychologists. These departments might seem more appropriate places for AI, but they don't tend to have their own computer systems. Not yet, at least.

AI AND THE HUMANITIES

The conversations between AI and humanities departments aren't always constructive. There is a great deal of hostility among humanists toward computers, technology in any form, and science in general. It is easy to show that all the ills of the world can be traced to the alienating, dehumanizing progress of technology and the industrial revolution, or to the callousness of sciences that purport to comment on objective reality while contributing to the subjugation of people by machines. It requires a little more thought to see that where people have been alienated and dehumanized, it has been at the hands of their fellow humans, or through the failure of their own institutions, ideologies, and abstractions. Scientists, at least those who conduct pure research, have rarely advocated the negative or dehumanizing uses of their discoveries. We can't blame Einstein for discovering the laws of physics that enable today's technicians to build nuclear warheads. He didn't make his discoveries by envisioning mushroom clouds and dreaming of Mutually Assured Destruction; nor did he develop the political systems that deploy today's nuclear bombs in such vast numbers. These are the inventions of people who *weren't* scientists.

In the same vein, it requires a little sophistication to see that AI researchers aren't trying to subvert the humane arts. We don't intend to replace Bach and Mozart with a computer program that can make up fugues or symphonies. Nor do we hope that poetry someday will be written only by computers. AI does not attempt to colonize the mind or to subordinate it to the computer. It need not even be based on the idea that *every* aspect of human thought can be modeled on the computer.

If, as Socrates maintained, the unexamined life is not worth living, then AI has made an important contribution to many people's lives. As people discover what AI is all about they begin to notice the complexity of their own thought processes. They become aware of their amazing ability to make connections and associations. They begin to analyze their thoughts and to examine their use of language in novel ways. Intelligence and indeed the whole learning process seem to be bound up with asking questions about what one thinks and says, and reflecting upon one's assumptions about the world.

Over the past decade AI has caused a wide range of people to ask some very interesting questions about language, reading, and understanding. It has spurred the public's growing interest in the mind and all its processes. It is difficult to imagine another discipline capable of doing this on so grand a scale. AI has brought some of the central questions that span philosophy, psychology, linguistic and literary criticism into the public awareness. This much can't be disputed. The simple fact that you have read this far in this book, never mind whether you agree or disagree with the views it expresses, probably means that you have thought about language and thinking on a very deep level, and that you will continue to do so throughout your life.

In trying to model our thought processes on computers, we continually learn more about what it means to be human. Far from dehumanizing us, AI research has compelled us to appreciate our human qualities and abilities. A great many people in the humanities have seen this. Humanists who don't feel threatened by the progress of AI have made significant contributions to the field. And AI researchers, with their novel approaches to the question of how knowledge of any kind can be represented, organized, and stored, have contributed to a wide range of disciplines.

AI AND PSYCHOLOGY

AI has contributed more to psychology than has any other discipline for some time. In the past ten years psychologists have paid much attention to AI research, and a great many valuable psychology experiments have been based on questions that AI researchers first proposed and began to work on. At some universities, psychology had actually joined up with AI in an area called cognitive science. Psychologists have taken notice of AI developments in part because experimental methods in psychology have been restricted in scope ever since the advent of behaviorism. Although behaviorism contributed to our knowledge of the mind, its adherence to certain methods has caused researchers in psychology to look elsewhere for interesting questions and experiments.

In addition to providing fresh ideas for psychologists to ponder, AI also will enhance their ability to model human cognitive functions on the computer. Psychologists have been using computers for decades to conduct statistical analyses. In a few years, however, psychologists will be building far more sophisticated models of human behavior. They will be able to model entire scenarios of group interaction and decision making that heretofore have only been modeled in the form of mathematical probabilities.

COMPUTERS AND
THE SOCIAL SCIENCES

We have been using computers in economics, sociology, and political science for quite some time. They are used by universities, private corporations, and advertising agencies to conduct huge statistical analyses and make predictions of mass behavior. They are used to model everything from who will buy blue jeans in the next ten years to how the nation feels about body odor. Computers are used to calculate just how much the average consumer can be asked to pay for something that has been calculated to cost as little as possible to produce.

Computers have been used by environmentalists to show that the world may soon be a desert of toxic wastes, inhabited by a diseased and miserable population. Chemical companies have commissioned think tanks to develop models that show how government regulation of industry actually causes more "units of unfreedom" for the average American than do the pollutants he would drink if there were no regulation. Whole companies are devoted to the development of software packages for the social sciences, and these are bought like hotcakes by eager sociologists and economists. It might be very interesting to create a model of who buys statistical software for the social sciences and for what purposes.

Do these models and software really tell social scientists or economists anything about reality? They can predict only what happens in a pretend world where the average person has a cheeseburger for lunch 3.23 days a week and gets a headache 2.3 days a week. He only spends 8.5 afternoons a month with his 2.639 kids, but that's up from 7.2 because of adult male unemployment and the increase in male single parents.

The people who use these models usually know what they're after, and are going to do whatever they feel will achieve their goals. If a computer model can be made to parrot their views, thus giving them credibility, all the better. The chemical company executive doesn't care about "units of unfreedom," even if he really believes such units exist. He just wants less government regulation, and he's prepared to stand by any program that spits out a favorable answer. He might take out ad space in a newspaper to tell Americans that a computer says that in order to reduce their "Units of unfreedom" by opposing government regulation. He might look for a politician whose model of his constituency shows that he'll get re-elected no matter which way he votes on this issue, and take him out to lunch. The politician would be far more interested in the results of his own little model than in the chemical company's model. The problem is not really what these models tell these people to do or believe. The problem is what these people *want* to do or to believe.

People in powerful positions already use computer models to make very important decisions that affect our lives, the lives of our children, the welfare of entire populations and the future of the world. Up to now, they have only built statistical models that represent a few crude assumptions about people. It is not likely that we are going to convince everyone to stop using computers to build models of decision-making problems.

THE SOLUTION: MAKE THEM SMARTER

Since there is no chance of preventing computer models from being used for important decisions, we should concentrate on making them better informed about human desires and needs. If these models are designed to incorporate more knowledge about the people and institutions they involve, the decision makers who use these models will be better informed as well. The more realistic these models are, the better off everyone will be, if only because those who use them will have a better idea of the consequences of their decisions.

Conceptual models of politicians, governments, voters, consumers, corporations, unions, and so on have not seemed even remotely possible until very recently. In a few years, AI will be able to offer the social sciences far more complex and integrated models of human behavior. Sociologists, economists, and political scientists soon will be able to build complicated models that can test better whatever ideas they may have. Models of corporations could interact with models of consumers or shareholders. Models of governments could interact with each other and test various scenarios.

These models will not provide the answers to all our problems. We will not have to start believing everything they say once they are smarter. Executives don't automatically do what their human advisers tell them to do. Political science professors don't imagine that their graduate students will find the answer to the problems of terrorism or Third World development any more than they believe a computer model will. These aren't the kinds of problems for which there are easy answers or even right answers. Most of the time we are just trying to find out what might happen in a given scenario.

Perhaps the ultimate function of AI in these areas will be to make humans better informed about other humans. A program that has the patience to read every terrorism story that ever comes over any news wire might just be able to figure out something new that will help people battle terrorism.

AI'S DAY IN COURT

By the time intelligent social science models start to appear, we will start to see AI-based judicial systems. A large part of a lawyer's basic task is to search for past cases that relate to a current one, and then analyze them in terms of certain particulars. Much of this work could be done by an intelligently programmed legal adviser. An intelligent legal adviser would have a knowledge of all the past cases and be able to relate this knowledge to a particular case. It would seek out cases with similar charges, sentences, judgments, comments by the judge and jury, and so on. It would analyze why a certain defense had failed in the past and explain how to make improvements. It could take into account a person's criminal record and compare it to the records of similar defendants to estimate a sentence. The system would have a knowledge of all the basic factors judges take into account when sentencing particular kinds of cases. These systems could advise everyone: the judge, the defense, and the prosecution.

AI also could produce an inexpensive legal adviser for use in the home. You just phone up and for a small fee your home computer is connected to the legal adviser. You type in *I want to sue someone*. The computer would ask you all the details and see if there were any similar cases around, whether they were thrown out of court or not, how they were settled, who won, and how much. It could tell you what claims or defenses worked and which ones failed every time they were tried. It could even estimate the legal fees. In 20 minutes, for perhaps a few dollars, the adviser could tell you whether your case was worth the financial risk of seeing a real lawyer.

Lawyers already have access to huge computerized law libraries, but these systems aren't very intelligent. They can't perform any cognitive tasks when searching for a certain brief or a clause. They are keyword-based systems that only scan the titles of briefs or index entries for subjects. If the brief that would save your case hasn't been indexed under a keyword that relates to your case, it's certain that you'll never find it. You might read a 100 briefs under a particular keyword entry and find only one brief similar to the case you are working on. If the sentence in the brief was twice as long as you had hoped to find, you would want to look for the exact same kind of case, but with a much lower sentence. You could tell an intelligent system to search for the whole set of particulars and details of the case, and tell it to give you the briefs with the lowest (or the highest) sentences. The librarian would search and find you only the cases you wanted. If you knew that the judge presiding in your case was especially responsive to a certain issue, you could see whether anyone had ever brought up the issue in a case similar to yours.

DISAPPEARING AI

Ultimately, AI will be assimilated into every other discipline. People in every field will start asking themselves AI-type questions about how they use this knowledge, and how they can model the knowledge in their field in the form of an understanding system.

The three or four top AI departments have students working on systems in a wide range of fields. There are people at Yale developing legal systems, medical systems, and economic systems. They may one day teach courses in law schools, medical schools, and business schools, respectively, on how to build cognitive conceptual models of legal, medical, and economic situations. In a few decades, many AI experts will specialize in developing understanding systems in various particular fields. There will be doctors who write medical models, and law students who develop and analyze cognitive models of legal situations. These students will have started to ask what kinds of knowledge structures judges, doctors, and economists use to make decisions.

People in many areas will be able to test, for the first time, their principles with integrated world models and see where they lead. Economists, sociologists, political scientists, and foreign policy experts will create understanding systems for their fields of study. Medical schools will start to incorporate the creation of medical knowledge systems into their curriculum. The designers of such systems will not be AI people in computer science departments. They will have to be real lawyers and doctors who are able to analyze the knowledge and principles they use, and who have some grasp of how to embody them in an understanding system. The knowledge in these fields is constantly changing, and there will be a continuing need for people in these fields who can build cognitive understanding systems.

As AI disappears into the rest of the world of intelligence, it will start to change the way we look at things. AI will change the questions people ask and the methods they use. The ability to create better and better knowledge systems will allow people in every field to develop new ideas and to find new approaches to their oldest problems. AI will encourage a renaissance in practically every area that it touches.

What other field can match AI in terms of its relevance to other disciplines? The only real candidate is, of course, philosophy. Philosophy, the love of wisdom, is the one other field besides AI that has developed general theories of mind and thought. AI is actually the newest development of a 3,000 year effort to describe what goes on inside our minds, a sort of modern-day epistemology. It is not surprising that of all the experts in fields that relate to AI, it is often philosophers, particularly philosophers of mind, who hate AI the most. (Of course, there are some important exceptions to this.) AI takes a process-based view of how we formulate responses, how we make connections and formulate abstract ideas, how we get reminded, how we learn a new domain of knowledge, and even how we make mistakes. This is not the way traditional philosophy has approached the problem.

AI, to some extent, flies in the face of traditional philosphers of science as well. The traditional view of science tends to demand that theories have certain structures, and that they will be either right or wrong. AI people have theories too, but they evolve bit by bit, or chunk by chunk. They are rarely either right or wrong. An AI person might have a very general theory that we have to look for conceptual representations in order to model human understanding processes. The theory is that we need such representations, not that a particular set of representations should be more "right" or canonical than another set. We choose the representations that get the job done, that work for a given task or body of knowledge. AI is at an exploratory stage, looking for the representations that seem to work. The theory is simply that some representation, any representation, will work. The theory is really developed by what works in practice.

AI AND THE WORLD

The ultimate question about the impact that AI will have lies not in its effect on academics but in its effect on the real world. I have explained some of the problems AI must face as it continues to evolve, whether in its product-directed or theory-directed mode. We can make some predictions about how AI will affect the world over the next few years. To talk about this, let's divide the future into three main parts:

SOON—the next two or three years
MID-RANGE—ten years after SOON
LONG-RANGE—within most readers' lifetimes

We will see steady improvement in overcoming the learning problem and the domain problem over the next two decades. We are already starting to develop experientially based learning systems, but there are many years of work ahead for anyone working on this problem. While it is easy to stifle AI research, or take it too far down a wrong track, there isn't much one can do to speed up its course. In AI there are no easy answers, and no sure-fire scientific or logical methods. As with any form of pure research, a vast coordinated effort on the part of government, universities and private industry is really no more likely to produce quicker or better results than just passing out unrestricted funds to any bright, hard-working people in any area of AI, and buying good computers for them to tinker away on. New or creative ideas can rarely be planned for in advance, budgeted, or regulated. It is a contradiction in terms to *plan* to make new discoveries.

SOON

We will see the emergence of advisory systems, such as the financial advisor and medical advisor, soon, in the next two or three years. Computer banking virtually necessitates that some understanding ability be built in to accommodate the growing need for customer service. Intelligent banking systems may soon field basic questions about interest rates, loans, insurance, IRAs, taxes, and investments of every kind. There must be millions of people who might save or invest in small amounts but don't because they can never get a banker. Intelligent banking and financial systems will streamline banking operations and reduce the cost to the customer while increasing profits for the bank.

The systems of the very near future will have narrow, fairly low level domains of knowledge. They won't have to form abstract generalizations or modify themselves on the basis of experience. They will simply have to be able to understand and answer basic questions in their field. They will rely on the knowledge structures we discussed earlier: scripts, plans and goals. The banking advisor will have expectations about deposits, withdrawals, interest rates, and loans. It won't have to know about Mexican cooking.

MID-RANGE

As for cooking, in the future we will see such sophisticated learning systems as the computer chef. A program like the one described in Chapter 2 currently is being written at Yale. There won't be a good market for such home systems until people can hook up their personal computers to the large computer time-sharing networks that such systems require. There really is no point in trying to cram enough computer power into a personal computer to support such big programs. People will just hook up to a network that offers services they need—cooking, home finance, household repair, education, preventive medicine, and other such understanding systems. In 10 to 15 year's time, such networks may indeed spring up, in which case there will be a flurry of activity to create learning systems for stockbrokers, doctors, librarians, and business management for use in the home.

Learning systems will make possible the development of extremely complex economic and political models. Corporations will be able to create models of their consumers and their competitors, as well as their own management structures. Whole economies could be simulated in microcosm, with companies interacting with consumers and the government. Integrated models of social behavior could be used to test out ideas in a number of fields.

LONG-RANGE AND BEYOND

Perhaps within the next 50 years, integrated world knowledge systems will be developed. These will be intricately woven systems that can learn new domains of knowledge by asking questions and reading new material. They will be able to understand very high levels of abstraction, and make general analogies that span entire domains. A useful idea typed in by an anthropologist might be met with an analogy from the work of a psychologist who had interacted with the system a few months before at another university. The most effective role for these systems will be as librarians and consultants to anyone who is studying something in depth and needs help in reading through massive amounts of material. These systems could be told to read massive amounts of material in search of certain concepts or ideas, not just certain strings of letters or keywords. Such cognitive abilities, together with tireless speed and infinite patience, will enable them to amass a general knowledge of a new domain faster than the average human.

We cannot say with any certainty that such systems can be built, what they actually will do when they are built, or when they will be finished. But we are trying to build them. Systems such as these would radically alter the way we approach books and written information of all kinds. People who would never think of going to a library to find out more about an area of interest would be able to do in-depth research in a single afternoon. Suppose you suddenly wanted to learn all about solar energy. You could sign up at a university and take introductory physics and earth science. If you were interested in solar energy because you wanted to build your own collectors, you might also want to take an engineering course. If you were designing a solar greenhouse, you would have to learn something about construction and carpentry. If you were a disciplined worker and knew how to use a library well, you could read on your own. But either way, it would take you many weeks to become well-versed in solar energy. You might spend a whole week just looking for a few books that introduce the material at a level of detail that suits you. However, if you worked with an intelligent world knowledge system you could conceivably learn what you needed to know about solar energy by interacting with an automated teacher who could assess your knowledge, find out what you needed to know, and figure out the right way to explain it to you.

These systems are not just around the corner. They are a considerable way off, but they are possible. We have no theoretical basis for ruling them out altogether, and until we find such evidence we can look forward to what they can contribute to our lives. The predictions and estimations put forth here are very loose, and are meant to put the current work being done in AI in perspective. In three years' time an entirely different set of possibilities may be in view. Three years more, and again, the scene may have changed completely. Change and constant evolution are the only rules governing AI research. We cannot become preoccupied with any given program because we are interested in all possible programs, as well as what seem to be the impossible programs. The only thing we can be certain of is that our perception of computers and of what they can do is going to change radically in the next decades. This will be accompanied by an evolution in the way we look at ourselves and the nature of knowledge and intelligence in general.

CHAPTER ELEVEN

THE WORLD OF THE FUTURE

Some day, intelligent machines finally will arrive. Machines that understand natural language will allow people access to information that they never had access to previously. Anyone will be able to get information that today is only available to specialists. Just as the public library system was seen in its initial concept as a boon to democracy, so it will be when computers are accessible to all. One of the byproducts of the information age will be an opportunity for the creation of an informed populace.

The real advantage of machines that are easy to communicate with is their usefulness for people who need information but who cannot program. Since the first owners of the new English-language accessible computers will be the industries that can afford them, we can expect banks, insurance companies, brokerage houses, and such to have them early on. These institutions will use their computers as a way for them to provide reliable information to their customers. The advantage of these English-speaking machines to such institutions will be the competitive edge they provide. We can expect that the general public will soon be acquainted with machines that understand a limited amount of

English, at least enough to provide specialized information easily to anyone.

Intelligently programmed computers will begin to perform simple banking and financial counseling, approve loans and sell insurance. This will naturally require that the computer understand the domains of banking services. But the knowledge needed to deliver those services is not that great. Selling insurance is considerably less complex than modeling the thinking of political leaders. Computers will begin to take over certain tasks where the knowledge needed for them is not tremendously complex and the need for the service is great.

Imagine a computer travel agent that understands natural language. You would be able to walk up to it and type, *I'd like to go to Jamaica.* The computer will respond, *When do you want to leave?* You might have a dozen things to consider, so you might just say them all sloppily: *Well, I want to leave in late December and stay five days, but if I can get a cheap economy fare for seven nights, I'll stretch my vacation. Also, if the fares are more expensive near Christmas, I'll go a few days earlier. Oh, and also, I don't want to fly in a DC-10, if possible.* The computer would understand all this and make the best fitting suggestion, given your particular travel plans. A human travel agent might spend 20 minutes searching through lists of flights on a computer, and making adjustments to all your needs, but an intelligently programmed travel agent computer system would do so in a fraction of a second. But speed isn't the only advantage here. You might be too shy to admit your fear of a certain aircraft to a human travel agent; you wouldn't want to be thought of as bothersome. But you wouldn't care what a computer travel agent thought of you.

Because so many things we do involve transfer of information, the possibilities for applying AI to our everyday lives are almost unlimited. Once there are intelligent systems that can teach and give advice, people will find it very easy to become do-it-yourselfers in everything from home and auto repair to finance and medicine. (If you could describe the symptoms that your troubled car had to a computer that knew all about cars and was located in your own home, it is hard to believe that you would prefer to call the tow truck.) People will be more informed about the world around them. They will interact with each other in new ways and have more to say to one another.

THE FINANCIAL WORLD

Banks exist because of the wealthy people and large corporations that keep their money in them. A bank wants to do business with people who can deposit or borrow huge sums of
money. Banks are not interested in processing hundreds of
thousands of little checks for under $100 written by people who
keep under $5,000 in the bank. They don't really care about these
small accounts, and when they have to cut corners it's the small
customer who has to pay the monthly service charge as a penalty for not having lots of money. Banks take care of small customers largely because they are required to do so by govern-
mental agencies.

Most importantly, banks do not offer the small customer
adequate financial advice in any area, even though the small customer's $5,000 is just as important to him as $500,000 is to the
big customer, if not more. And the larger world of advice and
counseling—stockbrokers, commodities traders, and bond fund
managers—is all but closed to the person with under $20,000 to
invest. People with only a small amount of money to invest simply will not be able to get the information they need to do so,
but they have every right to invest their money however they
wish.

Some people believe that the poor waste what little money
they have (perhaps even government money) on Cadillacs and
expensive televisions. According to the stereotype, people in the
lower income bracket tend to gamble on horses and to play lot-
teries. They tend to waste their money on liquor and drugs.
Whether these forms of waste are practiced more widely by the
poor than by anyone else is an open question. But what right
does anyone have to blame people with little money for their
wasteful spending when they have no access to the information
that would show them how to invest the $500 or $600 they might
spend on a big color television on something more productive?
One thing preventing people with small savings from making
profitable investments is the lack of good information. Rich people can find out all sorts of ways to make their money grow. Rich
people have access to newsletters, brokers, advisors, lawyers,
and other areas of expertise to help them grow richer and richer
and to keep their riches from the IRS. But why should only rich

people have access to financial information and financial expertise? Intelligent computers can radically alter this state of affairs.

Intelligent banking systems will enable more people to have access to financial information. People already ask other people for information. Asking your neighbor is a good way to get information, but your neighbor might give you the wrong answers. With a computer banking adviser, anybody could have top of the line banking information tailored to their incomes. The man with a thousand dollars could have the same quality of advice as the millionaire. Computers can be the ultimate in democracy.

Imagine an intelligent computer financial counselor that knows more about every kind of banking and financial service than any human banker could ever remember. It understands English nearly as well as a banker does (within the financial domain). You could walk up to it and say, *Hi, I've got $700 to invest. What can I do with it?* The computer responds *Do you have anything in mind—penny stocks, blue chip stocks, options, or futures?* You don't know what any of these things are, so you ask, *What are options?* and the system explains to you what options are, showing you examples of what to look for when buying them, and how to tell when it's time to sell. After ten minutes, if you paid close attention, you might know to ask, *What options are available with a 1:4 leverage factor or greater and more than 18 months to maturity?* The computer would give you a list, perhaps. You might look at the list of companies with such options available and then ask for information about a particular company. You ask the computer, *What do you know about Westinghouse?* and it reprints a series of articles about recent events at Westinghouse.

After an hour of careful study of all the information at hand, you might decide to risk buying 100 two-year options on Westinghouse stock at $22 a share, costing $2 each. Two hours ago you wouldn't have even known what this meant, let alone have been willing to risk $200. But now you know that if Westinghouse stock goes up to $26, an 18% rise, your warrants will be worth more than twice as much as you paid for them. You would know that 100 shares of Westinghouse at $26 that could be purchased at $22, or $4 under the current price, would be valuable.

Think of the small banking customer who wants a loan. Few banks consider it worth the trouble to lend small amounts of money, and bank officers don't take an interest in borrowers unless they want huge sums. Imagine a computerized loan officer who examines your loan request and verifies all the information you have given it and then decides whether or not you get a loan. It can't discriminate against you because of how sloppily you are dressed or what race you are. If it approves your loan, the money is immediately deposited in your account and you are automatically billed for payments. As long a you meet the payments, the computerized loan officer may approve you for other loans. The bank saves money on the time-consuming administration of small loans, and the customer feels less fearful about asking for a loan. He is only asking a machine, after all.

COMPREHENSIVE MEDICAL SYSTEMS

Once everybody has access to a computer in or near their home, we will see systems for emergency medical advice and initial diagnosis. You might wake up in the night with a horrible pain in your stomach, a cold sweat, dizziness, and nausea. You might recover in 24 hours and never know what hit you. But if you had a home computer and a modem, you simply could dial the number for the emergency medical diagnosis system installed in a hospital near your home and tell the system all about your problem.

The medical system would have access to your medical records and would survey them for crucial information such as your age, any medicines you had been prescribed, any chronic ailments or disabilities you had, and what medicines you were allergic to. It wouldn't forget a single detail, and would scan the entire record to make sure there were no drug interactions, no possible side-effects of any drug you were taking or might take in the future. It would know to check for certain life-threatening signs and follow them up rigorously if you appeared to have any of them. The medical system would ask you several questions in order to evaluate your problem. If it thought you might have a life-threatening disease, it might connect you to a doctor or call an ambulance. If it thought the problem needed attention but was not an emergency, it could make an appointment with a specialist for you during clinic hours. Finally, if it thought you had a case of food poisoning or flu, it would give you some instructions to follow, tell you whatever home remedies and therapies would lessen your pain, and urge you to call again if any new symptoms appeared or if your condition worsened.

It would add all this new information to your medical record, and even send a message to your doctor about the problem, if you wished. He could look at the message when he came to his office the next day and learn all the crucial details in a few seconds, without having to call you in for a half-hour just to have you undress and repeat what you have said to the medical system. Your doctor might know something that isn't in the records, or have some reason for wanting to change your therapy. He could send you a reply with new instructions, or just a cheery hello and get well message.

All of this would take a few minutes, cost relatively little, and would not require you to leave your house. You would not have bothered your doctor with a phone call in the middle of the night, nor would you have taken up expensive office time. A huge number of medical visits involve minor ailments for which the only treatment necessary is home care. Think of the number of times you go to the doctor with what seems to you a fatal illness, expecting him to prescribe all kinds of harsh drugs and therapies, and all he tells you to do is go home, get lots of rest, eat bland foods, and drink a lot of fluids. You return home in disbelief, expecting death. In two days you are on your feet again.

People, in general, are frightened to ask questions. They don't want to appear to be stupid, they don't want to bother an expert with a silly question, and they don't want to pay for advice that seems obvious after they hear it. One big advantage of the kind of medical system we are discussing is that it would eliminate much of the potential for anxiety and friction between doctors and patients. Shy people who live in more or less constant anxiety about their health could obtain constant medical advice without wasting a doctor's time. Mothers could treat most infant colds and flus without having to bundle the baby up to go to the hospital. Such systems could save lives, too. Imagine the fast-track senior executive who has had pains in his chest for a few months. He would only ask a doctor about it at a cocktail party, but the medical system would tell him firmly and urgently to have a check-up and an EKG taken. And if he woke up one night with a severe chest-crunching pain and numbness shooting down his arm, he might be tempted to think of it as indigestion or tennis elbow. He might sit there hesitating, when he should be acting. People die in such situations. If he told the medical system these symptoms, it would tell him that he was probably having a heart attack and to call an ambulance immediately. We are very close to having systems that could analyze an EKG taken in the home and make an emergency diagnosis.

With the advent of such a comprehensive medical system for home use, the family doctor will take on a much more effective role as a reliable counselor and expert on the total health of each member of the family. The general practitioner (GP), the more human, compassionate kind, might well reemerge.

GPs today are less respected than a few decades ago because they have not kept pace with society's needs and with medicine's expanding knowledge. They don't provide truly general service any longer. A healthy middle-class family is very likely to have three or four doctors: a GP for checkups and general advice, a pediatrician, a gynecologist, and perhaps a specialist in cardiology. Routine care in these areas has become the province of glamorous and expensive specialists. GPs should be able to handle routine questions and problems in all these areas without having to refer the patient to a specialist. We shouldn't have to see a specialist unless we're severely or inexplicably ill with respect to some special area of medicine. But the average GP today simply doesn't have the time to prepare himself to advise on routine problems in gynecology, pediatrics, and cardiology—three very complex fields that involve a great number of routine patient visits.

If general practitioners were supported by a comprehensive medical system that handled most of their patient's routine needs, they could afford to take the extra time and training needed to prepare for pediatric and gynecological general practice, and perhaps even general cardiology. GPs would be compelled to provide far better service, and to forge a more substantial relationship with their patients. A doctor who didn't follow up on messages from his patients or ignored their queries would lose many of his patients. Doctors who couldn't handle routine questions in some area would not impress a patient. Today, doctors don't really have to compete for their patients. In the future, doctors who want to be successful will have to start offering superior service and advice. General practice might become a difficult and challenging field again, with its own rewards and glamour. It would become more, not less, humane. The doctor will be less alienated from his patients and will not rush them through the examination room, giving them second-rate attention on the way.

With computers taking over the technical aspects of a profession, the human aspects will remain. Teachers and doctors will be prized for how well they deliver the human aspects of their service. The technical aspects, ever enlarging in the modern world, will be under their control instead of overwhelming them.

REDISCOVERING HUMAN VALUES

With all these exciting possibilities on the horizon, people nevertheless worry that computers are going to affect their lives in negative ways. First of all, people worry about losing their jobs. There are quite a few jobs that can and probably will be handled by computers in a very few years, for example, the directory assistance department of the phone company. Computers will have dramatic effects on the work that people do. Many jobs will disappear and new ones (possibly fewer new ones) will open. The social impact of computers will be large. We must take care to consider the social dimensions of such change. We want computers to make the human world better. But what could be more cruel or alienating than to be replaced by a machine?

Anyone who has ever been a directory assistance operator or who has one for a friend probably knows that it is one of the most alienating and dispiriting jobs there is. The directory assistance department at the phone company is as close to an electronic sweatshop as we have yet come. Computers are already used to distribute calls so uniformly and efficiently that directory assistance operators never go for more than four seconds without a call. Many callers are obscene, abusive, or inappropriate. Operators who are abusive in return or who neglect to follow the proper protocols for handling a caller are given "faults" that affect their pay and promotions. When an operator wants to take a break or freshen up, he must get permission from the manager and take no more than four minutes. There probably are people who would like to remain directory assistance operators all their lives, but there is no strong argument against entirely automating directory assistance and finding other jobs for all the unfortunate people who will never get the chance to be a directory assistance operator.

Won't callers be alienated by the synthesized voice? Not likely. Few people depend on dialing information as their only contact with other humans, and in any case, directory assistance operators aren't allowed to be humane over the phone. Synthesized voice quality is also getting better and better, and people will be less annoyed by the automated operators.

As computers take up advisory and support tasks in medicine, finance, business, education and other areas, we will discover things that robots or computers presumably *could* be made to do, but which no one would *want* a computer to do. We will put human values in a new perspective in the process of finding out what things we want machines to do for us. We're not impressed that a machine can throw a football perfectly or hit a baseball a mile. We want to see *people* do these things. We aren't going to put Hollywood out of business with robot actors. We don't have to worry that one day all doctors will be computers. The great impact of this new computer technology is that it will make automated doctors available to people who cannot afford human services. Anyone will be able to call up the automated doctor for routine advice.

All the worry about computers dehumanizing society tends to miss the fact that our society is already rather dehumanized. A great many jobs are boring and routinized, products of the first two industrial revolutions. The third industrial revolution should finish the job of the first two and completely dehumanize many jobs. The difference is that this time, humans will not even perform them. What will happen? Massive unemployment or rehumanization of values? In the short run the answer depends on how governments and corporations respond to the new possibilities. In the long run, people decide what to value—military heroes, government leaders, football players, scientists, or whatever.

In our modern society, the general populace has come to place less and less value on artists, poets, philosophers and their creations. There have been times when people never failed to consider the artistic merits of even their most functional creations.

Today no one has the time. Our priorities change largely as a result of new demands or new innovations. The first skyscrapers were veritable works of art. They were both beautiful and functional because they were a new product of a human imagination. They were the embodiment of someone's dream. But in a society where speed counts, where the ability to build buildings faster, taller, and cheaper, is of the greatest importance, functionality wins over beauty. One thing that intelligent machines will buy us is time. If computers can do it efficiently, then we will come to value how one does something with style. Human values are constantly changing, but one thing we tend to be consistent about is the devaluing of the abilities of machines.

The computer can bring us closer to an appreciation of our own creative and intellectual abilities. As our progress in getting computers to perform intelligent tasks continues, we will approach a more refined view of human creativity and imagination. Things a machine can do will be seen as insignificant, precisely because a machine can do them. Solving the same equation a million times a second or welding the same spot on a car aren't artistic or creative. The human calculators and assembly line workers who did these things for a living suddenly appear to have been doing a robot's job all those years before the computer came along. The computer will help us eliminate the least humane jobs in our society.

The surprising effect of intelligently programmed computers will be to put back an emphasis on human styles and activities that have been forgotten or devalued in the evolution of the machine age during the last half-century. We will rediscover the arts, architecture, farming, and conservation on a widespread and popular scale. We will take a "softer" approach to technology. We will concentrate on integrating *software* with human values and lifestyles, rather than molding our lifestyles around *hardware*. We will make new discoveries. We will start to work for the enhancement of human values—something that has been sorely lacking in the postwar years.

There have been periods of time where human values were stressed in certain fields, such as architecture. America made some of its greatest architectural strides during the depths of the Great Depression, when we were all unemployed and looking for something to do. Human values were all that mattered then because no one was rushing to do anything. Some of the most valuable artistic creations in everything from sculpture and painting to writing and city planning were achieved under the Work Projects Administration. People weren't making money at rapacious rates, and took time and care in carving stones, painting bridges and writing books. In contrast, American architecture and city planning during the fifties and sixties—times of relative over-production and squandering of resources—has turned many an active city center into a dull, inhumane cement ghosttown.

Must we fall on hard times for our creations to embody human values instead of paving over them? Not necessarily. There have been times and places when people did their best and took pride in what they were doing, when they worked not to get something done the fastest or to make the most money, but to make it the most beautiful—the Gothic cathedrals of Europe, the Renaissance in Florence, Paris from the gay nineties to the 1920s. When we start writing intelligent programs that are practical as well as human-oriented, we will be able to devote more of our energies to the preservation of our humanity, the creation of new things and institutions, and to the improvement of society. We will become better educated, healthier, and more informed.

THE BIG BROTHER ANXIETY

No concept sends chills down our spines faster than that of a dictatorship using a computer to watch over, control, and manipulate an entire population. Our world is primed for Orwell's *1984*, but not because of the computer. Orwell's book is not so much a prediction as it is a careful study of history. Orwell didn't know about computers; he knew about people. The rhetoric of *doublethink* has characterized politics ever since man decided to live in groups rather than alone. Thought-police have been around in various forms since ancient Greece and Rome. Socrates, perhaps the most famous thought-criminal of all time, preceded Orwell's Winston Smith by 2500 years. He was tried and executed by the city-state of Athens for what he *thought*.

Man has accomplished much evil without the aid of computers. The guillotine required no programming. The Ottoman empire did not need a data base for its genocide of the Armenians. A computer didn't order millions of men into machine-gun barrages in World War I; nor did it suggest efficient methods to enable Hitler to exterminate millions of Jews in concentration camps. The USSR reached its totalitarian peak without any significant computer sophistication (nor was life all that pleasant for most Russians under the czar). People in powerful positions thought up these atrocities, not machines.

While we have not yet created the world that Orwell predicted for 1984, the decade that follows 1984 may well have significance in the history of the world. Intelligent machines, albeit simple ones, have become a widespread subject of conversation in the calendar year of 1984. They are currently being used for benign purposes. But they can be very powerful tools for both good and evil. We must make sure that this positive use continues to be the case in the future by keeping an eye on what government says and does. If we want to remain free, we have to watch governments and large corporations, not computers.

It is difficult to prevent the erosion of our freedoms. The history of many totalitarian regimes is full of the gradual loss of freedom, privacy, and individuality. Americans always have resisted too much prying by governments into private affairs, yet governments have been snooping on people for a long time. We do not have identity cards or police who are empowered to search without a warrant. We don't have to ask permission to have an art exhibition, to read poetry, to travel from place to place, or to leave the country. These sound like trivial things precisely because we have never had to worry about them and can't really imagine a society where these things are true. We have to hope that no one in our society would tolerate such incursions or approve of laws that permitted them.

Although computers themselves will not diminish our freedom, our laws currently have little protections for those of us who have voluntarily entered important private information in computers. We don't realize the potential erosion of freedom that the increased use of computers (whether or not they are intelligent) for our daily needs and convenience may bring. Today the information we volunteer in order to get insurance, mortgages, credit cards, driver's licenses, passports, loans, medical treatment and so on is entered in computers. Yet 15 or 20 years ago, this was not the case. The likelihood that such information might be used by someone who we never intended to have access to it has increased dramatically.

America is primed for a dramatic increase in government surveillance of private citizens. There have been long periods of increased government surveillance in the past, during the McCarthy era, the Civil Rights movement, and the Vietnam War. At the moment, with no major crises or large movements sweeping the nation, we do not notice, or care so much about, the continual erosion of our privacy. Even without a major national emergency, the implication that a popular movement is really Soviet-controlled, that terrorism is on the rise, or that we may have to issue identity cards to everyone to keep illegal aliens out of the country all can serve as excuses for increased surveillance.

Computers aren't the problem here, but they will make it much easier for there to be a problem. Surveillance generally conjures up stereotypes from the past—steaming open people's mail, standing outside someone's house, following cars, illegal wiretaps, Watergate burglars, infiltrating campus groups, and breaking into psychiatrist's offices. But surveillance of the eighties and beyond will not require any of these extreme and arduous activities. The surveillance of the future will be carried out at a computer terminal in some air-conditioned office.

As an example, computer-based surveillance has been employed to track down teenagers who refuse to register with the Selective Service. Student loans have been denied to them and various government data files from unrelated agencies have been opened up in order to locate nonregistrants. The point here is not the "crime" involved. The point is that if this kind of computer surveillance can be done for nonregistrants, it can be done for any group at all—Jews, Blacks, Cubans, homosexuals, Republicans, Jehovah's Witnesses, truckers, Kurt Vonnegut readers, etc. This last item may seem silly, but it is not. It used to be difficult to find out who reads what. But today books are ordered from general warehouses of booksellers who tend to keep their records on computer. How hard would it be to determine which bookstores sold the most copies of *Slaughterhouse Five* last year? Change *Slaughterhouse Five* to *Das Kapital* or any other book associated with a clear radical movement and suddenly the idea of surveillance of this kind doesn't seem so far-fetched. And if some bureaucracy decided to audit the property taxes paid by the bookstore in an effort to close it down? How hard would it be to get a copy of every single check or credit card transaction used by the customers of that bookstore? *Not hard at all.* All of this information is on computers.

The Nazis began simply by telling Jews to *register.* After registration it became more and more difficult to escape the chain of events that the identification process made possible. *Access to information is a powerful thing.* If we face a clear and present danger, it is that we will let our freedoms and privacy be diminished, slowly or overnight, by our own politicians, political institutions, and large corporations. If business or government begin to use information about us that is already available on computers, can we prevent it? How many more forms are we willing to fill out?

KEEPING THE MACHINE
IN PERSPECTIVE

I suggested before that the way to insure that this nightmare doesn't come true is to keep an eye on the *people* who would put computers to nefarious uses, not the computers themselves. New technology does provide new avenues for these people, though, so in order to safeguard our freedoms, we must be aware of what new threats to look out for. New information resources will be made available. Who will get them and how much will they cost? All sorts of data will be gathered, analyzed, and disseminated. Data about what (or whom)? Who will get to use that data and for what will it be analyzed? How can we make sure it isn't wrong, misleading, or unfair? How can we make sure that everyone gains access to important information?

In some sense, the electronic library I described already exists. There are thousands of data bases available to anyone with a modem, patience with thick manuals, and enough money to pay the (often high) price. AI will replace the thick manuals with software that can find out what you want, but that will not make the information free. Until now, our public library system has been the mainstay of our ability to get information free of charge. We expect to be able to find out the voting record of a presidential candidate, the Consumer Reports rating of a new car, or the details of an important news story, all without having to pay. That may not be true in the information age. The electronic library will charge for its services. Some publicly accessible data bases now charge as much as $75 an hour, and there are no free rides anywhere. We, as a society, need to consider the importance of free public access to certain kinds of information. If AI is to help us become a more informed populace, we must insure that everyone has access to the information. The *public* library must be brought into the information age.

Public libraries are not the only place where the cost of information is significant. Access to lots of timely, accurate information is expensive. Although the price will drop, there will be increasing disparity between those who can afford the new power that AI offers and those who cannot. AI is not the cause of these problems, but it is a part of the society around it, and will reflect a great deal of that society. I have explained how computers have the potential to heal this division by making previously unavailable information accessible to nearly everyone. We should be aware that they also have the potential to make it worse by reserving important knowledge for a privileged few.

The biggest institutions in our society are the most powerful, and they will be the first to put AI to use in harnessing huge amounts of raw data. Already our governments and businesses have incredible amounts of information about each of us stored in their files. Currently it is very difficult for them to put all that information together—the IRS has as much trouble finding out the names of people who own expensive yachts and paid no taxes as the airline that wants to find out how many discount fares it sold in December. It seems likely that public libraries will be the last government agencies to get AI programs to help them. In the long run, I believe that cheap AI will make our society more fair; in the short run, however, AI may be expensive.

We have allowed the government and other large organizations to collect a wide variety of different data on us. We assumed that the information would be used only for the purpose it was collected. We don't expect our elementary school to tell our math grades to the IRS so they could audit people who are bad at addition. We don't expect an ad agency to get our children's birthdays from the vital records office to make special pitches to them so they will ask for expensive toys when they are most likely to get them. Unfortunately, the power of AI data bases make those abuses possible. Information that was gathered for one reason can easily be used for another. We must keep a careful eye on powerful institutions to make sure that they use the information that we have given them the way it was intended to be used.

When computers can easily tell us about investments or book our airline travel, the people who sell these services will want to influence what exactly the computers tell us. The intelligent machine is a powerful sales tool. It can be used to convince us that we should spend our money in a particular way or invest in a particular stock. We should be careful to evaluate computer advice the way we would any other advisor who might have a stake in our decision. Some people will put too much faith in computers, believing that their advice is somehow infallible. Computer advice will be a good source of information, but it will be no substitute for common sense.

Computers are machines that do one thing well—they run programs. They don't write their own programs or form their own committees, and are therefore unable to take over the world. They don't fancy that they know anything more than what they have been programmed to know. They aren't going to conceive of a Thousand Year Reich, a Five-Year Plan, or a Great Society. If the world is ever turned into a huge dictatorship, it will be by a group of humans who are just plain power hungry, or who actually fantasize that they know best how to run everyone's life. And even if this group of people decides to use computers to control entire populations and to track down dissident poets and ballet dancers, instead of just concentrating on tracking down every tax evader, draft dodger, parking violator, antinuclear demonstrator, and nude sunbather, the computer still will not be at fault.

When the computer emerged as a reality in the late 1940s political man already had demonstrated that barbarism of horrendous proportions comes so naturally to him that it would be absurd to blame an entity as inert and lifeless as a computer for the results of this native capacity for violence. Indeed, to imply that computers are somehow going to take over, run our lives, or create an electronic serfdom, dividing those who can log in from those who can't, is to make the age-old error of attributing to our creations a life of their own. If computers could speak, they would say, "The instructions we carry out are not part of us. They are given to us by humans. What is a part of us is our ability to follow these instructions. Humans tell us what to do and we do it." Computers depend on us for their existence. We build them. We program them. If they run anything at all, it is at our decree and convenience. We rule them. They do things because we ask them to.

A person who answers, "I did that because you asked me to" when he commits a dastardly deed, may or may not be considered responsible for his crime. We would expect him to have some concept of morality, but we often do not prosecute the actual person who pulled the trigger. Intelligent computers should also have some concept of morality, but as we have seen, even much simpler concepts are very difficult to build into a computer. Until computers do have such morality we are dependent on the people who write the programs (and run them) to be careful of the orders they give, and of the way they use these computers. The only way computers can pry into our lives is if we let them. Smart machines and understanding systems will not become despotic dictators who will take over the world and keep us as playthings. AI programs aren't going to run our lives. They will increase the ability of computers to do what we tell them to. We will understand what the computer says and it will understand what we say. They will be able to do what we ask them to do. We therefore must think very carefully about what we ask them to do.

DEMOCRACY: AN AI PERSPECTIVE

In an age of intelligent computers, we also can elect programs, but those of the electronic variety. A politician is someone we expect will carry out our views, and if it is possible to elect a system that embodies our views rather than a person who will administer those views, then we should do so. Electing plans of action as opposed to actors will appear less radical as the possibility for such elections becomes more real. I only mean to suggest here that having intelligent computers around may allow us to be more innovative in deciding how the country is to be run.

I do not believe that we should vote on every action that our leaders take. In general, the populace is not well enough informed to decide whether we should invade a country at a particular time, or to decide how many weapons of what type we actually need. Nevertheless, we could vote for the beliefs on which we would like our leaders to operate. By this I mean that we could vote for the conditions under which an invasion should take place, in principle. We can make sure that our well-informed leaders have our goals in mind when they take action. This may seem a little whimsical, and perhaps it is, but the larger our government gets, the more it will be run by computers anyway. With all this reliance on computers, the idea of electing the computer's program may not be quite so silly after all. Who will tell the computer what to do? People who cherish their freedoms will have to think carefully about this question, no matter what kind of intelligent computers we create.

BACK TO THE CAR

I began this book with an analogy between the automobile revolution and the computer revolution. Going back to the origins of that revolution, consider the advantages that the automobile has over the horse. I don't mean to be facetious in asking this question because, in fact, there are a great many reasons to prefer horses over cars. Despite the fact that cars are faster than horses, they have, in general, one significant disadvantage with respect to the horse. Cars are stupid. Now, horses may not be the most brilliant animals on this earth, but they know enough to be more careful in the rain, not to go over cliffs, to jump over fences rather than crash through them. When there is a fire, they go in the opposite direction, if they can.

As we replace even moderately intelligent creatures by machines, we have to substitute our own intelligence. We have to think about every single aspect of a problem. We once let the horse do some of the driving, as it were. Once we use machines to get us from place to place, we have to be sure that we can tell them how to do every single aspect of their work. For cars, this means having the manufacturer design windshield wipers, headlights, and responsive steering. It also means that now the driver has to understand about not crashing into fences and being careful on wet turns. No matter what we do, modern cars will not drive themselves away from a fire.

Sometimes the use of unintelligent machines makes our task easier, since the machines follows our every command. Sometimes it makes our task harder—we wish we didn't have to tell it absolutely everything. We somehow expect our machines to be at least as smart as the animals or people they replaced. When they are not, a great many problems ensue.

The computer is, or rather eventually will be, the solution to all this. The computer will differ significantly from other machines when it becomes, in essence, a machine's person. Computers will fulfill their promise as they start to be capable of telling dumb machines how to behave.

Computers are everywhere, yet they really have affected our lives in only very small ways. Sure, our paychecks are printed by computer, we have small computers to play games on, and there are even small computers in some of the appliances that we use. But, in reality we have done little more than replace the horse and buggy with a mechanical horse to pull the buggy. A big step to be sure, but a long way from a 747.

Just as the automobile and the airplane developed side by side, but in different ways and with different effects, so will the computer. Today's computers, the ones we see in our daily lives, augment our world without seriously changing it. But tomorrow's computers will transform our lives in ways that we cannot yet imagine.

At just the time when our society has become so large as to be unmanageable, at just the time when the world we live in is most alienating and people feel most alone—it is the time when intelligent computers are becoming a possibility. Maybe they can help.

We live in an age when everyone simultaneously has too much information and yet has not enough. We hear a great deal about Afghanistan, Bangladesh, and other far-off places, but many people have no idea where these places are, or what the people there are like, or what they want, or why it matters. We hear about news events without fully understanding their impact on us or on those they directly affect.

We live in a time when many people have difficulty with basic math skills, yet many Americans must struggle annually with income tax forms that even the most educated cannot easily handle.

We live in a time when there are so many possibilities available, from different types of bank accounts to different types of vacations, that deciding intelligently can be quite an effort. Often it is hard to figure out whom to ask for help.

We live in a time when there are so many political issues about which we cannot possibly have knowledge, that we vote for candidates based upon how well they come off on TV. Even when we want to know where a candidate stands on an issue it is difficult to know how to find out.

We live in a time when we need more and more knowledge and yet the schools seem to be doing a worse and worse job of providing just the basic skills, much less the extra knowledge needed to cope in today's world.

Computers may be one solution. The more intelligence that is built into a machine that anyone can have access to, the more intelligence and knowledge we can secure. We have reached a time in history where there is so much to know that no one person can possibly know enough to be well equipped to function intelligently in all aspects of life. Books may contain a great deal of knowledge but that knowledge grows quickly out of date. Further, there are so many books that it is hard to know where to look for what.

What to do? We may be able to have intelligent companions who can advise on matters social and intellectual, spiritual and emotional. What happens to the people who do not have the courage or hope that it takes to write letters to Dear Abby? What happens to the student who cannot get to see his professor? What happens to the patient whose doctor cannot find the specialist who can advise on treatment in time? What happens to the child whose curiosity cannot be satisfied by his parents' limited knowledge, or whose teacher is too busy grading workbooks to answer a question?

Intelligent machines are coming. They aren't going to emerge suddenly from some laboratory; rather, they will evolve gradually over the next few decades, changing our world as they do. We shouldn't be afraid of them or of the changes they will bring about. We are at one of those crossroads in history where people have had to confront who they are and what they expect from society.

Computers will change the way we look *at* the world and the way that we live *in* the world. They will be our servants, our partners, and our teachers. When our machines begin to understand us, perhaps we will be on the way to understanding ourselves.

E P I L O G U E

THE
ENTREPRENEURIAL
UNIVERSITY

I have suggested that one of the most valuable uses of computers is to cause us to view ourselves, and the world in which we live, in a new light. When computers first came into the university they caused this same kind of rethinking there. Administrators worried over whether it made sense to have a university department devoted to the study of a machine which, they assumed, would come and go as did other machines. They argued that there were no departments of "automobile science" to be found in universities. Why then should there be departments of computer science?

Computer science departments were established nevertheless. Those universities that debated for too long failed to get established in computer science and are now suffering from their earlier decision, since computer scientists are in great demand and it is very difficult to establish a new department now.

Today's computer science departments are not, in fact, devoted to the study of machinery. Computer scientists are mostly concerned with algorithms. The problem is that the algorithms with which some computer scientists concern themselves can be

248

very different from those that concern others. Algorithms that tell us how the mind functions bear little relationship to those that tell us how to make power plants run efficiently. AI professors in a computer science department have little to say, from a research point of view, to most of the other members of their departments.

Computers have forced us to view so many things differently that they are causing us to radically alter our concept of the university as well. What computer scientists have in common is their method of research, not their field of inquiry. Departments at universities have traditionally been organized around fields of inquiry. Anthropology, psychology, literature, and so on use many methods to study the same subject. But in computer science we use one method to study many different subjects. Because of the interest of computer scientists in so many diverse fields, and because the computer is an increasingly powerful tool whose presence has just started to be felt, the model for research in computer science soon may affect other fields of inquiry.

There is a crisis coming in the universities that is an indirect result of the computer revolution. Computer science as an academic discipline is terribly unstable. We are unable to produce enough computer scientists, and we are unable to keep the ones we have in the university because of industry pressures. The role of the computer in changing the manner in which a country produces new technology and new scientists is an important part of the computer revolution.

THE CRISIS IN THE UNIVERSITIES

The current crisis involves the relationship between the university and the outside world, and has its roots in the changes that have taken place in our society over the last 30 years. Once upon a time, universities were ivy-covered towers that allowed brilliant minds to consider whatever they liked, regardless of its significance to the world outside. But with build-up of the military industrial complex in the fifties, spurred on by the success of defense-backed science during World War II, universities became increasingly dependent on the federal government for scientific research. Science is expensive and the government was prepared to pay for it, a bargain that was difficult for universities to refuse.

Universities and their funding problems may not seem like burning issues for the general public. But it is vital to the health of any society that its most creative minds be allowed to have the most possible freedom. We traditionally have thought of academic freedom as the ability to speak one's mind without fear of reprisal or censorship and the liberty to pursue whatever lines of thought one wishes. Universities like to think they protect the members of their community from the pressures and concerns of the outside world. They have done an admirable job at this for several centuries. But academic freedom is becoming harder and harder to maintain for a number of reasons, the most salient of which is the difficulty of financing research without allowing sponsors to control objectives and methods.

To develop a technologically advanced society, we must make sure that our most creative minds are given the chance to do research. Academic freedom means freedom to do what excites you, rather than what excites the sponsor of your research. As long as money and researchers abound, science gets supported. But when money is tight all kinds of headaches are created for the university and its scientific research programs.

Because there are so few computer scientists, the most creative minds in the university are also being called upon to lead the efforts to apply their ideas to the creation of new technology in the real world as well. This can create tremendous problems inside the university. If it were just a question of how the university is to cope with a changing world, we could leave this discussion to some academic journal. But, in fact, how the universities cope with this problem greatly affects how technological development will proceed in the future, and that affects all of us.

PROFESSORS AND THE UNIVERSITY

Professors are people who like to read, think, and create. Often, they are attracted to the academic life by imagining a detached, contemplative existence, free from the worries of the real world— a life concerned with ideas rather than money and profit. Students imagine that their professors are there to serve them, and that therefore their primary interest is in teaching. But teaching is in no way the professor's major responsibility, at least not at major research universities. Professors at the top universities are hired because of their status in their fields. They are expected by their university to be great scientists or scholars. It is also nice if they like to teach, but it is usually not critical. Most professors are primarily concerned with their own intellectual development. This doesn't necessarily conflict with teaching (indeed, teaching can greatly enhance a professor's intellectual development), but it tends to make them prefer teaching graduate students who are working on specific projects rather than lecturing to undergraduates.

A university depends on the reputation of its faculty. A research university expects its professors to be great researchers, first and foremost, and secondarily to be great teachers. Scientists are expected to be innovators in their fields, win prizes, and maintain a high standing in the eyes of their scientific peers. The best of the social science faculty will get honored with appointments to government posts, fellowships at elite think tanks, and grants for policy studies. The humanities faculty is expected to write criticism and commentary, to make major historical and literary discoveries, and in general to publish as much as possible.

Universities can attract top-flight professors so long as the university guarantees them equipment and freedom to do their research. Researchers tolerate being bothered only when they are praised, promoted, or given more funding. They cannot be pressured to do very much teaching or administrative work. A typical courseload for a science professor in a top university is one course per semester. If a university can provide these congenial conditions, it can hope to attract and keep bright professors and students. There was a time when a university that wanted to put itself on the map overnight in some discipline could attract superstar professors by offering large laboratories, chaired professorships, elite committees, and departments. Universities traditionally had the money this required, but this is no longer the case. Now industry is the main competitor for the innovative scientist by offering huge salaries to qualified professors.

As the materials necessary for basic research have become more complex, it has become more difficult to equip, renovate, or even maintain a laboratory without vast sums of money. Also, federal money for basic research has been cut back severely and restricted. There is a greater emphasis on research that yields short-term results; long, ten-year research efforts are much harder to finance. Universities have had to put more pressure on their alumni for gifts, but it is difficult to raise large chunks of money in a short period of time, and tax cuts for the wealthy have made charitable giving less attractive. Universities are becoming more and more dependent on the money they cajole out of both the government and private foundations.

Universities are having difficulty attracting and maintaining good faculty in a number of departments, but computer science is currently hardest hit. The demand for computer scientists in the private sector far exceeds the supply. Salaries are consequently very high. The effects of this labor shortage are that fewer bright students go to graduate school (a person with a B.A. in computer science can start at $25,000–30,000), and that a large percentage of the few Ph.D.'s that complete their studies go into industry. (A person with a Ph.D. in computer science can easily earn $55,000–65,000, and sometimes far more). We normally think that bright people and scholars don't feel comfortable in the corporate world, working for supervisors on mundane projects. Their natural place is in the university. We expect intellectuals in any field not to mind the low salaries of professional life too much, and to stay in academia. But the computer industry has been able to offer students and professors in computer science high enough salaries, and good enough research environments to lure some of the best minds away from the academy.

Professors who are devoted to academics and want to stay in the university have been put under unusual stress. They have had to do things they have never done before in order to keep their departments on a steady keel. No professor can do the research that is both his bread and butter and his intellectual *raison d'etre* without decent financial support for that research. The research money that a scientist obtains is what keeps his very department in existence. A professor with innovative ideas in the sciences must have laboratories and assistants. A professor requires graduate students to help with his research projects, and to do much of the teaching of first year graduate students and undergraduates. Graduate students cannot be expected to pay their own way.

Universities have never faced a situation like this before. A university administration that wants scientific superstars but can't afford to raise their salaries, or pay for their research, has a problem. What is the *only* course of action in such a situation?

The science professor has had to become resourceful enough to pay his own way. To survive in the modern university, today's scientists, even stereotypically absent-minded ones, have had to learn where the sources of money are; how to convince the controllers of that money to give it to them; how to manage the people and facilities that that money will buy them; and most importantly, how to sell new ideas and strategies for survival to the university administration which has ultimate veto power on whether a department grows or disappears. The computer science professor (and this is true for a great many other fields as well) has become his own funder. He has become a kind of entrepreneur.

With government resources for research dwindling, private corporations have gotten in on the act as well. Their view of research sponsorship is much more product-oriented than the government's. Both corporations and government officials like to think they are sponsoring a particular professor on a specific project or set of projects that accomplish some of their goals. They want to use the university for practical purposes. Before they give away big chunks of money, they have to be convinced they are investing in something very concrete and useful in the short term. There are a few enlightened supporters of basic research in the military and elsewhere, who are simply happy to do their bit for pure science in this country. They can only act on this desire when they have enough money and when the government is not pressing for applied defense-related research. The federal government provides most of the monetary support for high-quality research in computer science and especially in Artificial intelligence. And the U.S. government expects some return—*products.*

Because of this, the power of the university to control its own destiny is gradually slipping away. When the university starts to rely upon the federal government and the military to support science at the university, professors are under some obligation to ask students to work on research that relates to the grants and contracts that these professors have obtained. Students are often put in the situation of working on problems that have (often cleverly disguised) military applications. True, many research projects that are important as pure research also happen to have those applications. For the most part, the research for military applications in no way diverts the graduate student from whatever basic research he wants to work on. But like it or not, the university finds itself in a very "un-ivory-tower-like" situation when it accepts money from the government or from private industry.

In taking money for product-directed research, the professor is a little like the man who has sold his soul to the devil. This need not be cause for despair, because in this case, the smart professor holds the superior bargaining position! He has the knowledge, the connections and the qualified people to do stunning work in his field. The industry and the government know that the same quality of people and facilities would cost five to ten times more to establish and maintain in the private sector. What might cost twelve million dollars and take five years to accomplish in the private sector might be achieved with one million in two years in the university. No institution in the world can compete on a dollar basis with the major research universities in the United States for research in the fields of computer science, applied physics, engineering, molecular biology, and a few other disciplines. Government and the private sector have begun to see how much farther their research dollar will go in academia.

When a professor sees that industry and the government want him very badly to work on a specific area or project, he can easily make demands on them, such as allocating a large chunk of money to general theory-directed research in exchange for promising to do some more or less product-directed work. He can set time limits to keep his people from being pressured, and generally see to it that the free flow of ideas in his department is protected from the incursion of the short-term development ethos of the outside world.

Should the university take such grants? If we look at the traditional mandate of the academy, with its ideals of independence from outside influences and freedom from the prisonhouse of daily concerns, we can hardly avoid asking this question. This is really a new version of the question of the 1950s and 1960s, involving the issue of whether universities should engage in defense research. This raised serious ethical questions for universities. Now those issues relate to whether universities should build products for industry.

The unfortunate truth is that today's universities are not in the position to easily refuse any grant. Professors are applauded for *any* grants. As chairman of a computer science department, one of my major worries is to make sure that all the faculty and graduate students are adequately supported. Moreover, our computers are purchased with federal grants. Clearly the entire fate of my department depends upon the federal government and the grants we receive. If Washington should take a dislike to my department we would be virtually finished. Science departments live in the real world. The university, whether it likes it or not, lives there too.

The university learns about the outer reality that we inhabit from its most valuable resource: the students. In the end, it is the students, particularly the undergraduates, who dictate reality to the administrators, the alumni and, most of all, to the professors. If a department chairman wants more faculty and graduate students he must justify this need by pointing to increasing enrollment in the department's undergraduate courses. The arithmetic can be very simple: If fewer than three students show up for a course, it is cancelled. If a hundred students turn up at a class designed for 20 students, at least three teaching assistants will have to be found, and the following semester the class will be given four meeting times instead of one. A professor can turn away two or three students too many, but if a hundred students want to take a given class, it's a fairly safe bet that faculty will be found and more sections established, at least by the next semester. Departments generally seek to increase enrollments, if they want to grow, or to at least maintain enrollments.

Shrinking enrollment has never been a problem in computer science. The number of computer science B.A.'s keeps growing and we have to speculate why. Certainly, computers are becoming more widespread in our society and people feel a need to be educated about them.

But, more importantly, young people are choosing to major in computer science because private industry will offer them very good jobs with high salaries. We live in less idealistic and more economically-minded times than we did in the 1960s and 1970s. Students are interested in marketable skills. Five years ago students thought the marketable skills were in business and finance, and the economics department swelled to bursting with career-conscious undergraduates seeking to prepare for the business world. Today's job market is booming in computer science, so many career-conscious students tend to choose that as a major.

THE UNIVERSITY RESPONDS

Department chairmen know that if students make demands, something will happen. Universities live in a very competitive world. They must offer what the students want or the students will go elsewhere. Today's college students are very demanding, even if not always well prepared. When the administration hears that Yale's computer science department is recognized to be first or second best in the Ivy League, it is pleased. It responds by putting more resources behind its strength. A university's deference to such realities does tarnish somewhat the ivory-tower image of the university. But today's universities must respond to the pressures of the outside world, the effects of new technology, and the economic realities of our times.

The university also gets a stiff dose of reality when a significant portion of the faculty asks for higher salaries. These faculty members could easily abandon the university for well paid, if less stimulating, jobs in private enterprise. Money talks in a university, too. When a professor sees other people in his field getting better research facilities and twice the salary in private industry—a condition which is not uncommon—it is hard to justify staying at a university. Faculties in the professional schools have always had slightly higher pay. But in order to keep certain college departments from losing faculty, the university has had to break with the traditional principle that all professors should be paid equally. Universities have realized that a computer science faculty member has to be better paid than his colleagues in other departments or else he will work in industry.

INDUSTRY AND THE UNIVERSITY

The latest battle in the assault of the real world on the university stems from industry. As corporate America becomes wealthier, and as the federal government becomes more near-term oriented in its support of research, the university will have to turn more and more to industry to sponsor scientific research. A computer science department can afford to take very little industrial funding only as long as it is well funded from other sources. As of now, the federal government still considers computer science important. There is little doubt, however, that most faculties would be happy to take industry money if that were all that was available. When survival is at stake, professors vote with their research needs. After all, we must have computers and laboratories.

Naturally, we don't want industry to dictate to the university whom to hire as faculty, whom to admit as students, what areas to work on in research, and who gets the ownership and the right to disseminate research. We don't want such restrictions from industry any more than we want them from the federal government. The federal government has tried to influence such decisions in the past through affirmative action policies, harassment of communists in the 1950s and of leftists in the 1960s, and its general pursuit of research with military applications. It is reasonable to assume that our relationship with industry, the likely sponsor of research in the 1980s and 1990s, will go along parallel lines *if we let it.*

It may be difficult to resist efforts by industry sponsors to control whom to hire and whom to admit. It may also be difficult to resist attempts to restrict the dissemination of research findings. Ultimately, we will have to defer somewhat to the sponsor's wishes for what research projects we undertake. Industry will want its needs addressed just as the government does. And professors who have no other source of funding will have to be willing to work on those needs. We must be prepared to let them sponsor research because we have no other choice. We live in a world dominated by industry, and universities must reflect its needs if we are to survive. We can hold fast to certain principles regarding our integrity, but ultimately we will have to attend to the needs of our sponsors as universities have done since the Middle Ages.

PROFESSORS IN PRIVATE COMPANIES

While the prospect of taking industry sponsorship is in many ways even less attractive than taking government sponsorship, there is a roundabout way in which the university could resolve a number of its money problems while maintaining a maximum amount of control over its own destiny.

Many professors have themselves become entrepreneurs in the process of surviving the research game and have founded their own companies while remaining professors. Some universities have treated this new phenomenon as an even greater threat to their traditions than the demands made by government and private industry sponsors. And yet professors who take on the dual role of conducting pure research and running private companies could end up playing an important part in helping universities to reclaim some of the self-sufficiency and independence that have slipped away in the last 30 years.

Many science professors in large universities are taking on the ultimate entrepreneurial duty of starting and managing a company in order to do applied research and development work for profit. University administrations have become more and more concerned with this involvement of professors in industry, particularly professors who have a sizable financial or management position in their companies. The university administration worries that being part of a private company can take time away from the professorial duties of teaching and research. University officials are also worried that conflicts might develop in the serving of two masters. When a graduate student sees that his work relates closely to work being done in a company owned and run by his advisor, he begins to think of business and not of science.

These legitimate concerns are cited by university officials who sincerely wish to safeguard the best interests of their university. Some of the more prestigious universities have been very reluctant to allow their professors to have controlling positions in private corporations. I believe, however, that the solution to the problem of professors with private companies has to be more sophisticated than making blanket prohibitions. Professors have always, at least tacitly, been permitted to have consulting positions with corporations. Indeed, the university likes to maintain certain formal ties to corporations. It is only recently that universities have had to take a strong position on professors who want to start their own companies. Five or ten years ago, this phenomenon was less pervasive and so it was more easily tolerated. But the state of the economy, the lack of professionals available to industry, the increased cost of research, and the decreasing number of federal grants have started to change all that. Professors with AI companies present a special case of this new phenomenon.

AI is a subject whose very essence is grounded in producing the technology of the future. It is both a theoretical inquiry into the workings of the mind and also a producer of computer models that can program some very powerful functions. AI's *theory-directed* approach may produce even more sophisticated products than its product-directed approach. It is an academic discipline in which the theories almost *have* to result in new products with each new stage in their development. (We have to implement our theories to demonstrate that they will do what we say. It may be a short step from that implementation to an actual product.) In the theory-directed approach, these implementations are never fully developed systems that could be marketed and make millions in profits. At each stage, theory-directed AI produces the mere bare bones of a program that models a few more elements of human cognition than the previous program. While each program teaches us what the next program we should work on will be, each now implementation also presents interesting possibilities for use in the real world.

The point is that theory-directed AI research creates the most interesting products only when it is done in an academic spirit, a spirit of free inquiry and expression. All the "hard" sciences are actually like this, but the realities of our economy have carved a huge gulf between pure and applied research. This gulf cannot be created in AI. If we just go after products, we can make no theoretical progress whatsoever. And to ask a theory-directed AI researcher not to come up with any useful products would be like telling a chemist he has to make great discoveries without ever mixing a solution or setting up a chemical reaction. The implementations are what tell us where to go with our theories.

The theory-directed AI researcher who wants to see his products used in the real world, and who doesn't want to leave the academy, will have to start his own company. There is no way to develop products for direct application to the outside world in an academic research laboratory. To do so would be an even greater violation of a graduate student's academic career than if the graduate student merely has to tolerate a professor who spends some of his time at a private company. It is precisely because such direct applications do not belong in a university that an AI professor must at least have partial control of an outside corporation in order to develop useful products. Indeed, in terms of the ideals of the university, a computer science department that just goes about the dull routine of cranking out B.A.'s who only want cushy jobs in industry is being far more mercenary than a department that encourages theory-directed AI research and allows its professors to do product-directed research outside the university.

The U.S. Defense Department, the major supporter of AI research in this country, has complained about the lack of AI in the *real world*, the lack of *products*. They are not just complaining that there aren't AI weapons systems. They are complaining that AI hasn't yet been applied in any major real-world situation. They aren't sure we can deliver. Critics of AI complain that it never actually produces what it promises. By and large, this is true and this fact alone has kept many major institutions from undertaking the very kind of AI research that might make such products possible. Few major computer companies are doing any AI research. Until recently, very few universities with growing computer science departments actively sought out AI people as new faculty. AI requires a major investment in both hardware and in people capable of running a large laboratory.

As an AI person, I am not very product-directed. My principal field of study is the human mind, not the creation of new technology for today's world. My research has been directed toward finding out how humans understand language by modeling understanding systems on a computer. My current interest is how human memory changes with experience to produce learning. My theories are tested by building precise models on the computer. Yet even when these models produce humanlike understanding we have not "proved" anything. We don't proclaim that this is exactly how the mind works, to the last detail. We create models of processes, not the processes themselves, just as biochemists can create models of cellular functions but not the whole cell. The attempt to model the understanding process gives us some very valuable insights into the workings of the mind, insights that have already been used in the fields of cognitive psychology, and that have the potential to be of use in almost any field.

It will take many years of hard research before highly sophisticated models of the human mind have been built and tested. It may take much more time than one generation. I am not satisfied with arguing with colleagues who do not agree with my theories; nor am I satisfied with building half-finished models that show what we could do technologically if we ever completed the task.

Science can be seen as a subject that can be studied for its value in shedding light rather than its potential in the creation of new technologies. But computer science is different from pure science. We are concerned with the potential *use* of a machine. AI is also concerned with the nature of mind, but as AI is also a part of computer science, it is incumbent upon AI researchers to create and complete AI programs that have a benefit to the world. AI people have to be interested in seeing their models provide some new service or opportunity to the culture. The ability to model certain understanding processes on a computer is bound up with the goal of getting computers to contribute to the society in important ways.

The work of getting computers to understand English sentences well enough to be useful was basic research only ten years ago. But it is now development work that can be done as a practical application at a private company. The current academic work on language understanding involves memory, reminding, and learning and this work could be yielding useful products in five to ten years. Where will this development work be done? Industry is not prepared to do it, and as we have said, the university is simply not the place for product development.

In a university we could not possibly pay competitive salaries, nor offer shares in the profits of the products created, to the people who must do the work. We could easily get grants to sponsor product development, but that conflicts with the idea that a Ph.D. student should be doing creative and original work. A graduate student should not be working on real applications of the research of others. He should be working at the leading edge of research, creating ideas of her own. I do not believe that graduate students should be the employees of the private companies that AI people create in order to apply their ideas to the real world. I do believe that it is important for AI professors to start such companies. AI product development will help the academic field of AI to gain the prestige and respect it needs to go on with its work.

Private companies started by professors are the inevitable result of having professors whose specialty is fast becoming a new technology. It is a natural part of their research career and of their wish to maintain the federal government's faith in the ultimate utility of their research. AI researchers along with other computer scientists who have ideas that they want to turn into new technology, are in the same position as the molecular biologist who wants his research to bear fruit. There is an analogy between a professor who wants to see useful products from his best ideas and an architect who wants to see actual buildings constructed from his designs, a doctor who wants to actually treat patients, and an English professor who wants to write great books. George Bernard Shaw said, *He who can, does; he who cannot, teaches.* No research university wants its professors to be living proof of this saying.

Having professors in the dual role of professor and businessman does create difficulties for the professor and for the university. Mechanisms must be developed by which a university could take advantage of the need of some of its faculty to be productive members of society in the literal sense of *productive.* What looks to some like a *conflict of interest* could, if it were cleverly managed, be made to work very much in the university's interest. Today's university must find ways to harness the entrepreneurial spirit and technological innovation of its professors for the ultimate benefit of the university.

It is natural to assume that professors who start their own companies are only interested in money. Yet people who only want money rarely become professors. The road heading toward becoming a respected scientist in a university is too difficult for those whose true desire is to be rich. What a creative scientist primarily wants is to get his ideas out into the world in a way that makes sense to him. To do this today, he must learn quite a bit about marketing, sales, finance, and be intimately involved in the details of running a company. As a country, we want and need our best scientists to help get their ideas out into the real world. America's creative scientists should be helped to get their ideas out into the marketplace in a way that allows them some measure of control with respect to how their ideas turn out, without having to make businessmen out of them.

To contribute their share to the country's continued excellence in developing new technology, and to protect their own independence and self-directedness, American universities must find ways to allow their science professors to continue to train the future scientists while developing new technology at the same time. There is at least one way open for all this to happen. The university must become entrepreneurial itself.

THE UNIVERSITY AS ENTREPRENEUR

As more and more professors demonstrate that they are quite capable of shouldering entrepreneurial duties while maintaining the quality of academic life in their departments, it seems clearer all the time that a university as a whole could create and manage profit-making corporations that could exploit the knowledge and inventiveness of its professors. This might satisfy everyone involved. The university could afford to pay its scientists competitively with private industry, fund academic research in its science departments, and perhaps even contribute to financially ailing departments in the humanities. Professors would be able to develop their ideas into interesting products while being better paid. Industries would get comparatively low-cost top of the line research and development from the country's best minds, while contributing to the academic future of many fields.

Let professors with an entrepreneurial flair and a desire to see their ideas turned into useful products devote one or two days a week to what I will call university institutes. The mission of these institutes would be to seek cooperation with industry in the development and marketing of ideas thought up by the faculty of a university. Faculty members who participate in these institutes would receive additional compensation derived initially from the monies invested in the institutes by industry, and eventually from the profits earned by the products that they designed at the institutes. The institutes also could make far more intelligent decisions than other companies about supporting pure research in the university departments. The university would derive additional revenues from the institutes as well.

This is not really such a radical idea. Stanford and MIT have taken the idea of cooperation between universities and industry quite seriously and it is one of the reasons that those universities have prospered (both academically and economically) in the last 20 years. They continue to be the leaders in science in this country in part because of the numerous businesses that they have attracted to Silicon Valley and Route 128. I am not suggesting that other universities simply follow the lead of Stanford and MIT. It is far too late for that. But it might be possible for a university-owned institute to become an innovative leader in the world of the future.

Universities already negotiate licensing agreements with faculty for products that they have developed at the university and sometimes the university provides them with additional compensation for such products. The university cannot expect that a computer scientist who develops a new piece of hardware or software will just give it away. The place of the university institute is in between the university and the marketplace, without distracting or pressuring the professor/inventor. Universities already are negotiating cooperative agreements with industry. Through grants and contracts from the government, universities have always given special privileges to those who bring in money (by reducing a professor's teaching load, for example.) And perhaps most relevant here, universities have always had an investment policy aimed at making money for the university. Why not encourage universities to invest in their own faculty?

The survival of the university in the future means attracting the innovators of society who would like to *both* invent *and* teach. The university should not put itself in the position of saying to its innovators that they must somehow choose between the desire to create and the desire to be professors. That cannot be good for the universities in the long run, and it is definitely not good for the country as a whole. Universities that wish to be strong in the twenty-first century must marshal their resources now and forge ahead. They must look for ways to set up entrepreneurial Institutes. They must view professors who start their own businesses as a chance for the university to control its own destiny, to protect the ideals of the academy, and to lessen the impact of real-world problems on the life of the mind.

INDEX